Detained and Deported

Stories of Immigrant
Families Under Fire

Margaret Regan

BEACON PRESS, BOSTON

Beacon Press
Boston, Massachusetts
www.beacon.org

Beacon Press books
are published under the auspices of
the Unitarian Universalist Association of Congregations.

18 17 16   8 7 6 5 4 3 2 1

This book is printed on acid-free paper that meets the uncoated paper
ANSI/NISO specifications for permanence as revised in 1992.

Design and composition by Wilsted & Taylor Publishing Services

Some names and other identifying characteristics of people
mentioned in this work have been changed to protect their identities.

Library of Congress Cataloging-in-Publication Data

Regan, Margaret
  Detained and deported : stories of immigrant families under fire /
Margaret Regan.
     pages cm
  Includes bibliographical references.
  ISBN 978-0-8070-7983-6 (paperback)—ISBN 978-0-8070-
7195-3 (ebook) 1. United States—Emigration and immigration—
Government policy. 2. Immigrant families—United States.
3. Immigrants—United States. 4. Emigration and immigration—
Government policy—Case studies. 5. Arizona—Emigration and
immigration—Government policy. 6. Immigrants—Government
policy—Arizona. I. Title.
  JV6483.R44 2015
  325.73—dc23   2014031770

For my family,

Kevin, Linda, and Will Gosner,

with love

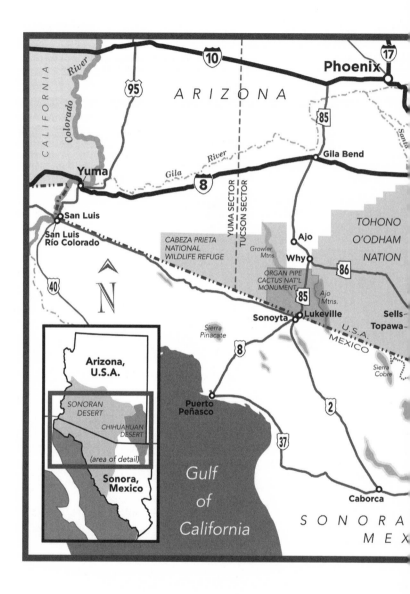

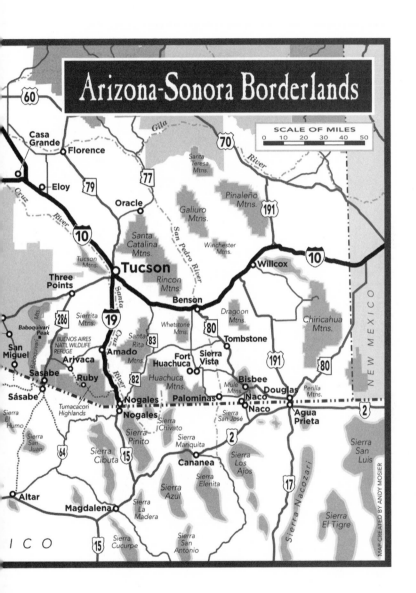

Arizona-Sonora Borderlands

Contents

Part Two: Deportation

Part Three: Resistance

Prologue

A man named Enrique was packing up his hot dog cart on Calle Internacional in Nogales, Sonora, on a hot summer afternoon. The United States had just erected a brand-new border wall across the street, dividing Nogales, Sonora, from Nogales, Arizona. Enrique looked up appraisingly at its steel posts. They loomed above him.

"It's *más* beautiful," he said, speaking in the Spanglish of the borderlands. Prettier than the old wall. Not everyone agreed. At the bus stop down the street, an older man shrugged. The two walls were *igual*, he said. Equally ugly.

The old wall had been a rough patchwork of used helicopter-landing pads, hastily cobbled together in the 1990s when migrants first began to surge in large numbers into Arizona. The US Army had discarded the flats after using them in the Persian Gulf and in the jungles of Vietnam and was only too happy to turn them over to the Border Patrol free of charge. Rising up twelve to fifteen feet—miniature compared to the big new wall—the landing-mat fence was colored the purples and rusts of a bruise. It was unapologetically ugly, and its battle history provided an uncomfortable metaphor for an international border between two nations at peace.

Even the Border Patrol didn't like it. Coyotes smuggling

migrants to the North routinely used torches to blast holes into its thin metal skin before hustling their charges through. No danger of that with the new wall, Steve Passement, a Border Patrol supervising agent, said proudly. The flimsy corrugated panels had been replaced by towering new poles that rose as high as thirty feet in some places. The massive poles, six inches square and filled with concrete, descended six feet into the earth.

The old wall had another flaw, Passement said. It was opaque, and agents couldn't see what migrants were doing on the other side. The new wall was see-through. The heavy posts were separated by four inches of open air, too small for a body to slip through but big enough for *la migra* to look south into Mexico.

"Our agents need to be aware of what's on the other side," Passement said. "There's always the chance of being rocked"—hit by rocks thrown from across the border. "The new [wall] definitely gives agents an awareness."[1]

But the open spaces cued in potential wall-crossers as well. As Enrique closed up his cart and prepared to head home, three likely migrants ambled down the street, equipped with telltale border-crosser backpacks. They could see right through the new posts to a Border Patrol agent stationed on the other side. They laughed when they saw him pacing just yards from the barricade they intended to cross; then they turned and walked off in another direction.

And enterprising families quickly found a way to convert the see-through wall to their own purposes. They transformed it from a divider into a connector. Days after it went up in 2011, families separated by deportation began staging cross-border visits through the bars, a tacit protest against the international laws that kept them apart. Mothers brought children to the wall to see their deported dads on the Mexican side. Husbands living alone in America slipped down to Nogales to see their families. Separated sweethearts held hands through the bars.

The new wall also developed deadly uses. On October 13, 2012, when it had been up little more than a year, a Border Patrol agent reached his gun through its poles into Mexico and shot a volley of bullets into the back of a sixteen-year-old Mexican boy. José Antonio Elena Rodriguez collapsed and died on the sidewalk in Sonora. His grieving family turned the barrier into a platform for protest. At a gathering marking the anniversary of his death, they reached through the bars to clasp hands with American supporters on the other side. And the poles were just wide enough to accommodate a picture of José Antonio. His mourners plastered images of his haunting young face on the wall all up and down the Nogales line.

In 2014, when eight Catholic bishops came to the border to call for immigration reform, they said a Mass in the shadow of the wall. Congregants gathered on both sides to pray together. Preaching to both nations, Cardinal Sean Patrick O'Malley lamented both the sufferings of families separated by deportation and the deaths of migrants in the desert. Invoking the memory of the Irish who died in coffin ships crossing the Atlantic, he reminded his listeners that America has always been a nation of immigrants. At Communion time he walked to the wall with the consecrated hosts, and the faithful in Mexico extended their hands through the bars for the body of Christ.

But even on ordinary days, when there were no prayers or protests, families kept coming to the wall. Just before Father's Day one year, a little girl dressed up in pink to see her father, come to visit from America. She sat by her mother, her legs dangling into the ditch that ran along the Mexican side. Her parents leaned into the poles, and her father listened intently as her mother spoke.

A few feet away, a little boy of about five or six had brought along a school paper—a drawing, perhaps?—to give to his father. The boy's arms were too short to get the paper across the divide into the United States, so his father thrust his own hand between the bars and reached toward his child in Mexico.

Introduction

What's new is that we're deporting people
who have been here for a long period of time.
When they cross back to the north, they're coming
home. They're coming to where their family is.

—*Kat Rodriguez,*
immigrant advocate

Yolanda Fontes sat in her prison scrubs and watched the
families gathered all around her. Husbands were reconnect-
ing with wives, sisters with sisters, mothers with children. It
was a sunny Sunday in April, and the families had flocked to
the Eloy Detention Center, a dreary for-profit immigration
prison in rural Arizona, to visit their detained loved ones. A
female prisoner sat with her small son on her lap, her arms
wrapped tightly around him, as if she were imagining never
letting him go. The aunt who had brought the little boy
spoke sorrowfully to her sister as the child snuggled in his
mother's embrace. Nearby, an imprisoned father sat across
a table from his wife, clutching her hand. They were trying
to talk, but their four-year-old daughter, hungry and tired,
fussed on the floor below.

None of the families in the packed room had any privacy.

An impassive guard presided over their melancholy reunions, keeping a close watch on the mothers and fathers dressed in jailbird scrubs. The visiting room was bleak and windowless, lit by glaring prison lights. It was a beautiful spring day outside, but no rays of sunlight pierced its cinder block walls.

Alone among the detainees in this stark space, Yolanda had no family visiting, just me, a writer who had come to hear her story. She was glad to be out of her prison unit, and she was full of smiles, determined to be cheerful. Yet her tale was grim, and she looked at the other detainees' kids wistfully as she recounted it. During the two years she'd spent locked up in Eloy, she'd seen her two little girls and her little boy only sporadically. The children, all American citizens, lived in a distant suburb northwest of Phoenix. They came to visit their mom only when a relative or friend could spare the time to drive the two-hundred-mile round trip to Eloy. The last time Yolanda had seen them was two months before.

Yolanda was thirty-two. She'd slipped into Arizona from Mexico seventeen years before, when she was just fifteen. She spoke flawless English and, even though she had no papers, she'd almost never had any difficulty finding a job. And until two years ago, she'd never had trouble with immigration. But the father of her two younger children regularly beat her, and one attack triggered a series of disasters that eventually landed her in jail and now detention.

The abusive ex had the two kids and Yolanda was facing deportation. She could have accepted "removal" to Mexico right away—and gotten out of Eloy—but if she were deported she would lose the children. So she stayed in the prison month after month, fighting her case, hoping to persuade a judge to overturn the deportation order, praying to get back to her daughters and her son.

Yolanda's spirits flagged just once during the two hours we talked. The last time the kids came to see her, she said, her five-year-old, Little V, had looked at her suspiciously. "He told me I didn't look like his mother," she said, her eyes filling with tears. Her own child was starting to forget her.

Down in Nogales, on the Mexican side of the border, Gustavo Sanchez Perez was just as worried about his kids. He was a twenty-five-year-old landscaper from Phoenix; I met him early one hot July morning at a Catholic *comedor* just steps from the international line. He was one of sixty deportees eating a hearty breakfast of beans and rice in a humble dining hall run by an order of Mexican nuns. Like Yolanda, Gustavo had moved with his family from Mexico to the United States as a child. Born in Veracruz, he'd come to Phoenix at the age of eight and lived there ever since. He spoke perfect English. He and his wife had two small children, a boy of four and a baby girl, both of them US citizens.

Gustavo had been arrested in Phoenix for riding his bicycle at night without a light and then detained by ICE. He'd rotated through several detention centers, in Arizona and in Colorado, before being tossed back over the border into Nogales. He'd always worked hard to support his children. What was their mother doing now, he wondered, without his wages coming in?

He was staying in a shelter, but he would have to leave soon. Nogales was reeling under a deluge of deportees from the United States, and the town's shelters didn't have the resources to house *los deportado*s longer than three days. Gustavo would have to move on. His mother in Phoenix had advised him to go back to Veracruz, but he had no intention of returning to a place where everyone was a stranger. He knew where he needed to be: with his children, at home, in Phoenix. The way to get back to them lay over the border and through the Arizona desert, but the journey would be perilous in more ways than one. He could die out there in the heat, as so many had done before him. And if he made it through, he ran the risk of arrest. "If they catch me," he said, "I get ten years in jail."

———

Yolanda and Gustavo were just two of the millions of undocumented immigrants who've been ensnared in the US dragnet of immigration detention and deportation. Since 2010, ICE, the federal Immigration and Customs Enforcement agency, has worked mightily to meet its goal of deporting 400,000 people every year. In 2012, deportations hit 419,384. And the annual tally of detainees held in the nation's detention centers soared past those deportee numbers.

In 2012, when Yolanda was still in Eloy, ICE admitted an astonishing 477,528 immigrants to detention centers around the country, outpacing what in 2011—Gustavo's detention year—had been a new record: 429,247.[1]

On an average day, more than 31,000 immigrants are held in some 250 detention centers scattered across the nation. Only nine of these lockups are owned and operated by the feds; the rest are inadequate rural county-run jails in need of extra income, and massive—and lucrative—private prisons like Eloy, run under contract to ICE.

The Global Detention Project in Geneva has called this motley collection of prisons the "largest immigration detention infrastructure in the world."[2]

As the numbers of detainees imprisoned in this infrastructure skyrocketed, human rights complaints likewise multiplied. Critics noted the racial dimension of the incarcerations. The vast majority of detainees were Mexican—64.4 percent in 2012—with Guatemalans coming in second at 10.6 percent, Hondurans next at 8.5 percent, and Salvadorans at 6.6 percent, for a Central American total of 25.7 percent.[3] And organizations from the ACLU to Amnesty International have cited physical, verbal, and sexual abuse of detainees, inadequate health care and food, use of solitary confinement as punishment, prolonged detention, and even an untoward number of deaths.

Arizona plays an outsized role in this human tragedy. One of twenty-eight states in the Union with detention centers within its borders, it has more than its share of the prisoners: some 10 percent of all immigration detainees in the United States are imprisoned in the Grand Canyon State. On any given day, Arizona's four detention centers hold some three thousand immigrants behind chain link, a 58 percent increase since 2005. Owned and operated by the for-profit Corrections Corporation of America, Eloy is the largest, incarcerating about half the detainees in the state. A fifth Arizona lockup, the notorious Pinal County Jail, once named one of the ten worst detention centers in the country, had its contract with ICE canceled in July 2014.

Arizona's high ranking in the detention sweepstakes is of a piece with the state's long list of dubious immigration benchmarks. Though Brooks County, Texas, is fast making inroads in the fatality rankings, Arizona has for years been first in the deaths of migrants. Between 2000 and 2015, some 2,903 bodies of border crossers were found in the state, lying withered in its parched deserts or decaying in its freezing mountains, dead of heat or cold or thirst. And during the great migration in the first decade of the twenty-first century, Arizona ranked first in the numbers of migrant apprehensions. Border Patrol in the Tucson Sector made 4.6 million arrests from 2000 to 2013.[4]

Arizona is both reviled and admired for a cascade of anti-immigrant laws, culminating in the infamous SB 1070, which not so incidentally helped fill its detention centers. Detention has been nothing but a growth business for Arizona. Located in the small towns of Florence and Eloy, the detention centers are major employers that help prop up a shaky local economy. Back in 1995, the fledgling Eloy Detention Center had just 395 beds. Ten years later, in 2005, its immigrant population had more than doubled, to 949; and by 2014 it had soared another 60 percent to reach 1,596 beds.

———

Americans have grown accustomed to the idea that the Land of the Free routinely incarcerates thousands of immigrants, sometimes for years on end. Yet detention centers on this scale are a relatively new feature in modern American life. Now remembered in the warm glow of nostalgia for our immigrant ancestors who passed through its portals, Ellis Island was in fact a detention, deportation, and processing center that operated for sixty-two years, from 1892 to 1954. But when Ellis Island closed, the old Immigration and Naturalization Service—precursor to ICE—announced that it would henceforth maintain just a few detention beds for hard-core cases. The Supreme Court applauded this evolution in the nation's moral development.

"Physical detention of aliens is now the exception," Justice Tom C. Clark wrote in 1958. "Certainly this policy reflects humane qualities of an enlightened civilization."[5]

Twenty-two years later, in 1980, that enlightenment principle was abandoned when 125,000 Cubans in flimsy boats landed on the beaches of Florida. Jimmy Carter, in the final year of his presidency, immediately freed many of the so-called Marielitos and held others only briefly before granting them permanent residency. Yet more than 1,500 others were incarcerated for at least five years in a maximum-security federal prison in Atlanta.

From locking up Marielitos it was an easy step to detaining Haitian "boat people." Beginning in 1981, under the Reagan administration, Haitians fleeing the dictatorship of Jean-Claude Duvalier were held in federal prisons and detention centers around the country, and even in an old missile base in a Florida swamp. In 1982 INS published new rules, over the protest of the United Nations High Commissioner for Refugees: from here on in, the detention of unauthorized immigrants would be the rule and not the exception.[6]

The race was on to build a massive detention infrastructure. Corrections Corporation of America, formed in 1983 to capitalize on the criminal incarceration boom, soon expanded into the immigration market and signed a contract with the INS.[7] President Ronald Reagan's 1986 Immigration Reform and Control Act, best known for giving "amnesty"—legal status—to certain immigrants, was the first law to define certain crimes as deportable.[8] By 1994, the nation held five thousand immigrants in detention.

Soon there were plenty more bodies to occupy the bunks. In a push-pull one-two, a thriving American economy welcomed waves of Mexicans and Central American workers in the 1900s, while NAFTA, the 1994 North American Free Trade Agreement, forced an estimated two million Mexican campesinos off their land. Under NAFTA, subsidized American corn was dumped into Mexico at such low prices that local growers couldn't stay in business. (CAFTA, a similar treaty with Central American nations, had a comparable effect.) These economic refugees fled north in search of work. But when they arrived at the border, they found new walls and more Border Patrol boots on the ground, courtesy of President Clinton's Operation Hold the Line in El Paso (1993) and Operation Gatekeeper in San Diego (1994).

The country was in the middle of a new Great Migration. During the twenty years between 1990 and 2010, twenty million immigrants poured into the country, legally or illegally, the same number, as writer David Bornstein points out, who'd landed on American shores during the forty years between 1880 and 1920, roughly the heyday of Ellis Island.[9] Now, as then, virulent anti-immigrant sentiment crested and harsh new laws were rapidly put into place. In 1996 a newly Republican House and Senate enacted the hard-nosed Illegal Immigration Reform and Immigrant Responsibility Act. IIRIRA, as it's known, dramatically upped the ante, establishing broad justifications for mandatory detention of immigrants and for subsequent deportations. Misdemeanor crimes were reinterpreted as "aggravated felonies" when they were committed by an immigrant, even a legal permanent resident. The newly defined felons were increasingly vulnerable to detention and deportation.

IIRIRA also broadened the powers of local law enforcement and of Border Patrol. Among its provisions, 287(g) deputized cops on the beat, allowing them to do immigration enforcement, and "expedited removal" gave the Border Patrol new authority to quickly remove undocumented immigrants found in the broad stretch of land within one hundred miles of the border.

After the 9/11 attacks of 2001, the new war on terror suddenly converged with border enforcement, blurring the "line between criminal and civil enforcement of immigration issues," as a *Frontline* reporter put it.[10] The old INS metamorphosed into ICE, which was incorporated into the new Department of Homeland Security. Border Patrol mushroomed, and the nation spent billions building miles more walls across the southwest border. In Arizona, the deaths of migrants trying to evade the border walls escalated, and so did complaints of Border Patrol abuses of border crossers. Borderlands residents quickly wearied of the Border Patrol's new highway checkpoints, the agents' routine incursions into private lands and fragile natural preserves, and the helicopters rattling over their rural homesteads.

Yet the nation clamored for more enforcement. Operation Streamline, begun in 2005, pulled randomly selected border crossers into federal court for mass hearings on criminal charges of illegally crossing the border. Secure Communities brought ICE's reach deeper into the country. Begun in 2008 by President George W. Bush and reformed by President Barack Obama in 2011, it had beat cops sending the fingerprints of anyone they picked up to a federal database. If an immigration match was found, ICE could authorize a "detainer" hold and dispatch officers to the jail to round the prisoner up. Sometimes the "crime" that triggered the cycle was as minor as a broken light on a bike. And sometimes that negligent bicycle rider—like Gustavo—was deported.

The furious step-up in immigrant enforcement was a marked change for undocumented immigrants like Gustavo and Yolanda who had lived and worked peacefully in the United States for years. Advocates lobbied for immigration reform that would allow the nation's estimated 11.5 million undocumented residents to live here lawfully. But bills offering a path to citizenship—as well as increased border security—crashed and burned in 2005, 2006, and 2007 under Bush and again, in 2013, under Obama. Even the Dream Act, aimed at young immigrants brought to the United Sates as children, was defeated four times.

Finally, in 2012, Obama used an executive order to institute Deferred Action for Childhood Arrivals (DACA), which allows young Dreamers who meet certain criteria to stay lawfully in the country for two years, with the option to renew. (By 2014, some 580,000 had signed up for the popular program, 20,000 of them from Arizona.) But the legislative trend against reform continued. Congress voted several times to shut DACA down, so far without success. And when unaccompanied child refugees from Central America surged over the border in large numbers in 2014, enraged politicians sought to weaken a 2008 bipartisan law that had given such children special protections.[11]

Even as immigration reform was debated, deportations continued apace.

The exact number of deportations under the Obama administration has been a point of angry dispute. Opponents on the right declared that Obama was deporting fewer unauthorized immigrants and playing semantics to hide it. Detractors on the left called him the deporter in chief and charged that he was on target to deport more people than any previous president.

The truth lay somewhere in between. Fewer people overall were being expelled from the country under Obama, but they were being deported in a far more punitive way and faced far more dire consequences—including lengthy jail sentences—if they tried to come back, as Gustavo had learned to his sorrow.

In the past, most border crossers were allowed "voluntary return" without further penalty, a practice many maligned as "catch and release." In 2000, in the last year of the Clinton administration, when migration across the southwest border was at its height, 1.6 million immigrants were voluntarily returned; just 188,467 were formally deported.

George W. Bush shifted that ratio in the last years of his presidency. Voluntary returns dropped and deportations rose, the better to punish those who came to the country unauthorized. In 2006, according to ICE's figures, Bush returned 1,043,381 immigrants, while formally deporting 280,974 immigrants. Two years later, the voluntary returns had dropped to 811,263, while deportations rose to 359,795.

Obama continued that trend. In 2009, his first year in office, the voluntary returns stood at 582,648, while the formal removals climbed to 391,932. In 2012, the ratio finally tipped, and for the first time formal removals (419,384) eclipsed voluntary returns (229,968).

Even as he pushed for immigration reform, Obama hit 1,951,400 deportations by the end of fiscal 2013. Though he now had fewer voluntary returns than his predecessor, he had tallied more deportations than any other president.[12]

———

The human impact of these deportations cannot be overstated. Families have been torn apart. Mothers and fathers have been turned into single parents. Breadwinners have disappeared. Children, many of them US citizens, have lost one or both parents, and some have ended up in foster care. In the first six months of 2011, the year that Gustavo, father of two, first turned up in Nogales, no fewer than forty-six thousand deportees were mothers and fathers whose children were left behind in the United States.

Activists and academics alike say that today's deportees differ dramatically from the migrants they had been seeing for years. These new exiles were more likely to have lived in the United States for a long time and to have been forcibly separated from their families. "What's new is that we're deporting people who have been here for a long period of time," as immigrant advocate Kat Rodriguez points out. "When they cross back to the north, they're coming home. They're coming to where their family is."

No More Deaths, which had long operated an aid station in Nogales for returned border crossers, first noticed the shift around 2009. "More often than not, the Mexicans we see now have been living in the United States," member Sarah Launius told me. "The people that just got off the bus typically have families in the US." No More Deaths changed their services to meet the new needs. "We help people make calls back home, mostly to the US."

As I was researching this book, I met many of these displaced people, both in deportee shelters in Nogales and in detention centers in Arizona. They were taxi drivers and fruit pickers, construction workers and fast-food servers, waitresses and hotel housekeepers. Some had lived like third world campesinos in the United States, speaking Spanish and living in wholly Mexican communities, doing the lowest of low-paid labor. Others were indistinguishable from American citizens. Dreamers, young and educated, had been in the United States since they were children and lived a more typically American life. They'd gone to public school, graduated from high school, and aspired to college. Then there were the immigrants who'd lived for years in Chicago or Florida or Virginia and got tripped up at the border after going back to Mexico or Guatemala to visit their families.

Saddest—and most determined—were the parents separated from their kids, the Yolandas waiting out detention, the Gustavos plotting a dangerous desert hike. I rarely saw the kids who'd lost a parent, but when I did it was painful.

The little girl I saw crying under the table in the family visiting room at Eloy haunts me still. Her name was Jacqueline, she was an American citizen, and she was four years old. It struck me that this tiny child was bearing the full burden of her country's immigration policies on her own small shoulders. And the weight of it was crushing her. Confronted with the scary jail, the angry guards, her unhappy mother, and the father who had become a stranger to her, she responded in the only way she could. She threw herself down onto the floor, clenched her fists, and wailed.

PART ONE

Detention

CHAPTER ONE

Yolanda in Limbo

She's been separated from her three children.
She was the primary caregiver. The children
need her back in their lives.

—*Nina Rabin, attorney for
longtime detainee Yolanda Fontes*

Drive an hour north from Tucson toward Phoenix, up past the craggy outlines of Picacho Peak, and you pass an innocuous sign for the town of Eloy.

Not many travelers flying up I-10 to the Valley of the Sun take note of the exit, and few have reason to turn off. The landscape here is pancake-flat, and the sleepy town looks like something out of a road trip movie about the desolate West. The houses are small and faded, and the worn-out cotton fields all around are bone-dry. During the monsoons—the desert's fierce summer thunderstorms—dust from the fields swirls up into deadly storms called haboobs. Great clouds of blinding dust whirl across the highway, sometimes taking the lives of motorists who can't even see the lights of the car ahead.

Even the name *Eloy* stands for despair. In the settlement's early days, shortly after the turn of the twentieth century, so the story goes, railroaders were so struck by the barrenness of the land that they named the new train junction Eloi, invoking Jesus's lament on the cross. "Eloi, Eloi, lama sabachthani?" *My God, my God, why have you forsaken me?*[1]

Only the occasional driver pulls off into this forsaken country, to buy a cold drink at the Circle K on a broiling day. Tourists do flock to Picacho Peak, south of town, a jaggedy lone mountain where, back in 1862, the westernmost battle of the Civil War was fought. (The South won.)

But most of these visitors aim their cars right back onto I-10 after they've had their fill of history and frosted drinks, speeding past Eloy as quickly as the freight trains roll by on the nearby tracks.

That's something the Corrections Corporation of America counts on. Because if Arizonans did wander into Eloy, and up the two-lane road past the outlying farmhouses and trailers, they'd come upon a gigantic immigration detention center that houses fifteen hundred souls.

Hidden away from the taxpayers who support it, the massive Eloy Detention Center—the third largest in the country—rises up in the rural flats like a nightmare mirage. A dozen two-story block buildings, colored an institutional shade halfway between beige and gray, sprawl over acres and acres of Arizona. Behind triple layers of chain link and coils of barbed wire, on the far side of its thick block walls, immigrants ensnared by Immigration and Customs Enforcement are imprisoned here for profit. Mothers and fathers, sisters and brothers, daughters and sons languish here indefinitely, unseen and mostly forgotten.

Undocumented border crossers, asylum seekers, workers who've lived for years in the United States, Central Americans waiting to be flown back home: all are inside, sharing space with immigrants who've already served prison time for crimes. Some of those with a criminal record are legal permanent residents who've been living in the country lawfully, but committed an offense, however minor, that landed them in mandatory detention and subjected them to deportation.

Despite appearances, Eloy is not a prison and nobody locked up there is now serving a prison sentence. The detainees, held under "civil" detention for immigration violations, are not supposed to be subject to punishment or harsh treatment. They're incarcerated only to guarantee their appearance at deportation hearings. The newcomers are awaiting their first hearing before an immigration judge or their first asylum interview. But the long-timers can while away the months, even years, while their appeals of deportation orders slowly wend their way through the immigration bureaucracy.

Yolanda Fontes was one of them.[2]

I first took the road to Eloy to see Yolanda in March 2012, on an unseasonably blustery and rainy Sunday, driving the sixty miles from Tucson. I had lived in Arizona for years, but until that day, I had never before ventured up Route 87 past Eloy. The rain had turned the brown soil a faint green, right in time for St. Patrick's, and dramatic blue-gray clouds clung to low mountains, a welcome relief from the strafed landscape along I-10.

Attorney Nina Rabin had filled me in on Yolanda's history. Yolanda had ended up in the private prison two years ago after a series of extreme traumas, starting with domestic violence and ending with sexual slavery. Her partner, the father of her two younger children, had beaten her and tried to strangle her, and she'd fled with all three kids in fear for her life. Desperate and vulnerable, she'd been ensnared by a prostitution ring; the operators coerced her into working for them, threatening to harm her children if she did not. An arrest for prostitution had gotten her thrown first into the Maricopa County jail in Phoenix, and then, after her conviction, into Eloy, where she'd been transported under threat of deportation. Detainees can hire an attorney if their families can scrape together the money, but most can't. And unlike criminal defendants, they're not entitled to public defenders. So most represent themselves, struggling to make their way through thickets of immigration law. At first Yolanda toiled on her own trying to put together a legal case that would stress the domestic violence that had triggered her train of troubles. After four months, she had the extraordinary, if unlikely, good luck to attract the attention of Nina, an attorney and law professor at the James E. Rogers College of Law at the University of Arizona in Tucson.

Nina was highly attuned to the particular woes of female detainees—she'd written two studies, one documenting the poor treatment of women's physical and psychological needs in detention, the other reporting on the ways detention and deportation separated parents and children.[3] She had become all too familiar with the domestic violence that was so often a factor in the detention of undocumented women. Nina took on Yolanda's case pro bono, through the law school's immigration clinic, and for more than a year and a half she'd been locked in combat with the ICE prosecutors who were doggedly pursuing the case.

She'd arranged for me to get into Eloy to talk to Yolanda. Like any friend or family member wanting to visit a detainee, I had to get a security clearance. I'd surrendered not only my name to ICE but my Social Security number and birth date. That week, Nina had called to tell me that I passed muster.

But it turned out to be not so easy to penetrate fortress Eloy.

It wasn't hard to find. Eight miles from the highway, the massive prison occupies a bleak tract of land scraped bare. A trademark Arizona saguaro is planted in the barren soil next to a sign announcing Corrections Corporation of America's dominion over the prison. A company flag—white CCA letters on maroon—flies beside the flag of Arizona and the Stars and Stripes, as if the for-profit prison corporation had evolved into a nation-state.

To get to the prison entrance, visitors must walk through a cage-like passageway enclosed by chain link and get buzzed through three separate doorways. A sign warns that everyone is subject to search, and another notice informs visitors only belatedly that their cell phones must be left in the car. Coats, jewelry, purses, money, even ChapStick, must be deposited in lockers provided free of charge. Women in clothing deemed provocative—short skirts, low-cut tops—are barred entry. Visitors surrender driver's licenses and car keys to the guard at the fortified desk. If someone has forgotten to take off a piece of jewelry, earrings, say, the guard confiscates them for the duration of the visit. Wedding rings are sometimes, but not always, exempt.

CCA is a stern nanny, and the rules are especially punitive for families with young children. Toys or books or art supplies to keep them entertained during visits are forbidden; so are healthful snacks from home—or homemade treats for the detained loved one. Any food has to be purchased from CCA, and the only fare on offer is overpriced vending-machine candy and chips. Families can't use regular money to buy this junk food. They have to know, somehow, to set up an account with CCA in advance and load money into it. And in thirsty Arizona, they can't even carry in a bottle of water.

While I waited my turn to take off my shoes and go through the airport-style screeners, I could see that the waiting room beyond was jam-packed with families. A few adventurous little kids ran around, but most clung to an adult's hand, spooked by the prison atmosphere. There were too few of the plastic foam couches to accommodate the Sunday crowd, and most people had to stand while they waited for the name of their family member to be called. Many had traveled far, and time was short; visiting hours were set to end within two hours.

Several would-be visitors complained. "I've been waiting more than an hour," one man said indignantly. The guard just shrugged.

Visitors are permitted only on Saturdays and Sundays, between 8:00 a.m. and 3:30 p.m., but unbeknownst to new-bies, there's a dead hour in the afternoon. The place goes on lockdown between 1:00 and 2:00 p.m., and all visits are abruptly stopped. These families had unknowingly arrived at the exact wrong time.

One little boy of six, bored by the endless delay, climbed aboard a metal exit gate and began swinging back and forth. A guard turned on the child angrily and barked at him to get down at once.

The staff member's nasty response to the kid's playfulness was of a piece with the unrelenting harshness of the place. Eloy was not supposed to be a prison, but the atmosphere was purely punitive. The guards themselves were brutalized in a way by the dreary conditions under which they worked, and they in turn were surly toward the prisoners—and visitors. This was Sunday, family time, and not one of the Eloy workers made the least effort to make the occasion cheerful in some small way. No accommodation was made even for the tiniest visitors, the children who would be reuniting with beloved parents. I saw no staff member greet a child indulgently or even politely, or help a frazzled mother.

I soon had a problem of my own. When the gatekeeper checked my paperwork and consulted her computer, she declared that I was not on the visitors' list. I protested that Yolanda's own lawyer had confirmed the visit and that I had cleared security. And I had traveled a long way. The woman glared at me, unmoved. I'd have to "get with Yolanda," she said, to clear up the misunderstanding. But Yolanda was unreachable, somewhere behind us in that locked prison. I wasn't getting in.

At Eloy, I was learning, families and friends are at the mercy of a capricious system. Hopeful visitors who've traveled long distances can be turned away at will. Worse, frantic family members often have no idea where their loved one is being held. An undocumented driver in Tucson with a broken tail pipe, say, can be stopped by police, swiftly transferred to Border Patrol, and transported to a detention center before the family even knows he's gone. The husband or father or mother could be in Eloy, or in Florence, Arizona, or even on the way to faraway Louisiana. Families struggle to track their loved one, calling their consulate, searching on the ICE website. Sometimes even lawyers who know the system need a week or more to locate a detained client.

At least I knew where Yolanda was. I was a reporter, and it was my job to try to break through bureaucratic roadblocks, but it took me almost two weeks, and many phone calls, to get permission—again—to see her. I could only imagine how much harder that task would be for an immigrant family who didn't speak English or feared the government. I had two strategies. One was to call Yolanda herself. Detainees can't receive direct phone calls, but callers can leave messages and the inmates can call back collect. Yolanda and I played phone tag for ten days before we finally made contact; she agreed to try to get my name once more on her visitors' list.

It was even more difficult to reach someone in authority who could help. My calls were passed back and forth from CCA to ICE and back to CCA again. Finally, after eleven days, I was referred to a Supervisor Galvez, a cordial ICE agent. He took my info, then called back at midnight to say he had found no reason that I'd been denied. He clicked on his computer and instantly authorized my visits. I was in.

Yolanda was a small, pretty woman with a cascade of black curls tumbling past her shoulders. During our two-hour visit, on April Fools' Day, she tried hard to be positive, despite her desperate circumstances. Even her clothes telegraphed her problems. In the color-coded Eloy universe, her blue scrubs branded her as a convicted criminal; the clothes were a highly visible and painful reminder of the criminal charge for which she'd previously served time in jail.

Initially, Yolanda tried to minimize her problems.

"I can't complain," she said to me in her excellent English. "I have people I like here."

She was trying to make the best of her time in Eloy. To keep busy, she'd taken a job in the prison as a "porter," cleaning the in-house ICE offices and the courtrooms for a dollar a day. She liked getting out of her cell, but the job was also a strategy. She believed that if the judge saw what a hard worker she was, he might be more inclined to let her out on bond—and be with her kids—while she awaited news on her deportation appeal. So far, all the mopping and dusting had failed to persuade him.

And for the first time in her life, she'd taken up art. She regularly made drawings to send to her kids, and she'd even won permission to paint murals in the depressing Eloy corridors. A long time later, after she'd gotten out of Eloy, I was back for an official tour and I saw one of her murals. It was a prisoner's vision of the outside world, filled with longing: orange flowers and a palm tree grew out of a sandy beach. A bright sun shone in the sky, and the ocean stretched out into infinity. Yolanda boasted that she had a special place in the hearts of the staff—she'd used her clout to get me sprung from the Eloy waiting room in record time—and one time she'd even wangled permission to make a microwave cake for her kids when they came for a visit. She took pride in her mothering skills and she kept up with the children's lives as best as she could from a distance. Her cousin brought the kids to visit when she could, but it was a long drive; they lived on the far side of Phoenix's sprawl.

"The last time I saw them was on the eighteenth of February," she said, her bravado faltering a little. Nor could she call them often. Prison phone calls were expensive, "and I don't have the funds," she lamented. With the children split between two households, even when she did have a little money, she could afford only one call. "I feel bad—I call one and not the other one."

With their mother effectively out of their lives, the children weren't doing all that well. Ten-year-old Janie, the oldest, lived with Yolanda's cousin Noemi. Noemi was kind—it was she who'd brought the children for that February visit—but Janie was "acting up," her mother said. "She's going down in her grades."

The younger two, Madelyn and Little Victor, were living not only with their dad, Yolanda's abusive ex, Victor, but with his new girlfriend, Yolanda's niece Lalia.[4] Yolanda hated that her niece was now the children's de facto stepmother. Seven-year-old Madelyn's health "was bad" in Lalia's care. She'd had a worrisome rash, and Yolanda didn't like the way her new "mom" fixed her hair, pulling it back so tightly it hurt. The baby of the family, six-year-old Little V, was having trouble in school; he was going to have to repeat first grade. The complicated family situation confused him, and he was no longer quite sure who his mother was; on that rough day more than two years ago that the police took Yolanda away, he had been just four years old.

Yolanda came north from Mexico at fifteen with an aunt.[5] As Nina recounted in a legal article on Yolanda's case, it was a rescue operation. The young girl had gotten mixed up with a man in the narcotics trade and the worried aunt whisked her away for her own safety. They slipped across the border undetected and made their way to Phoenix. Although Yolanda had no papers, she found work easily: she was smart and she worked hard. She hired on at restaurants and with a cleaning service, where she was so diligent that she was promoted to team supervisor. "I know everything about chemical cleaners," she boasted to me.

She gave birth to Janie when she was twenty-two; she met Victor later, and Madelyn and Little V eventually came along. Lalia came to live with the family as a teenager, and Yolanda's relationship with Victor soon began to deteriorate. As Nina wrote, Victor "became increasingly violent . . . much of his rage was fueled by the secret affair he was having with her fifteen-year-old niece."

Victor hit Yolanda and smacked the kids around too, Yolanda told me, her face tightening. "He was very bad. I will never forgive him."

The beatings escalated until the night that Victor nearly killed her. He squeezed her neck so hard he left a necklace of bruises on her flesh. In fear for her life, Yolanda fled with the kids. They were tiny. Madelyn and Little V were babies still, just one and two years old, respectively. Janie was five. After that, Yolanda's fortunes plummeted. She and the kids had to sleep in her car for a while, and then they bounced around, sometimes alighting at a friend's place, sometimes at a shelter for battered women.

It was 2008. The economy had tanked, and for the first time Yolanda had trouble finding work. She got a tip on a job at a cleaning service, her specialty, only to learn too late that it was actually an "escort service" run out of an apartment. It was a brutal operation that had a sideline in drugs. As Nina worked on Yolanda's legal case she learned more of the gruesome details. The "bosses" were armed men who accompanied the women—most of them immigrants, many only in their teens—to "dates" with men. Sex with the customers was required, and the armed guards threatened to hurt the women if they tried to quit or call the cops. After a night when rival gunmen broke into the apartment and forced some of the women to give them oral sex, Yolanda was so frightened she tried to stop working.

That's when she started getting anonymous phone threats, "telling her that she and her children would be hurt if she stopped coming to work," Nina wrote. The unknown caller started sending "photos to her cell phone of her, her children, and her babysitter, making clear that he knew where to find her if she didn't obey the managers." In fear for her family's lives, she went back to work. The police found out about the operation, and one day when Yolanda was there cops swarmed the place. They questioned her, asking whether she was there voluntarily. The bosses who'd threatened her were right there listening. Terrified of reprisal if she told the truth, she said yes.

Soon after, she quit for good; unbeknownst to her, investigators had filed a warrant for her arrest on charges of working for an "illegal enterprise." The police found her not long after. She had gone to pick up Madelyn and Little V from a visit with their dad. They were scheduled to go back home with Yolanda, but Victor and Lalia "were refusing to give my kids back," she told me, still upset by the memory. Then she made the mistake of calling the cops for help. They came, but they found the warrant for her arrest in online records. Yolanda was cuffed and taken to jail. She was charged with a crime related to her work in the brothel—"illegally conducting an enterprise"—and her undocumented status was uncovered.

Undocumented immigrants accused of a crime in Arizona are forbidden by state law to be released on bail, and Yolanda was held in a Maricopa County jail for two months before she even had her hearing. She pled guilty; the judge gave her a suspended sentence and a year's probation. An American citizen convicted of the same offense and given the same sentence would have walked out the courthouse door a free woman. But any conviction at all is a different order of magnitude for an immigrant. As Nina succinctly put it, Yolanda was now officially a "criminal alien." She was facing deportation, and with a crime on her record she was subject to mandatory detention. ICE took custody of her right after the court hearing; an agent showed up and took her straight to Eloy.

Had she accepted immediate deportation to Mexico, she would have avoided the long years of detention. But lost her kids.

"They say I'm a risk to flee," she told me, beginning to cry. "But how does that make sense? I've been sitting in detention for two years so I can be with my children. Why would I leave them?"

So Yolanda remained in Arizona behind chain link— it was the only way she could fight for her daughters and her son.

Every day that Yolanda sat in Eloy, pining for her children, was a day that the Corrections Corporation of America got another $122.

CCA is the largest for-profit private prison corporation in the United States, and Eloy is just one of fourteen immigration detention centers that it runs for Uncle Sam. The work pays nicely. In 2012 alone, Yolanda and the other Mexicans and Guatemalans and Salvadorans who ate the starchy meals and slept in the cramped cells in its ICE-contracted detention centers helped the corporation turn a profit of $206 million in its detention enterprises alone. CCA has a much larger business in for-profit criminal prisons, but the bull market in locking up immigrant mothers like Yolanda helped double its stock prices between 2010 and 2013.[6]

The US Congress has been more than helpful in furthering the private-prison-business boom. In 2004 the country had 18,000 detainee beds. Five years later, in 2009, lawmakers added the first-ever "bed mandate" to the Department of Homeland Security budget: ICE was now required to incarcerate no fewer than 33,400 detainees each and every day. That demand naturally sparked new efforts by ICE to find people to put in those beds. And in 2014, Congress tweaked the number up yet again, pushing the mandate to an even 34,000.[7] The majority of those uncomfortable bunks are in private prisons.

The bed bonanza doesn't come cheap. By 2013, the federal government was paying out $2 billion a year to detain the immigrants tossing and turning in those beds; the daily tab ran to $5.6 million. Immigrant advocates pleaded in vain for the nation to switch to cheaper—and more humane—techniques that would still guarantee that detainees like Yolanda showed up for their hearings. If she'd been allowed to go home to her kids in an ankle bracelet that kept track of her whereabouts, the feds would have shelled out a bargain $6 a day—the average cost of bracelet monitoring in 2012, the year I met her.[8]

Bracelet monitoring can't match detention centers for job creation, though.

Eloy is one of many small towns across America that have learned to love private prisons. If cotton once was king in Eloy, now it's prisons that rule. The Eloy Detention Center is the third largest in the country, second only to Stewart in Lumpkin, Georgia, and South Texas in Pearsall, Texas. And it's not the only CCA facility in Eloy. On the same dusty tract of former farmland where the immigration detention center stands, the company runs three medium-security prisons for men convicted of crimes. One is under contract with the state of Arizona, but the others, oddly, hold out-of-staters, men convicted in faraway California and Hawaii.

The stricter America's criminal laws, the more hard-core

its immigration enforcement, the more jobs Eloy gets. In the microeconomy of the city—population 17,448 in 2012—CCA is the largest employer. Despite record profits, the wages it pays for the dispiriting work of prison guard are not high: Eloy's median household income for 2012 was $30,583, well below the Arizona figure of $47,826.[9]

Even so, the jobs are welcome in a remote town with few other work options. The people of Eloy know the same thing that the CEO of CCA knows: the more detainees who come up I-10 in chains, the more money everybody—from the townspeople to the guards to the prison shareholders and even the ICE agents—stands to make.

Yolanda's conviction had immeasurably complicated her immigration case. The government has a list of "crimes involving moral turpitude," an old-fashioned label with more than a hint of Victorian prurience, that target immigrants. The list covers a surprising range of crimes. "If you have a waitress arrested for working illegally at a restaurant using false papers, she's charged with ID theft," Amber Cargile, a spokeswoman for ICE, told me. "At ICE, if we decide to prosecute, those are crimes of moral turpitude or CMTs. The waitress would face mandatory detention after serving time for a crime of moral turpitude."

Some offenses on the list are "clear-cut crimes of moral turpitude: molestation, indecency, and so on," Amber said. "Others are things like fraud or theft, things that implicate your moral character. The law was written that way: can we trust you if we let you out?"

Yolanda was in the same boat as that hypothetical waitress. Prostitution was definitely on the moral turpitude list, and her conviction was keeping her in the private prison under mandatory detention. While Yolanda was incarcerated,

Nina was researching the domestic violence angle. She made the case to the in-house immigration judge in Eloy that as an abuse victim Yolanda was entitled to relief from deportation under the Violence Against Women Act (VAWA). As Nina wrote in her article, "abusers can use lack of immigration status as an additional means of control"; as a result, VAWA gives particular protection to immigrant women who've been abused. Nina argued that since Yolanda had been pushed into her crime of moral turpitude by Victor's violence, she was entitled to a "waiver" of the conviction and a "VAWA cancellation of removal." In short, she didn't deserve to be deported.

Meantime, Nina was doing battle with the local ICE prosecutor. The ICE lawyer parried Nina's VAWA application by declaring that Yolanda didn't have the "good moral character" VAWA required. As proof, he produced an order from Maricopa County family court that had given Victor full custody of their two children. This was the first Yolanda had heard this bad news. As happens all too frequently with detainee parents, the family court had lost track of Yolanda's whereabouts when she disappeared into detention. The court hadn't been able to notify her of the custody hearing, and in a Kafkaesque twist, when she didn't show up, her absence was counted against her. She lost custody of Madelyn and Little V.

A pro bono family law attorney enlisted by Nina to remedy this injustice soon got the decision reversed. If Yolanda ever got out of detention, she would have primary custody once more.

Her immigration case wasn't faring as well. After "five months, four hearings, and multiple briefs," as Nina put it, the Eloy judge announced his decision: Yolanda's crime made her ineligible for VAWA relief. Nina appealed his decision to the Board of Immigration Appeals in Virginia, and simultaneously made the case to ICE that Yolanda should be granted "humanitarian parole" while she awaited the board's decision.

ICE's official policy, enunciated in June 2010 by then-director John Morton, was to concentrate on deporting dangerous criminals and people who were risks to national security. Prosecutors were to give low priority to parents, like Yolanda, who were the primary caretakers of young children. They were to use "prosecutorial discretion" in deciding the merits of each case. If ever there was a candidate for Morton's prosecutorial discretion, Nina argued, Yolanda was it. Her children were little; they were US citizens; and they needed their mother. She was a victim of domestic violence, and two of the kids, Madelyn and Little Victor, were in the care of the man who had abused her. She had committed no violence. She was most definitely not a flight risk.

ICE never responded to the request.[10]

So Yolanda waited out the days and weeks and months and now years at Eloy, cleaning and painting and trying to keep up her spirits behind block walls and barbed wire.

"You lose interest in food and sleep," she confessed. "It's boring. You lose interest in everything."

Eleven days after my April Fools' visit, Nina was racing up the highway to Eloy; law student Ben Harville was riding shotgun and I was in the backseat. We were on the way to Yolanda's hearing with US immigration judge James De-Vitto, a tough judge who has a 93 percent denial rate for asylum requests.[11]

The plan was to persuade Judge DeVitto to bond Yolanda out, and the two lawyers plotted strategy in the front seat. Nina tallied up the gender dimensions of Yolanda's plight.

"Her conviction is a direct result of the abuse she suffered," she said. "She was kicked out of the house. The people she was working for are connected to drug cartels. They threatened her and her kids when she tried to leave. She deeply regrets doing it and she has paid dearly for it."

And at Eloy, she had chalked up an outstanding behavior record. "She has been nothing but a model detainee."

Nina plotted tactics with Ben. "You need to say: There are serious humanitarian issues. She's been separated from her three children. She was the primary caregiver. The children need her back in their lives."

At Eloy, we met up with two of Yolanda's supporters, her cousin Noemi, who was hoping to bring Yolanda home that day to her own house, and Nelly, a family friend. All of us—even the legal team—had to go through security; then a guard escorted us down a hallway to the in-house court-room. Yolanda was in the corridor waiting to confer with her attorneys. When she saw her three visitors trotting along behind them, her face lit up. We returned her smile, winning an angry rebuke from the bailiff.

"This is not a family visit," he snapped. "If you even look at the defendant or smile, you will be asked to leave."

Inside, the deep blue courtroom looked like any other court of law. At the far end, beyond rows of chairs, an American flag was on display. The judge was seated at an elevated bench.

Another hearing was under way when we entered. A woman in blue scrubs sat all alone, huddled in a chair. Like most detainees fighting their cases, she had no attorney. She was trying to represent herself and she struggled to under-stand the proceedings. She spoke no English. An interpreter was translating as the judge explained that he had some le-gal papers for her—in English—that she needed to read and study. He asked if she'd like a stay, a delay in the proceed-ings, so she could get the papers translated into Spanish. She agreed, took the papers, and shuffled out, looking hopeless and scared.

Yolanda was next up. The battling attorneys sat on opposite sides of the courtroom—Nina and Ben at the table on the left, the ICE prosecutor on the right. Ben stood up and pleaded with the judge to let this mother go home to her children. She had a place to live, with her cousin. She was a victim of domestic violence. And she had already been incarcerated, two years to the day.

The ICE attorney argued back hard, returning again and again to Yolanda's crime of "moral turpitude." Judge DeVitto slumped over the bench, head in his hands, the very picture of a world-weary observer who already had seen far too much human tragedy and folly in his courtroom.

He looked up and raised his eyebrows. "And what was the sentence for this 'crime involving moral turpitude'?" he asked, sarcasm giving an edge to his voice.

There was only one answer possible. "A year of probation," the attorney replied sheepishly.

Judge DeVitto parroted his response. "A year of probation." He nodded, then issued his decision. He'd found a loophole. In their zeal to throw the book at Yolanda, her prosecutors in state court had charged her not with prostitution per se, but with "facilitation to commit/illegally conducting an enterprise," apparently trying to cast her as a leader of the prostitution ring. Judge DeVitto declared that the vague "facilitation" was not a crime of moral turpitude.

He made his ruling: Yolanda could leave.

The catch was that she had to pay a $5,000 bond. It was a stiff penalty, but Nina knew that with the criminal conviction, that was as low as the judge would go. Yolanda had a whispered conference with the attorneys, then gave her assent.

She was going home.

Noemi and Nelly raced out of the prison. To get Yolanda home that day, they needed to get a postal order for $5,000 and have it back at Eloy by 3:30 p.m. It was already 11:00 a.m. The two women charged out to the parking lot and worked their phones, calling every Yolanda supporter they could think of, then dashed up to Phoenix to collect the cash. And they pulled it off.

In a matter of hours, they rushed back to Eloy, down the highway, across the railroad tracks, past the dusty farms. They had the money and they were on time. But there was a glitch. The ICE attorney had already told Nina he was filing an appeal of the judge's bond decision immediately, with a goal of sending Yolanda right back to Eloy. Accidentally or not, he failed to sign off on that day's court papers. Without his John Hancock, Yolanda could not be freed. She had to spend one last night in detention while officials sought his signature. Noemi would not be bringing her cousin home that day.

The next morning, Yolanda made a grand exit.

"Yolanda was unusually beloved in the facility," Nina recounted later. "She said everyone came out to clap and cheer for her—some ICE people, some CCA people."

After two years and one day in detention, Yolanda Fontes marched out into the sun.

Nina was still worried. The ICE prosecutor had made good on his vow to appeal the judge's bond decision. If she lost, Yolanda could be hauled back to Eloy. And Nina might still lose that VAWA appeal at the Virginia court. She started working every possible legal angle.

First she wrote to the ICE legal team, asking them to drop their appeal of the bond. Once again, she tallied all the factors in Yolanda's favor: she was a victim of domestic violence, the caregiver of young US citizen children, and she had not committed a violent crime.

"Yet within hours, ICE denied my request," Nina recalled. "ICE has said they only use their resources for serious crimes. But they denied my request the same day."

Nina saw a clear disconnect between ICE's stated policies

and its actions on the ground. "There was nothing to account for the vehemence of ICE's prosecution," she later wrote, "other than a pervasive, deep-seated belief that immigrants 'like her' were criminals, and the ICE trial attorney's role was to deport them."[12]

Despairing of ICE, Nina began to see her way to make a different case. She had learned more about Yolanda's "crime" in the last months, when she was gathering information for the bond hearing; before that, Yolanda had been too embarrassed to say much about her time in the brothel. The fact was that Yolanda had been coerced into prostitution, by criminals who had threatened her and her children. In short, she had been a victim of human trafficking, defined by the Trafficking Victims Protection Reauthorization Act as, among other things, "sex trafficking in which a commercial sex act is induced by force, fraud or coercion."

In September, Nina filed an application with US Citizenship and Immigration Services (USCIS) arguing that Yolanda was entitled to a T visa, granted to immigrant women and children who had been victims of trafficking. If she could get the visa, Yolanda could stay in the country.

In October, the board in Virginia denied Yolanda's appeal; the board agreed with their Eloy colleagues. In spite of the domestic violence she had suffered, Yolanda's subsequent crime made her ineligible for a VAWA waiver. Nina immediately filed an appeal with the Ninth Circuit; the appeal allowed Yolanda to remain free for the time being.

Then in January 2013, a decision came down from USCIS finding that Yolanda had indeed been forced into the sex industry by human traffickers. She could have her T visa. She could stay in the United States. She could stay in the home she'd returned to that May. She would not be going back to Eloy, ever.

Nina was struck by the clash of the two enormous federal

bureaucracies. "ICE saw her as a criminal," she told me. "And the CIS saw her as a victim."

Nina kept her appeal on mandatory detention open with the Ninth Circuit. Maybe, just maybe, the judges would see Yolanda's VAWA case the way she did, and a precedent would be set that would help other immigrant women who'd been beaten—or strangled. If Nina hadn't come along with her free legal help, there was no telling where Yolanda would be now. Still locked up in Eloy, maybe, like that other woman we saw in court, with the rest of the detainees who have no lawyers to lead them through the twists and turns of immigration law. Or she'd be in Mexico, a deportee living in a country she hardly knew. In either case, she wouldn't be raising her children.

Now she was. She was home, back with Janie, Madelyn, and Little V, loving them and scolding them and singing them to sleep, making sure they did their homework, dabbing salve on their rashes, and fixing their hair exactly the way she pleased.

CHAPTER TWO

Suicide

We have mental health issues here.
Most have anxiety, and some are depressed.

*—Shane Kitchen, Eloy's ICE detention operation
supervisor, speaking of detainees at Eloy*

The chapel at Eloy is a windowless cinder-block room, just one more anonymous space in the vast prison. Only the crucifix on the wall signals its heavenly purpose. On a blistering day in July 2013, the chapel was as full of heartfelt prayers—and grief and longing and despair—as any stained glass cathedral.

Several dozen men in green scrubs were singing and weeping and wailing. One prisoner strummed a guitar and another rattled a tambourine. Near the cross, a big-bellied minister sweated and shouted out one *corazón*—"heart"—and Alleluia after another. The detainees thrust up their arms to give praise to the Lord, and four fell to their knees. The minister bowed and patted the heads of the genuflecting men. "No pierdan esperanza, mijitos," he said. *Don't lose hope, my sons.*

Locked up, far from home, separated indefinitely from their families, these jailed evangelicals regularly channeled their anguish into religious fervor. The minister came from the outside to lead them through the rituals and to ask God to ease their pain. They weren't the only detainees who turned to religion for respite. Catholic priests, Muslim imams, Jewish rabbis, and at least one Mennonite minister from Tucson also came to Eloy to soothe its suffering souls.

"We have mental health issues here," acknowledged Shane Kitchen, Eloy's ICE detention operation supervisor, who was taking me on a tour of the prison. "Most have anxiety, and some are depressed. Their family might be in Honduras without a phone, for example," and the locked-up son or sister can't speak to them. "The ladies, especially, form little families. They cry together."

Not for nothing was Eloy named for Jesus's cry of despair. A flyer hanging in a day room in one of the women's units addressed the prison's forsaken, echoing the minister's words: "Don't Let Go of Hope," it read.

Three months before, two Guatemalan detainees had taken their own lives in Eloy's cells.

Elsa Guadalupe-Gonzales was the first to die.

She begged off from dinner late on the warm Sunday afternoon of April 28, 2013, and stayed in her cell. The other women in her unit, Bravo 200, were marched out under guard to the chow hall.

Once everyone had left, and she was locked into her cell, Elsa sat down on the lower bunk and pulled the laces out of her sneakers. She knotted them together into a circle, looped the string around the top bed frame, and tied it. Finally she climbed up onto the bottom bunk, circled the noose around her neck, and stepped into the air.

She was twenty-four years old.

Next was Jorge Garcia-Mejia, age forty. Two days after Elsa's death, Jorge followed her example and hanged himself in his cell.

The deaths threw all of Eloy, staff and inmates alike, into a panic. Mariana Rodriguez, an eighteen-year-old detainee from Tempe, Arizona, was living in the same building as Elsa, but in a different unit, Bravo 100. While Elsa was making careful preparations for her own death, Mariana was eating her dinner in the dining hall, with the other women of Bravo.

As always, they had only twenty minutes to eat. "I'd joke to the officers, 'You're gonna make us choke,'" Mariana told me after she'd been released. They wolfed the food down—at least as much of it as they could stomach; the meals were universally despised. After the rushed meal, Mariana and the others walked back to Bravo as usual. Suddenly they realized that something was very wrong.

"Out of nowhere an officer was there," Mariana said. "We heard screaming on the radio, people yelling, 'Emergency!' The officer right there was shocked. They were saying, 'Get back in the cafeteria!' I was the only one who spoke English, so I asked the officer, 'My gosh, what's wrong?' She said, 'I'm not supposed to tell you. But I think someone committed suicide.'"

The women were herded back to the chow room and locked up for two hours. In another sign of the chaos, a cluster of male guards supervised them: usually Eloy was strictly sex-segregated. And when the women finally got back to their "pod"—the residential unit—they weren't allowed to hang out in the big common space as usual. Everyone was sent straight into lockdown.

"Nobody could go out," Mariana said. "One of the regular female officers told me the ambulance was there. She was scared."

From her cell Mariana could still hear the frantic conversations crackling over the guards' radio. "I heard: 'She's not responding. The ambulance is here.' The other girls didn't speak English. They didn't know, and I didn't tell them."

Eventually Mariana fell asleep, but her bunkie—prison-speak for cellmate—couldn't sleep. A Guatemalan like Elsa, the roommate kept watch, peering through the tiny window of their cell. Hours later she heard a commotion and saw a body being carried out in a bag. Though Eloy officials never formally told the detainees what had happened, Mariana and the others soon learned the gruesome details from Elsa's bunkie. Back then, at the time of the suicides, inmates could skip meals if they chose, but they had to be locked in and monitored regularly. The guard on duty apparently had checked on Elsa, as the rules required, peeking through the window of the cell door.

But Elsa was tiny, short enough to die by hanging from a bunk-bed gallows. The guard saw her upright body and "thought she was just standing there," Mariana said. It was not until her bunkie got back from the dining hall that the truth was discovered. The roommate found Elsa's lifeless body suspended from the bunk. "She saw the shoelaces and screamed for the officer."

The guards called 911. "Emergency medical technicians responded to the scene, but were unable to revive Guadalupe-Gonzales," an ICE press release reported. "She was pronounced dead at 6:06 p.m."[1]

The next morning, Mariana said, the graveyard-shift officer who had been at Eloy overnight told the Bravo inmates, "Something really bad happened. I want you to be really nice to the girls in Pod 200. Make them happy, pray for them."

Jorge's death by hanging was eerily similar to Elsa's. He too was alone in the cell, though his body was found by an Eloy staff member making a routine check. The guard called 911 at once, but the EMTs who rushed to the detention center were unable to revive him. He was pronounced dead at 2:45 p.m.

Neither of the two dead Guatemalans had been in Eloy long. Elsa had been held thirty-nine days, and Jorge thirty-eight. Elsa crossed the border near Nogales, Arizona, in March, but she didn't get far; on March 18 the Border Patrol picked her up close to the line. She arrived at Eloy two days later, on March 20, and petitioned for asylum. Jorge had been arrested on criminal charges of assault by the Phoenix police and then brought to Eloy by ICE on March 23.

Elsa and Jorge had undergone the two standard routine physicals all newly arrived detainees got, and neither had asked for treatment for any medical or mental health problems, the ICE news release said. Attorneys from the nonprofit Florence Immigrant and Refugee Rights Project were scheduled to meet with Jorge about his immigration case on the day he killed himself. They hadn't had any contact with Elsa.[2]

Eloy had "a lot of women from Central American countries seeking asylum," Charles Vernon, an attorney with the Florence Project, told me. "There are a lot of indigenous Guatemalans in Eloy," with "horrific" tales of what had happened to them back home.

As Americans would learn in the late spring and summer of 2014—when Central American women and children poured over the border in unprecedented numbers—the people of Guatemala, El Salvador, and Honduras had suffered agonies for years. In Guatemala, decades of a murderous civil war had given way to an uneasy peace, and the nation was still dangerous. All three countries were stricken by poverty and plagued by violence from gangs, drug cartels, and corrupt police and military. The US State Department issued a travel warning against Honduras in 2013, noting that it had the highest murder rate in the world.[3]

Like Elsa, the other Central American detainees in Eloy applied for asylum on the grounds that they face "credible fear" in their homelands. Asylum was no easy thing to win, and many of the asylum seekers "have lost their cases and appealed, but the appeals drag on for years," Charles said. "They can stay in detention for two or three years." And if they ultimately lose their appeals, they face the horrifying prospect of being flown back to Central America, to the place whose terrors they had fled.

Shaken by Elsa's death, Mariana and the other Bravo women kept asking themselves why she had taken her own life. She had been in Eloy less than six weeks, but "her friends told me she was tired of being locked up," Mariana said. "She had had enough." Still, Mariana was puzzled. Elsa had already had her asylum interview and "she was supposed to get an answer that week." Why, she wondered, didn't Elsa wait to find out if her request had been granted? What had gone wrong?

The outside world wondered too. Two suicides two days apart incensed critics of immigration detention in general and of Eloy in particular. Detention Watch Network, an organization that regularly monitors conditions in detention centers nationwide, called for the private prison to be shut down.

Eloy was already notorious. It had the dubious distinction of more known inmate deaths than any other detention center in the nation: from 2003, the year ICE was created, to 2012, ten Eloy inmates had died. (In the same period, ICE's records show the deaths of a total of 131 detainees in its own centers or its contract facilities.) Eloy's casualties died either behind its walls or after being taken to a hospital when already desperately ill.[4] Now the suicides of Elsa and Jorge had pushed Eloy's death toll to twelve. At least two of the earlier Eloy deaths were also suicides; others had been triggered by poor or negligent medical care.

In 2009, journalist Nina Bernstein reported in the *New York Times* that the government's own investigative teams had twice denounced the center's poor safety record. One of the earlier Eloy suicides, José Lopez-Gregorio, a thirty-two-year-old Guatemalan, had been on suicide watch, but when he asked for medical help he was ignored, Bernstein wrote. Alone and distressed, locked up in an "isolation cell," he hanged himself on September 29, 2006. After looking at the lead-up to José's death, investigators wrote a scathing report. "Medical care in this facility does not meet ICE standards," they said, ". . . detainee welfare is in jeopardy."

A few months later, on December 13, 2006, a twenty-seven-year-old Colombian, Mario Francisco Chavez-Torres, died after undergoing a seizure that went unnoticed by Eloy officials. Medical staff had ignored Mario's headaches, dizziness, and vomiting—possible symptoms of a brain bleed. After his death, a second investigative team concluded that the "facility has failed on multiple levels to perform basic supervision and provide for the safety and welfare of ICE detainees."[5]

Between 2007 and 2011, four more inmates died. In 2013, after the back-to-back deaths of Elsa and Jorge, ICE officials acknowledged that Eloy was not conforming to the federal agency's current detention standards. Formulated in 2011, the new ICE rules had added a number of provisions to help prevent suicide. Training of workers was to be ramped up, for example, and twenty-four on-call experts were to be available to staffers worried about a despondent detainee.[6] But Eloy was operating under an outdated set of rules from 2008—without the extra suicide precautions.

ICE had the power of the purse, paying CCA to house its detainees, but the agency had not forced the prison corporation to comply with the rules. Instead, as Amber Cargile, ICE press officer, told me in July 2013, "We're in *negotiations* [italics mine] with CCA to bring it up to 2011 standards."

Meantime, ICE made some tepid pledges, promising to conduct a "thorough assessment" of the latest suicides and to provide group counseling sessions for detainees and training for staff. An ICE news release stated that CCA would "conduct an internal review of its suicide prevention policies and practices."

No mention was made of revoking CCA's contract on the grounds of poor performance.

Instead, the ICE statement concluded by reiterating the status quo. "ICE contracts with CCA for the operation of the Eloy Detention Center, under ICE oversight."[7] As Detention Watch angrily pointed out, there was no "independent oversight" of the cozy relationship between the government agency and the for-profit prison corporation.

It was not until December 2013, nearly three years after the 2011 standards were drawn up—and eight months after the deaths of Elsa and Jorge—that CCA put the new, safer practices into place.

Three months after their suicides, I got deep into Eloy for the first time, going beyond the visiting rooms and the courtroom. Photographer Jay Rochlin and I were accompanied on our tour at all times by no fewer than six officials, several armed guards among them.

Once we got past security, the first thing we saw was a dismal waiting room jam-packed with Central Americans. Dozens of brown-skinned men, many of them *indígenas*, or Indians, slumped in their seats, their faces despondent.

The men were awaiting their asylum interviews, trying to document the fears and dangers that had pushed them from their homes, Shane Kitchen, the in-house ICE supervisor, told me.

Eloy's inmates had a surprising variety of histories, all of them reflected in their color-coded prison uniforms, Shane explained. Recent border crossers and asylum seekers—like Elsa and these sad men—were the lowest level of offender; they wore green scrubs. Next rung up the hierarchy were the Level Twos, the khaki-wearers, who had committed mild criminal offenses. The Level Threes, dressed in blue, were seen by ICE as the most incorrigible: the Yolandas who'd been convicted of acts of moral turpitude. Orange was reserved for those consigned to solitary, to the dreaded *el hoyo*, or hole.

Not all the detainees were undocumented. Marco Juarez-Pelayo was a legal permanent resident who had been in the United States since he was twenty-three days old. He'd gotten into a legal dustup as a young man and been charged with misdemeanors for marijuana possession. His green card couldn't save him. Under the far-reaching Illegal Immigration Reform and Immigrant Responsibility Act of 1996, even legal permanent residents can be deported if they're convicted of certain crimes. The day before I'd arrived in Eloy for my tour—with plans to interview him—Marco had been deported.

Eloy started out as a real prison, designed and constructed for hardened criminals, Shane told me, as we walked through the cheerless corridors of the main building. Now, the former Bureau of Prisons lockup had metamorphosed into a detention center and, as Shane was eager to point out, "detention centers are held to a different standard" than regular prisons. The detainees were not supposed to be punished the way criminal convicts were; anyone here who had committed a crime had already done their time. At Eloy, as I'd been reminded time and time again, inmates are being held only to guarantee they'll show up at their immigration hearings.

"It's *civil* enforcement," Shane stressed.

Still, the detainees led the regimented lives of prisoners, subject to orders from the stern uniformed guards I saw in every corner. They were roused from sleep before dawn and marched in groups to the dining hall under guard. They were routinely locked up in tiny cells, and they had little privacy. They were punished for infractions of the rules, with the worst *castigo* being solitary confinement. Detainees thrown into *el hoyo* were isolated for up to twenty-three hours a day, sometimes in the dark. Gay detainees complained of being thrown into solitary for their own "protection."[8]

Men and women were strictly segregated, and if a husband and wife were detained at Eloy at the same time, they were allowed to visit just once a week. Many inmates didn't even have the relief of family nearby. ICE crisscrossed detainees across the country to assorted prisons, picking them up in one state and detaining them in another. Eloy held flocks of Californians.

And if Eloy acted like a jail, it looked like one too, inside and out, from its minuscule cells to its dreary cinder block walls. There were few windows to let in the bright Southwest sun. Here and there in the main building, prisoners had painted murals on the walls in an effort to brighten the place up. When I asked about Yolanda's painting, Shane led me straight to her sunny beach. And he remembered her affectionately. "She was a very nice young lady," he said.

Shane was a genial man, and he was compassionate when he brought up the detainees' tough histories. He was an ICE supervisor, though, and as he led me around, to the chapel, the library, the medical clinic, he spoke of Eloy's virtues in glowing terms. Yet nearly everything he told me about the treatment of the detainees contradicted what the inmates themselves described.

Eloy's residents had plenty of complaints about poor medical care, from enduring long waits to see a nurse or doctor to having their ills minimized or dismissed. When Shane turned down a corridor where patients were sitting on chairs awaiting appointments, he tallied up the services detainees received. All newcomers got a health screening, including a chest X-ray to check for tuberculosis. Plenty of them were the walking wounded, migrants who'd just crossed the desert and hobbled into the detention center on crutches; staff regularly treated their broken ankles and their dollar-sized blisters. The ICE Health Service Corps ran the operation, staffing the place with a doctor, a nurse-practitioner, certified nursing assistants, a dentist, and mental health specialists.

"We make diagnoses of diseases people don't know they have," Shane said proudly. "Diabetes. HIV. High blood pressure." For some third world villagers, he added, "it's the first time they've seen a doctor."

Shane was proud of the library too; located near the chapel, the book-lined room was a pleasant space. Two lively young women, both detainees, were working the desk. One of them smiled at me and said, "Tell everyone we need more books." The wares on their shelves were battered paperbacks in Spanish, in English, in Korean, in Russian, most of them romances and thrillers, from what I could tell by their colorful covers.

"They can check out one book at a time, two on weekends," Shane said. If they want, "they can request extra time in the library."

One book on the shelves was *Desperado*, a Stephen King novel translated into Spanish. Called *Desperation* in English, the 1996 novel seemed an eerily apt choice for Eloy readers. As King's website explains, Desperation is both a place and a state of mind: "Located off a desolate stretch of Interstate 50, Desperation, Nevada, has few connections with the rest of the world."

At the far end of the library, a female detainee was working on one of the eight desktops. The computers were preloaded with LexisNexis software so the prisoners could do legal research, and a word processing program allowed them to type up their findings. Thick tomes on immigration law stood nearby, and the copy machine was gratis. But the computers were not linked to the Internet—meaning no emails to family or friends. They gave detainees no more connection to the outside than they'd get in Desperation, Nevada.

From the cool of the library, we headed out into the blazing July sun—and the 109-degree heat—to survey the lay of the Eloy land. A dozen separate buildings were connected by walkways. Half of the structures were cell blocks housing the massive prison population of 1,550; there were beds for 494 women and 1,056 men. Each of the six residential buildings was divided into five single-sex pods, each housing around 50 women or men.

We went into a pod in the now-infamous Bravo building, where Elsa had died. Its large common room rose up two stories, accommodating two tiers of cells. We climbed up the metal stairs to the second floor to inspect a typical cell. It was equipped with a bunk bed for two, a sink, and a toilet; the women who lived here had lined up their toiletries in a row, adding a tiny personal touch to the institutional space. The showers were downstairs and curtained for privacy, but the toilet stood in full view in the middle of the cell, with no partition or even a drape for privacy. Prisoners were forced to perform their most intimate bodily functions in view of their bunkie.

The cell windows were painted black. Only a narrow strip of clear glass was left unpainted at the top to let in a ray or two of light. The windows had been clear once. According to Shane, "The women were exposing themselves to the men walking by." Eloy's solution was to punish all the women by blackening every window in all the women's pods; the men's cells were not similarly blighted. Darkened by black paint by day, the cells remained lit at night by dimmed electric lights. The brightness allowed guards to check on inmates at night, but it made sleep difficult.

Downstairs, small clusters of women were sitting around long tables, on uncomfortable-looking backless stools. A puzzle they'd been working on, picturing the snowcapped Rocky Mountains, lay abandoned, only half-finished. Several women were in headphones watching one of the two TVs; one played Spanish programs, the other English. A few were alone in their cells, catching a private moment to doze or read.

The Bravo dorm had an oddly empowering name—it

came from the military phonetic alphabet, Alfa, Bravo, Charlie, but in Spanish it means either "strong" or "angry." The Bravo women looked neither that morning. It was only nine thirty and already they were listless. They were facing a long day of little to do but worry, about their kids, about their immigration cases, about the future. Without the classes or training programs that state and federal prisons offer long-timers, Eloy inmates struggled to fill the day. Later some women would exercise to a Zumba video, and others would immerse themselves in the calming old prison craft of paper weaving. Women at Eloy spent hours working on their *papelitos*, cutting up paper into strips and fashioning them into tiny paper baskets or birds. Yet the days were long.

"Occasionally we show movies with popcorn," Shane said. "We try to have extra activities." He paused. "A busy detainee is a happy detainee."

The forbidding architecture of Eloy had one plus. The separate buildings were scattered across the property, and inmates had to walk outside regularly, to get to the library, the chapel, the visiting room, the infirmary. Many of them had prison jobs and left the pod to wash floors, do laundry, or prepare food. Some detainees took the jobs to get out of the cell or, like Yolanda, worked to impress the authorities with their diligence. Yet critics pointed out that low-paying detention jobs exploited inmates and bolstered CCA's already high profits. A *New York Times* investigation found that sixty thousand immigrant detainees a year work for as little as a dollar a day, saving the prison corporations the cost of the federal minimum wage of $7.25.[9]

All the detainees, employed or not, were marched over to the freestanding chow hall three times a day. It wasn't much of a destination. The gloomy room looked like it had been lifted from an *Orange Is the New Black* episode. The backless metal stools and table were welded together and bolted to the floor, evidently to ward off any detainee attempts to hurl the chairs skyward. Trays of food were delivered anonymously by fellow inmates through a narrow slot in the wall. Notwithstanding the complaints of every detainee I talked to (one woman described wet lettuce that tasted like chlorine), Shane boasted of the cuisine. One Eloy staffer, he said, was charged with eating it three times a week. And that taster was a stickler who wouldn't let deficient meals pass muster. But the posted menu shored up detainees' criticisms that the food was heavy on starches and light on fresh vegetables and fruit. The lunch the day I was there was to be the classic cafeteria combo of Salisbury steak, mashed potatoes, gravy, peas, bread, margarine, and pudding. And for dinner: turkey creole, steamed rice, cooked cabbage, and bread with margarine.

The freest part of the detainee day was the hour of outdoor recreation in *la yarda*, a dusty field to the north of the complex. Out there the prison walls vanished, and detainees could take in the wide-open spaces of the West. To the southeast, there was a distant view of the Picacho Mountains, and above, the changing drama of the Arizona sky. The men shot hoops or played soccer, while the women typically socialized or prayed together under the shade structure. Yet the summer's heat and winter's cold often kept them indoors. And if they couldn't go to *la yarda*, they got locked up again in their cells.

After the suicides of Elsa and Jorge, a few things changed around Eloy. Now no inmate, sick or not, was allowed to stay behind in a cell, alone, when the whole pod was herded someplace else. And authorities swooped in and confiscated everyone's shoes. Until then, the detainees could wear their own lace-up sneakers or boots. Now they were issued flimsy new canvas slip-ons in screaming orange and turquoise. There were to be no more suicides by shoelace.

On the plus side, the warden allowed activists from Casa

Mariposa in Tucson to come up during the week, outside regular visiting hours, to give comfort to the lonely and stressed. The inmates noticed something else too: the guards toned down their yelling. The verbal abuse had been so bad before that Mariana had complained to the "detention counselor" assigned to monitor her case.

"The officers were rude to the girls," Mariana told me after she was released from Eloy. "Most of the officers didn't speak Spanish." They'd get frustrated when detainees couldn't understand orders in English. In an escalating loop, a guard would scream at a detainee, fail to be understood, get mad, and then just scream louder.

Now the whole place was under investigation by higher-ups from ICE. And the Bishop—the nickname given to the Bravo supervising officer—had admonished the guards to knock off the bad behavior. In her remaining few weeks at Eloy, Mariana noticed them easing up. "I did see them start changing their attitude," she said.

The kinder, gentler Eloy didn't last long.

Three months after the deaths, the day of my tour, a long-time detainee named Diana Margarita Ramos told me that some of the worst guards were still verbally abusing their charges. She was a fifty-year-old woman from El Salvador who'd been locked up for two years and five months. A campesina from the Salvadoran countryside who crossed the border with two young daughters in 2003, she'd made a big-city life for herself in Phoenix. She'd worked for years *sin papeles*—without papers—as a fast-food cook, at Sonic Drive-In and elsewhere. Then she'd created a job where she was her own boss. She'd become a *taxista*, ferrying fellow immigrants around Phoenix in her own car for a fee.

Then one night in January 2011, "*la migra* came to Mesa." She was arrested at her usual pickup point, a gas station, and slapped with a felony charge of smuggling "illegal aliens." Her public defender pled it down to the misdemeanor of "eluding inspection by immigration officials," and Diana was ordered deported. She'd filed for asylum on the grounds of domestic abuse by her partner—he beat her and the kids—and pervasive violence in El Salvador. She'd been in Eloy ever since.

In the long lonely years that she'd been confined, she'd had plenty of time to observe conditions at Eloy. She was a devout Christian, and when I interviewed her in a private conference room—with two armed guards posted outside the closed door—at first she spoke only politely of the staff.

"There are good people here," she declared. "There are always good people and bad people." Like Mariana, she'd noticed a few changes after the suicides. "The guards are not as aggressive," she said.

As she warmed to her subject, she acknowledged that the worst of them still screamed. "Some are racist," she said, and continued to get angry with inmates who didn't understand English. And out of spite, guards meted out *castigos* that cast inmates in a bad light and could even harm their legal cases.

"When we get in trouble they tell us, 'We're going to put you in the hole.'" The so-called troublemakers could be locked up in *el hoyo* for three to five days.

She hadn't known the woman who'd committed suicide—Elsa had been in Bravo 200 and Diana was in 300—and she was sorry about her gruesome death. She was unhappy about the policy mandating the flimsy new shoes, though: they gave no support to her fifty-year-old feet.

"I don't like the shoes," she said. "They're not comfortable."

And, she said, smiling at her own complaint, she didn't like the colors. The shoes came only in two shades, and it was the blinding orange that fit her.

Except for the aches they gave her feet, the radioactive-looking shoes were a minor irritant. Contrary to ICE's assertions, the medical care was poor, she said. Staff dismissed detainees' complaints routinely, suggesting drinking water as a cure-all panacea for whatever ailed them. "If something hurts, they tell us to drink water," she scoffed.

Diana's eyes were sore and red the day I met her, and they'd been that way for ages. "For two months I made requests" for an appointment, she said. "After two months, I saw a doctor and got antibiotics." She took the meds, but the pain and redness did not recede. All evidence aside, the medical staff insisted she was fine. Case closed; no further treatment would be forthcoming.

She also took exception to Shane's praise for the fine food, which she'd now eaten day in and day out for—by my count—867 days. "La comida es fea," she declared. *The food is ugly.* "Every two weeks we get chicken. But it's old and bad. There's almost no salad, fruit, or fresh vegetables. Once in a while we do get oranges." As a Christian, she didn't believe in wasting food. But she couldn't help it.

"Father, forgive me," she said, invoking the Lord. "I don't eat it. I don't want to."

The worst part of detention by far, worse than the yelling and the threats and the bad food, was the separation from her family. The little daughters who'd crossed the Arizona desert with her years ago were now young women, nineteen and twenty-one years old. They lived in Phoenix, but they were undocumented; for a long time they couldn't visit their mother. "For twenty-five months I didn't see them," Diana lamented in Spanish. *Hace veinticinco meses que no las vi.*

In the happiest change of Diana's dreary stay, her daughters just months before had won permission to stay at least temporarily in the United States. Under Deferred Action for Childhood Arrivals (DACA), an Obama program begun in 2012, young immigrants who'd been brought in as children were given the right to live and work in the United States for two years; the waivers were renewable. Now the girls could visit; Arizona law didn't permit DACA recipients to drive, but a minister from church took them to see their mom every Sunday. Grown as they were, they still needed her, Diana said. She had no intention of accepting deportation and leaving them in Phoenix, or taking them with her back to dangerous El Salvador. For them she stayed in Eloy.

"Sometimes I have bad thoughts," she said, her sore eyes filling with tears. "I've been here two and a half years. I don't know when I'll get out. My task is to wait and hope. With the favor of God, it's going to turn out well."

A year later, Diana was still asking God for help. In October 2014, more than three and a half years after she was first incarcerated, she was still in Eloy.

By the time María Antonia Díaz Rodriguez arrived in Eloy, five months after the deaths of Elsa and Jorge, the slight reforms that Mariana and Diana had noticed had vanished. By then, in her telling, the detention center was rife with abuses of all kinds.

María was sixty-one years old, and in her six and a half weeks behind bars, she suffered terribly from the constant screaming of the guards, the inedible food, the poor medical care, the lockups in her small cell, and the bitter cold of the air conditioning.

"This was psychological abuse," she said, months after she got out. "I told my lawyer, get me out of here."

Critics make the case that poor conditions are deliberately imposed for this exact purpose: to persuade detainees to drop their appeals and choose deportation over continued incarceration. María did just that.

I'd first met her in April 2013 at a migrant shelter in Nogales, Sonora. She and her daughter, Adriana, had lived undocumented in Phoenix for twenty years, and after a failed return to María's hometown of Mexico City, they were trying to figure out how to get back to the United States. I didn't see María again until after her Eloy nightmare. It was February 2014 and she was back in Nogales. She poured out her anguished story to me in her bedroom in a community center where she'd been living ever since her deportation in November 2013. María had presented herself at the port of entry in Nogales in September 2013. She'd slipped across the border without papers years ago; this time, she said, "I wanted to enter legally and ask for permission."

Adriana was already back in Phoenix. She'd departed two months earlier, crossing *al Norte* with a group of Dreamers—young immigrants who'd been raised in America—in a highly publicized event. After a short stay in Eloy, a judge had accepted Adriana's claim of credible fear if she were returned to Mexico and released her to her older brother in Phoenix to await immigration hearings.

María didn't fare as well. From the minute she stepped up to the US Customs and Border Protection officers and asked for asylum, she said, she was treated like a criminal. For the ride up the highway to Eloy, she was handcuffed and shackled. And the detention center felt like a criminal prison in every way. The AC was cranked up to frigid, and by day she was forbidden to wrap herself up in the lone blanket she'd been issued. *Las vigilantes*—the name she gave the guards—claimed the low temperatures had a medicinal value. They told her, "The cold is to kill viruses."

The food was virtually inedible. Fed breakfasts of watery oatmeal and lunches that tasted like dog food, "I was hungry all the time," she said. "I lost weight." Going outside to *la yarda* each day was nice, she said, with a slight smile, but it only made her want to escape into the wide-open country around it. Otherwise there was little to do. It cost money to watch the TVs in the day room; María paid twenty-five dollars for the necessary headphones. And by the time she got to Eloy, the women could no longer while away the time by making *papelitos*, the tiny paper sculptures. The reason given: too many women were turning important legal papers into art.

María couldn't tolerate the guards' constant screaming. As Mariana and Diana had found, the guards treated all the detainees badly, but "the people who spoke only Spanish were treated worse." Sometimes the guards would jeer at the inmates in English, not knowing that some could understand. "They would say, 'What are you doing here? You should go back to your own country,' insinuating that you weren't worth anything."

Women would be punished for the slightest of infractions—"if they didn't get up right away when they were told"—and once she witnessed a woman "thrown in the hole for defending her friends." The officers "took revenge against her." One, and only one, guard was compassionate toward the prisoners.

Worst of all was the claustrophobia. María was incarcerated in a tiny single cell, without a roommate, and her room was even smaller than the norm. Like the other detainees, she was locked in for an hour at a time periodically throughout the day and at 9:00 p.m. "enclosed for the whole night." Four days in, behind her closed and locked door, María was convulsed with her first-ever panic attack.

"I was alone in the small room," she said, shaking at the memory. "There was only a little ray of light. I started having fright spasms from being closed in, and I began shouting and trembling. The guards noticed and took me for medical help."

The docs gave her an antianxiety med, but it didn't take away her fear. She couldn't sleep. She begged *las vigilantes* to leave her door ajar at night, but they refused. And the meds quickly triggered a serious case of hives. "I really swelled up," she said, with a rash that looked like mosquito bites all over her body.

She returned to the clinic more than once, until a doctor

told her, "I can't do anything for you," and ordered her back to the pod. To their credit, the pod guards could see that María was in bad shape, and they took her back to the clinic. This time a nurse threatened to throw her in *el hoyo* if she bothered the medical staff again.

"The nurse told me I'd be locked in a room that was dark and had padded walls."

The supervising guard called a psychologist, who gave María a new prescription. This drug got the rash down but didn't do much for the anxiety. She began pacing the perimeter of her cell in the darkest hours of the night and walked frantically around the common room by day.

By this time, María was desperate to flee. She accepted deportation, and she was once again shackled hand and foot for the ride down the road to Nogales. Detainees are given a clear plastic bag to carry all their worldly goods, and an ICE officer noticed contraband inside María's. It was a tiny paper swan that María had contrived to make—against the rules—and smuggled into her bag. The ICE guy pulled the swan out and crushed it under his boot.

Months later, back in Mexico, María was still wounded by her Eloy sojourn. ICE and the CCA both benefit financially from the detention system, she said; CCA rakes in profits and ICE gets an ever-escalating line in the Homeland Security budget.

"They think of the undocumented as money," she said. "The undocumented are kept in prison so they can earn a lot of money. I think that's wrong.

"It's inhumane for them to do this. They don't know the suffering of the people in there."

CHAPTER THREE

Purgatorio Arpaio

I was saying, God, if something bad ever happens
to me, prepare me for that moment.

—Mariana Rodriguez, detainee in the
Maricopa County Jails

Mariana Rodriguez grabbed her backpack and hurried out
of Tempe High. It was 3:10 p.m. Classes were done for the
day, but she had a long night ahead. She was still a student,
a senior in high school, but she'd already worked for three
years nearly full-time at a Subway restaurant. A palm-tree-
lined town best known as home of the mammoth Arizona
State University, Tempe was just east of Phoenix, in Maricopa County, fiefdom of the infamous Sheriff Joe Arpaio.

The money Mariana earned slicing up Subway rolls and
piling them with tuna or ham was "for the house," for the
family, she told me later, much later, after she'd made a long
odyssey through Arpaio's prisons and the Eloy Detention
Center.

Ever since she could remember, her mother, "Lidia," had
worked hard, chopping food in restaurant kitchens, cleaning
houses. But three years earlier Lidia had begun to feel ill. She
was tired all the time and losing weight.

Fifteen-year-old Mariana took up the slack. Her father had abandoned the family when she was too little to remember him, and her two older sisters were already married and out of the house. It was up to Mariana, a high school freshman, to keep an eye on her younger brother and take care of the family's bills.

"I was working and going to school at the same time," she said, earning $500 to $550 every other week. "I was paying everything. The rent. As much as I could. I worked thirty-seven or thirty-eight hours a week."

Mariana and her family were devout Christians, and between school, work, family, and church, she had little time to herself. She'd go right home from school each day, drop off her books, and then rush out to work. At eighteen, Mariana was a Subway favorite. She could assemble sandwiches at lightning speed, and her sweet smile had won over boss and customers alike. The manager even had her train new employees.

Something was amiss, that February afternoon in 2012, when she walked into the restaurant. "Two people were sitting in a corner," she said. "They called, 'Shannon, come over here. We need you to sit down with us.'"

Mariana was alarmed. She was undocumented, and "Shannon" was the name on the fake Social Security card she had used to get the job. The man and woman at the table were in street clothes, but when Mariana approached, they flashed their badges: they were officers with the Arizona Department of Public Safety, the state agency that not only patrols the highways but tracks down high-level criminals. Drug dealers. Identity thieves. And forgerers.

"We know your name isn't what you say," one agent said. "We need to know everything about you. Your real name."

"I was scared," Mariana remembered. "I'd never had to deal with officers. My mom had always been scared of them, and I got that fear from her."

She told the agents the truth: her name was Mariana Rodriguez and she was eighteen years old—a legal adult. The man took in this information, pushed back his chair, and walked over to the counter, where freshly cut veggies gleamed behind glass. He told Mariana's boss, Wendy Wang, that she was going to need a new sandwich maker. "Shannon" was not her star employee's real name, and he was going to bring the young girl in for questioning.

Wendy was horrified. "She's the sweetest person," she protested. "She's a great worker, very reliable." In front of the customers, the female officer led a mortified Mariana out to the car, patted her down, and snapped handcuffs onto her tiny wrists. "She started asking me questions. How long had I been working? I said, 'Don't I need a lawyer?'" The agent put her off. "If you want," she said, according to Mariana, "but these are easy, basic questions." Not knowing her rights under the law, Mariana obediently told the woman everything she wanted to know. With no lawyer present, the officer recorded her answers.

The two agents drove Mariana to a station in downtown Phoenix, where she was fingerprinted and ushered into a cell. She begged to be allowed to call her mother. The answer was no. "The lady was a little rude. She said, 'You're eighteen. You don't have to call your mom.'"

Alone behind bars, Mariana began singing hymns in Spanish and praying out loud. "It made my faith grow bigger," she said. "I was saying, God, if something bad ever happens to me, prepare me for that moment."

When the female officer came back to get Mariana, she heard the girl's prayers, sung and spoken, and her manner softened. "We're going to let you go for now," she told her, more gently. Mariana would be getting a letter from the court with a date for her hearing. "You'd better go to court," the woman warned. If Mariana missed the hearing, she'd be in even bigger trouble.

By now it was dark. Going against protocol, the woman told Mariana she would drive her home. "I don't want you on a bus in the middle of Phoenix," she said solicitously. Her partner looked up, alarmed. "Cuff her," he snapped.

The woman ignored him. She spoke kindly to Mariana in the car, telling her that perhaps the arrest was "a blessing in disguise." Maybe it would lead to her getting papers to stay legally in the United States. Mariana thought she might be right. "I told her, maybe this is God's plan."

A year and a half later, Mariana sat back in her seat at a McDonald's in north Phoenix and smiled. It was a torrid July day, and McD's full-blast AC had reeled in families and boisterous kids, nearly all of them Spanish speakers in this heavily Mexican neighborhood. Nothing seemed to faze Mariana. Not the children kicking her chair, not the responsibilities that had taken over her teenage years, not the fact that she had spent the previous night on the floor of her mother's hospital room.

She had a slight frame and long, light-brown hair, and she was wearing a cool pair of horn-rimmed glasses. But the most striking thing about her was her heartbreaking sweetness, the sweetness that had won over her Subway customers and softened the tough DPS agent. The word "blessed" was spelled out in silver studs across her gray T-shirt, just above a quote from the Bible: "It is more blessed to give."

At the moment, she and her family were living in a dark apartment in a shabby complex on a frontage road, in the shadow of I-17. The Rodriguezes' circumstances had been badly reduced since the day Mariana had been arrested at Subway. Two branches of the extended family were jammed into one small apartment; when I came by to pick her up, her brother-in-law was babysitting a gaggle of toddlers in the crowded living room. Lidia was in the hospital—again—and everyone's anxiety was palpable.

It was high noon, lunchtime, and I had driven Mariana to McDonald's, down a boulevard shimmering in the 108-degree heat. At first, she politely declined to eat. Only after I insisted did she allow me to buy her a small sandwich. She was happy to tell me her story, she said, on one condition: she had to be home by four. There was late-afternoon dance ministry at her church, and there was no way she was going to miss anything at all at her beloved Iglesia Ciudad Sión Evangélica, the Evangelical Church of the City of Zion.

Mariana had always been a city girl. She was born in 1993 in the colonial city of Guanajuato, Mexico, four hours north of Mexico City. An amber-colored basilica dominates the hilly town, and the winding streets are so steep that some of them are more staircase than *calle*. In Spanish times, the nearby silver mines poured unimaginable wealth into the city. Nowadays it's a World Heritage Site, and tourists flock to see the elegant casas that silver built.

Not much of this wealth flows down from the hilltops to the working people. Mariana's mother, Lidia, grew up in the countryside, on a *ranchito* outside own. Her childhood was poor, and hard. Her own mother left the family when Lidia was twelve, and as the second oldest she took on the burden of caring for seven little brothers and sisters. She married at sixteen and left home, thinking, Mariana said, that life as a wife would be easier. But before too many years had passed, her husband abandoned her and their two little girls. She had two more children, Mariana and her little brother, but neither of their fathers stuck around either. Lidia tried to support her brood by cleaning houses in Guanajuato, but grand as its mansions were, she never earned enough. She finally decided to try her luck in the North, in Arizona.

In 1996, Lidia headed to the border with three-year-old Mariana, leaving the other three children with an aunt. "My sister always said I was her favorite child," Mariana said with a wan smile. Crossing was easier back then, when the border was not so strongly fortified. Smuggling fees now run into the thousands of dollars, but Lidia paid only a few hundred to a coyote to get them across. Mariana had no memory of the trip—or of Mexico—but she knew by heart the story her mother had told her. "We were running at night in the desert," she recounted. "We were really tired but some guys carried me on their back." Mariana had absorbed the lessons of the journey: the trek was hard, but the travelers helped each other.

Mother and daughter settled in Guadalupe, an impoverished town just south of Phoenix. It felt like home. Their neighbors were mostly Mexican and Indian; Yaqui Indians fleeing persecution in northern Mexico had founded the postage-stamp-size municipality in 1907. It even had a village plaza with a whitewashed mission-style church—Our Lady of Guadalupe, patroness of Mexico—where the Yaquis performed their traditional Easter ceremonies. When Sheriff Arpaio conducted a "crime sweep" of Guadalupe in 2008, complete with helicopter, deputies on horseback, and officers on the street stopping brown-skinned residents at will, the furious locals held up hand-lettered signs: "You're on Indian land. The only illegal here is Arpaio."[1]

In the 1990s, Arizona's fury over immigration had not yet erupted, and Guadalupe was peaceful and welcoming. After two years Lidia returned to Mexico to fetch her two older daughters, leaving Mariana with a friend. Months later she arranged to have her little boy brought *al Norte*. Reunited, the Rodriguezes settled into their new American life.

"All those years we had no trouble with Immigration," Mariana said. The family made no particular effort to live inconspicuously, and all four children went to the Tempe public schools. "We'd go out everywhere, parks, movies," Mariana said. "I didn't know I was illegal."

Lidia was undocumented, but she found jobs easily.

"She made up her Social Security number," her daughter said. "They didn't have E-Verify then." That changed in 2008, when Arizona began requiring employers to use E-Verify to vet job applicants. Under the system, bosses punch a prospective employee's personal information into a federal online site—and learn almost instantly whether the applicant is documented. Lidia never tried to get a green card; she was afraid even to make the attempt.

Mariana didn't learn the truth about her own status until her mother's illness sent her out into the workforce at fifteen. She knew only that she'd been born in Mexico. Now she found out that she and her mother had crossed over without papers, and that she didn't have the Social Security number that she needed to get a job.

An aunt who knew her way around the black market went out and bought her niece a fake Social Security card and birth certificate, she said. Mariana Rodriguez metamorphosed into Shannon Graf. The newly minted Shannon applied to a number of fast-food joints, and Subway bit. Before she could start working, Mariana was required by law to get an official food handler's card. She went down to the Maricopa County Department of Health, took the test, got her picture taken, and fatefully signed her official new ID with her new name.

On the February day that Mariana was hauled away from work in handcuffs, her mother had a feeling of dread. Normally she didn't bother her daughter at work, but that afternoon she was so anxious that she called Subway. A coworker of Mariana's told Lidia what little they knew: Mariana had been cuffed and taken away.

By the time Mariana arrived home in the dark, in the DPS car, "My mom was hysterical. I heard her crying. She came running to me. I felt so bad."

Mariana was safe for the time being, but the family was in bad straits. Without her Subway wages, they could no longer pay the rent. Mariana, her brother, and their mother moved in with one of Mariana's older sisters, to an apartment in the same complex. The sister and her husband were crammed into a one-bedroom with their two small children, but they opened their door to their displaced *familia*.

"We were all in there," Mariana said. "My brother slept on the couch. Me and my mom were in a bed in the living room. My sister and her husband and the kids were in the bedroom."

The DPS officers had given her strict instructions to report any change of address, and Mariana dutifully called them to let them know she'd moved. Then she set about supporting her family. Still going to Tempe High each day, Mariana picked up work cleaning houses after school. The pay was $60 a house, nowhere near what she'd been making at Subway. With only three clients, she was bringing home about $480 a month, less than half of the amount of her old paycheck. The family pooled resources: her sister cleaned houses too, and her brother-in-law worked construction. Despite her tough workload, Mariana graduated from high school right on schedule in May 2012. She was dreaming of becoming a dental assistant or a minister or even a police officer. For now she was dusting and mopping. One late afternoon in early September, when she was out scrubbing a client's kitchen, two detectives showed up at her apartment complex. They called on the manager, Jim Stapleton, showed him Mariana's picture, and demanded to know if he knew her. Jim was a friend of the family, a fellow Christian, but he had little choice but to cooperate. He sent them to her sister's apartment. Mariana's brother-in-law was at home, and the detectives told him to have Mariana call them right away. It was urgent.

The brother-in-law telephoned Mariana in a panic. "Call them quick," he said. "It's really important."

"I was scared," she told me. It was after hours, and no one answered when she dialed the number. "The next morning I called them again and they said, 'You're in trouble. You haven't responded to the court.'" An important letter setting her hearing date had apparently been sent to her old address, and Mariana never got it. She told the detectives that she had reported her new address, but all that mattered to them was that she had failed to respond. Half an hour later, they turned up at the apartment with a warrant for her arrest.

"I threw stuff in my bag, my Bible. But they wouldn't let me take it. They cuffed me and took me to the Fourth Avenue Jail" in Phoenix. In her rush, she forgot her eyeglasses.

At the jail, three ICE officers grilled her: "What are the last four digits of your Social Security number?" "Where are you from?" "How old were you when you were brought to the United States?"

One ICE officer taunted her, "You think you're going to get legal? You're never gonna get legal."

Even then, "I wasn't scared," Mariana told me. "I kept up my trust in God." She began singing Spanish hymns, and a guard scolded, "You shouldn't be singing or happy." Mariana replied that "God is going to help me." But the guard was right: there wasn't much to celebrate.

Mariana was being charged with two Class 4 felonies: forgery and taking the identity of another person. If even one of the felonies stuck, she would be a surefire candidate for deportation. And since ID theft is rated a "crime involving moral turpitude," she'd be looking at mandatory detention until her immigration case was resolved. If somehow she escaped deportation, a felony conviction would prevent her from taking advantage of Deferred Action. Only young immigrants with clean criminal records were eligible for DACA, which gave certain undocumented young people a waiver to stay in the country. (Unhappily for Mariana, she was arrested just months before Obama initiated DACA in June 2012.)

At a brief hearing, a judge ordered Mariana to be held in jail until her next court date. In Arizona, criminal defendants who are suspected of being undocumented can't be let out on bail, no matter how minor the charges. This time there was to be no respite, no quick return to the arms of her mother. This time eighteen-year-old Mariana Rodriguez—faithful Christian, high school graduate, family wage earner—would be imprisoned for months in the Maricopa County prisons, run by the man who proudly calls himself America's Toughest Sheriff.

Before Sheriff Joe Arpaio started his all-out war on undocumented immigrants in the early 2000s, he'd already weathered any number of controversies, most notably over jailing prisoners in his outdoor Tent City. Cynics charge that he settled on illegal immigration as a hot issue that would divert attention from his other scandals. In the years since he embarked on his campaign, he'd staged multiple sensational raids on Hispanic neighborhoods. Like the Guadalupe sweep in 2008, they typically included helicopters, horse-mounted deputies, many boots on the ground—and plenty of TV cameras. Born in 1932, he was eighty years old the year Mariana landed in his jails, and he remained a popular political figure. His get-tough immigration policies had won him election after election.

In December 2011, a few months before Mariana was arrested, the US Department of Justice issued a damning report concluding that Arpaio and company practiced "unconstitutional policing," engaging in racial profiling, targeting, and discrimination. In response, then-secretary of Homeland Security Janet Napolitano terminated the federal government's 287(g) agreement with the Maricopa County Sheriff's Office. A provision of the harsh 1996 IIRIRA law, 287(g) is a controversial program that pays ICE-trained local cops and deputies to do immigration work in the course of their regular police duties. Like Arizona's SB 1070, it allows officers to question people about their status during regular police stops. But the finding that Arpaio's troops were doing racial profiling—partly on the feds' dime—was an embarrassment. Napolitano moved swiftly to expel Arpaio from the program.

Around the time of Mariana's high school graduation, in May 2012, the US Department of Justice followed up with a formal lawsuit against Arpaio, making the same claims and pointing out that Spanish speakers in particular were mistreated in his jails. An ACLU class action suit, *Melendres v. Arpaio*, brought on behalf of Latino drivers and passengers who said they had been racially profiled and unlawfully detained, wound its way through the courts for years. While Mariana was still in Eloy, in May 2013, a judge ruled that Arpaio and the Maricopa County Sheriff's Office had violated the Fourth and Fourteenth Amendments. That fall, Judge G. Murray Snow followed up with specific orders for reform, and Arpaio appealed.[2]

In still another lawsuit, this one most relevant to Mariana's immediate future as an inmate in Maricopa County jails, the US Court of Appeals for the Ninth Circuit in October 2010 slammed the sheriff's practice of giving pretrial detainees too little to eat, and providing food that was "overripe, moldy and generally inedible." The appeals court also upheld a lower court's finding that Maricopa County jammed way too many prisoners together in overcrowded holding cells. The court found that both practices constituted cruel and unusual punishment, forbidden by the Eighth Amendment.[3]

Nearly two years later, when Mariana entered the Maricopa labyrinth, she found these same punishments were alive and well and still being meted out to prisoners.

On her first day in an Arpaio jail, in the short-term holding pen at Fourth Avenue Jail, Mariana was locked up with twenty other women, most of them older than she was and a lot tougher. None of them had been convicted: they were being held for trial, innocent until proven guilty, but no one would guess that by the treatment they got. Mariana was in the packed cell from ten in the morning until eleven that night, and the only food she and the others got all day was a small bag of peanut butter—an Arpaio specialty—and bread and juice, delivered at 6:00 p.m. There was a single toilet, in a bathroom that had no door. The walls and floor were concrete, and the only furnishing was a concrete bench that was part and parcel of the wall. The bench wasn't big enough for all the women, and many of them spent the day shivering on the cold floor, chilled by AC in overdrive.

"It was really, really cold," remembered Mariana, who was dressed that day for the Arizona summer heat, in a light dress, leggings, and sandals.

Mariana and sixteen of the others eventually were chained hand and foot, marched into a bus, and driven to Estrella, the jail that would be their long-term home. Its name—the lovely Spanish word for "star"—was no match for its harsh conditions. Estrella sat on a vast tract of land in southwest Phoenix, along with three other Maricopa County prisons. One of them was the notorious Tent City, where Arpaio housed up to 2,126 inmates in outdoor tents, in the cold of the winter and in the heat of the Phoenix summer. Estrella held a thousand inmates, most of them women, divided up into dormitory-style pods, ruled by a cadre of tough guards.

Their first order: strip. The women were taken in groups of four to a separate room and ordered to "take off everything," underwear included. "It was something so embarrassing to me," Mariana said. "I don't even change in front of my mom. It was four girls all naked." But it got worse. The guard barked, "Turn around. Bend over and open up your cheeks and cough."

Mariana winced at the recollection. "It was so bad for me, humiliating."

The women next donned the striped prison garb worn by all Arpaio prisoners. Designed for maximum mortification, the black-and-white-striped tops and pants look like old-fashioned jailhouse wear. (Male prisoners, famously, are given pink boxer shorts.) Maricopa County even distributes postcards of prisoners in these uniforms to the inmates to send to their families. "They give out five postcards a week to write to your family if you don't have money on your account" to buy stationery, Mariana said. That postcard ensured that the mail carrier and neighbors would know that a family's loved one was in jail.

The women were assigned to beds segregated by the seriousness of their criminal charges. The prisoners in "minimum" were accused of nonviolent offenses; "medium" was for violent crime; and "maximum was if you killed somebody," Mariana said. "I stayed with the minimum girls."

Mariana's K dorm was a single large room, lined with sixty double bunk beds. Eighty-seven women were packed into the place, watched over by guards who sat in a space that was more wire cage than office. The toilets were in a separate room but had no doors—and no privacy—and the showers blasted out water that was unbearably hot. The prison issued soap, "bad toothpaste," and menstrual pads. Tampons were forbidden, and if women were caught fashioning them out of toilet paper "they'd get in trouble," Mariana said. Anyone who wanted shampoo had to pay for it in the prison canteen, which also sold more-palatable toothpaste, conditioner, and deodorant. Twice every day the women were required to clean up their quarters: mop, sweep, clean the bathroom, showers, and wipe down the sinks.

The Estrella food was both skimpy and bad, and Mariana was hungry all the time. Breakfast was at eight: two pieces of hard bread, a bag of peanut butter, and two small milks. There was no lunch. Dinner was colorless "slop," Mariana said, "maybe soy meat stew with something else hard. Maybe there'd be one stalk of broccoli, rice or beans, or mashed potatoes. But no salt or flavor." One day a reporter turned up at the jail. He tried to eat the evening meal, Mariana said, but couldn't. He declared it the "nastiest" thing he'd ever tried.

Sometimes family or church friends would put money into Mariana's account so she could buy chips or tuna at the canteen. When she was flush, she'd save the hard bread from breakfast and feast on a tuna-fish sandwich for lunch.

Though Maricopa County asserts on its website that Estrella has "outside areas for recreation," the "rec yard" adjacent to K dorm wasn't a yard at all. It was a small, walled, windowless room with no ceiling or roof; wires were strung across the top to prevent escape. The prisoners were allowed there briefly at 7:00 a.m. each day. They could look up through the wires, Mariana said, and "sometimes see the sky."

At first, Mariana was too scared to talk to any of her fellow prisoners. She was the youngest, and she kept to herself in the back of the room, in top bunk number 104. Eventually she ventured to speak to some of the other Latinas; plenty of them, she learned, had also been jailed—and charged with a felony—for using a fake name to work.

Her bunkmate below couldn't stop crying, and Mariana tried to calm her. "As a Christian, I'd ask, 'Are you OK?' I don't like people to be sad. I'd ask, 'Do you want me to pray for you?' She'd say, 'Yeah.' I held her hand and prayed."

One night, lying in bed, Mariana closed her eyes and "saw girls standing in a circle and praying, holding hands. I didn't know if it was a dream." Dream or not, the prayer group soon turned into reality. When she saw a circle of real-life women standing together another night, Mariana joined them. Holding hands, together they walked into the little TV room, turned off the noise, and prayed.

From then on, Mariana was part of the prayer circle; eventually she led two groups every night, praying with women in English and in Spanish. Even the toughest women started softening around Mariana. A prisoner who looked like a gangbanger—all tattoos and attitude—began to pray with the others, and from time to time she let a smile creep across her hard face.

"They called her Loca. She had problems with everyone else. Others would say to me, 'Be careful, she could hit you.' But she'd say to me, 'I can't cuss in front of you. You're a little angel.' I'd talk to the troublemakers, try to calm them down."

In one of the few breaks to the oppressive monotony of the Estrella days, clergy came to minister on Tuesdays, a spiritual respite Mariana looked forward to. But for all the comfort religion brought her, the prison was a hellhole. The guards were forever shouting. "They yelled and screamed every day," Mariana said. Even a command as simple as "Move down the hallway" was delivered at high volume and wrapped in anger.

They leveled punishments for the slightest of infractions. One time, all the prisoners had been ordered to stay in their beds. Mariana sneaked out from under the covers to go to the bathroom, and made the mistake of flushing the toilet. "It was really loud. The officer yelled, 'All of you! You're going to be on lockdown all day.'" Mariana was horrified that she had triggered the punishment of all eighty-seven women.

The guards routinely checked the beds for contraband, and on one occasion they told all the women to put their property on their bunks. When some prisoners yelled in protest, the whole dorm was put on lockdown. "We had to stay in bed, no talking, no showers, for three days," Mariana said. "Everybody got punished."

Some prisoners were addicts going through a tortured withdrawal from heroin and meth. "They were kicking, vomiting, shaking," Mariana said. "I'd never seen anything like that." Even then, the guards were cruel. Mariana saw one young addict lying in her bed, looking "like a zombie. The officer was screaming, 'You have to get up. You think I feel bad for you? This is what you wanted. You took that stupid decision to take drugs.'"

Worse than all of it—the confinement indoors, the lousy food, the verbal abuse, the lack of privacy—was the painful separation from her mother and siblings. "I was missing my family," she said. They couldn't visit, because they were undocumented themselves, and phone calls were expensive: three dollars for just fifteen minutes.

Mariana got only hints of the difficulties at home. She found out later that her mother had become hysterical when she learned that her daughter had been taken once again. And a month after that terrible day of Mariana's arrest— around the time that she marked her nineteenth birthday, in jail—Lidia's chronic illness suddenly turned critical. The pain in her back grew so intense that the family rushed her to the hospital. The doctors first suspected bone cancer, but the final diagnosis was equally grim: leukemia. Mariana knew something was wrong, but no one told her that her mother had a life-threatening cancer of the blood. On the phone from the hospital, Lidia would tell her, "It's nothing bad."

With so little to go on, Mariana worried. "I told God, 'Lord, you keep it under control.'"

The Maricopa County prosecutor was refusing to budge on Mariana's legal case; he wouldn't hear of a plea deal that would reduce her felony charges to misdemeanors. Not long after Mariana's court hearing, Stephen Lemons of the *Phoenix New Times* broke the news that ICE attorneys regularly train Maricopa County prosecutors, teaching them the best strategies to make a felony stick to immigrant defendants—and ease the way for deportation. As a result, Maricopa's prosecutors were less likely than others to negotiate.[4]

Mariana was entitled to a public defender for her criminal charge—not for her immigration violation—but the first lawyer she was assigned just threw up his hands and told her to plead guilty to both felonies. She knew what to do.

"I prayed for a better public defender," Mariana said.

Sure enough she got a new one, Christopher E. Manberg. "He tried for me, but he said my case was the hardest he'd ever done. He told the judge how unfair the justice system was to me."

Chris labored mightily on the case; he argued that her statements to the state police officers the day of her initial arrest should be considered involuntary, given her youth and lack of familiarity with the law. And he emphasized that the only reason she used a fake ID was to support her family after her mother fell ill. At a very young age, she had managed to carry the whole household while still going to school.

The attorney collected a sheaf of character testimonials—from everyone from Mariana's Subway boss and a higher-up Subway exec to her minister, her apartment manager, and a fellow inmate at Estrella. The Subway division manager, Jesse Vasquez, wrote that Mariana was one of the top five employees among the hundred he supervised. "Our customers loved to see her," he said; she "always greeted them with a smile."

Wendy Wang, Mariana's immediate boss, called her exceptional, a hard worker who was always reliable. Wendy had planned to promote her to assistant manager, she wrote. "If I could, I would rehire her."

In a note, the fellow prisoner said that Mariana "has been

such an inspiration to each and every one of us in Estrella Jail. Her smile and constant reassurance has helped all of us.'... Her nightly prayer circle keeps us all hopeful."

The prosecutor was unmoved both by evidence of Mariana's character and the suggestion that her actions were undeserving of a felony conviction. The most he would do was drop the felony forgery charge leveled against Mariana for signing the food handler's card and downgrade her impersonation of Shannon Graf to a Felony 6—six was the lowest level of felony but a felony nonetheless.

Chris told Mariana that if she pled not guilty and tried to fight her case, she'd have to stay in Arpaio's purgatory another year awaiting trial. Mariana was trapped. She knew she couldn't stand a whole year of the screaming guards, the revolting food, the confinement indoors, the crying women, a year of not seeing her mom.

"The place was really bad," she said. So she gave up and pled guilty to the felony.

Four days before Christmas, the day of her sentencing, her lawyer excitedly told her, "There are thirty-five people out there!" Mariana walked into the courtroom and saw for herself. "My whole church came," she exclaimed later, beaming at the memory. Her family was there too. It was the first time she had seen them since September. A bailiff caught her looking over at them and reprimanded her.

"If you smile at them," he warned, "I'll tell them to leave."

For her grievous crime of moral turpitude, pretending to be Shannon Graf so she could work at Subway, Mariana was sentenced to time served. She'd been in prison three and a half months, one hundred and seven days, to be precise, already well over the ninety days normally meted out for a Felony 6.

"Chris told me, 'Game over. You signed the paper. You're going to get deported right away.' I was prepared in my mind."

She was brought to Lower Buckeye Jail to be released and transferred, then shuttled to the ICE office in Phoenix. But she was surprised by the kindness of the ICE officer who interviewed her.

"She was really nice. Not the usual. She really listened to me, to everything I said. She said, 'I think there's a chance for you.'"

On Christmas Eve, instead of gathering with her family to celebrate Navidad, Mariana was driven south to Eloy, sixty-five miles from her loved ones in Tempe. On the day before she'd celebrate the birth of Christ, she was imprisoned once again.

Eloy was not Estrella. She could go outside and breathe in the country air in the big rec field, and take in Arizona's pink-streaked winter sunsets. Instead of sleeping in a noisy room with nearly ninety women, she was in a double cell with one bunkie. And though the food was *fea*, as Diana Margarita Ramos so memorably said, at least there were three meals a day.

One thing was the same: Eloy's guards were as angry as Estrella's and they directed their rage particularly at Spanish-speaking detainees. Fluent in both English and Spanish, Mariana played peacemaker and soon found herself becoming a go-between between jailers and detainees. Before long, she organized a Bible-study group.

Because of her felony conviction, Mariana was housed in Level Two and issued khaki scrubs to brand her with her criminal status. But she played by the rules and after two months with no write-ups, she was downgraded to Level One and given a green uniform. Now, she said, "I was with the girls who had just crossed the border."

Mariana's bunkie, "Flora," a twenty-one-year-old Guatemalan, was one of the border crossers. Flora had made it as far as Phoenix before she was caught; she was charged not just with illegal entry but with felony "solicitation of human smuggling." This ingenious twist on the law was dreamed up by the Arizona legislature in 2005: border crossers were charged with conspiracy to smuggle, but it was themselves they were accused of smuggling. The inventive new tool converted many border crossers into full-fledged criminals. County prosecutors ignored it in much of the state, but Maricopa County embraced the novel interpretation, which helped increase the census of Latinos in its jails.[5]

Flora was one of many newly defined smugglers to be held in Arpaio's domain, but she'd fared even worse in his jails than Mariana had. She was held in "protective custody"—a nice name for solitary—and allowed out only an hour a day to shower and go "outside"—to the walled room open to the sky.

The young woman didn't understand anything about her rights, Mariana said, and her "public defender didn't help her."

Mariana's own legal case remained fraught. At her first hearing at Eloy on January 16, the judge was accommodating enough, asking if she had any family members who were citizens, or any children. He told her if she took voluntary departure she could escape the onus of a deportation on her record. But Mariana didn't want to go back to Mexico, a country she barely remembered. The judge ordered her removed—deported—and then explained that she had the right to appeal his decision.

Mariana worked on her appeal with the help of another detainee and sent it off to the Board of Immigration Appeals, in Virginia. A month later, she got a response: the board wanted an official legal brief. Other women in her pod told her about Charles Vernon, a lawyer with the Florence Immigrant and Refugee Rights Project. "They said he was really nice."

Eloy inmates could make free legal calls on the telephones in their unit, and Mariana contacted Charles. He came to see her, and looked over her case. He told her he would try to help her, but with that guilty plea to a felony on her record, he didn't think the case would go anywhere.

Charles began counseling Mariana on what to do if she got deported. He suggested returning to her birthplace of Guanajuato, or to the neighboring city of San Miguel de Allende. Both were picturesque tourist towns, filled with Americans, and with her excellent English and Spanish skills he thought she could get a job.

"I lived with this fear," she told me, her eyes filling with tears. "I would say to myself: I'll just give up. Just get deported."

Then Charles came to see her again. Something had changed, he told her. ICE was talking to the attorneys at the Florence Project. The lawyers had invited ICE to take another look at Mariana's case. If anyone ever qualified for leniency, Mariana did. She'd been brought to the United States as a toddler. When her mother fell ill, Mariana had supported her whole family, balancing high school classes in the day with sandwich making at night. She had no priors, not even any disciplinary infractions at school. And at this moment Mariana's mother was in the hospital once again, dangerously ill with leukemia.

"I started praying," Mariana said. "I knew God could do it. The next week, Charles told me, 'They decided to let you go!'"

ICE agreed only to close the case administratively, an action that left Mariana in legal limbo. She wouldn't be allowed to work, and ICE officials could reopen her case later if the spirit moved them. Still, the decision was enough to get her out of immediate deportation proceedings—and out of Eloy.

"I couldn't believe it," Mariana said. "I didn't tell my mom in case it didn't happen. I got my stuff all ready. I waited weeks to hear my name."

On May 23, almost five months to the day she arrived at Eloy, Mariana was in her room praying. "Then I heard my name called. 'Rodriguez!'"

A guard came and told her to collect her things.

"They took me inside a room at 5:00 p.m. There were other girls there getting released on bond asylum. Around eight o'clock ICE came and put us in a van and drove us to Greyhound in Phoenix. They put our stuff on the street. Then the ICE guy says, 'You can go now.'"

Simple as that.

Mariana borrowed a phone from a passenger in the waiting room and called the mother of a friend. The woman started crying and told her, "We'll be right there." The family rushed to pick Mariana up and drove her directly to the hospital. Lidia had no idea that her daughter was on her way. Earlier that day, she had truly believed that she was dying, she told Mariana later. But she held onto one thing.

"She said she had a dream—or a vision—of me moving into the room and smiling."

That night the vision was made flesh. Mariana tiptoed into Lidia's hospital room. Mariana hadn't seen her mother in nine months and the change in her appearance was hard to bear. Lidia was thin and bald, and she was hooked up to tubes and beeping machines. She lay back weakly against her pillows. She turned her head and caught sight of her daughter. Mariana walked slowly toward the bed, leaned down, gently lowered herself into her mother's arms and wept.

"Everybody cried," Mariana said. "She cried. I cried. She said she felt so much better after that. She's strong. I know she'll get well."

CHAPTER FOUR

A Tale of Two Towns

I see this as my home. I remember one or two years
of school in Mexico, but it's so long ago it's like a
dream. My memories start here.

—*Alma Hernandez Rodriguez,*
a Tucson mother sent to detention

In the little town of Florence, just two dozen miles from the
Eloy Detention Center, the Pinal County Historical Society
and Museum has everything you might expect in a small-
town Arizona collection: a table and chairs handcrafted from
saguaro cactus ribs; cowboy saddles and shirts; old Indian
artifacts. The prize piece is a bone incised by a Hohokam
Indian more than a thousand years ago.

In a far corner, past these dusty relics, is something unexpected and distinctly grisly: an exhibition on the executions
that the state has carried out at the nearby Arizona State
Prison. Twenty-three nooses—the ones that actually killed
the state's early criminals—are displayed on a wall, each one
coiled around a portrait of the person who hung from it by
the neck until dead. Even the old trapdoor the condemned
fell through is there. Then there's a double gas-chamber chair,
complete with straps to tie the prisoner down; it was first

used in 1934 to execute a pair of Mexican teens, Fred and Manuel Hernández, who'd been convicted of murder. The gas-chamber era was ushered in after the last hanging, in 1930, was flubbed. When Eva Dugan was strung up for the murder of her boss, the rope snapped so violently that she was decapitated, and her head rolled over to the feet of the horrified witnesses.

H. Christine Reid, a researcher and guide at the museum, stiffens when visitors head straight for the gruesome death display. "The prison came in 1908," she told me, "and there was a lot of history before that came along."

She was right. Florence was part of Mexico until 1854, and in the town's National Historic District old Mexican-style adobes from the 1860s and 1870s stand side by side with brick Victorians and bungalows. In the late nineteenth century, canals dug from the Gila River north of town watered the cotton fields, and the nearby Silver King Mine, one of the richest lodes in Arizona, brought prosperity. A couple of movies have been filmed here, and south of town, in a stretch of Sonoran Desert thick with saguaros and prickly pears, western-movie fans still come to pay tribute at the Tom Mix memorial. A black, iron riderless horse marks the spot on Highway 79 where the silent-movie cowboy star was killed in a single-car accident in 1940.

Yet there's no denying that Florence went in for prisons in a big way, early on. "Something always comes along to save Florence," Christine said, and after the mine went bust in 1900, the town clawed its way back up by winning the plum territorial prison. The old jail in Yuma was shut down and a new one built in Florence, beginning in 1908. Four years later, in 1912, when Arizona became a state, it was renamed the Arizona State Prison. The hangings began there in 1910, and executions continue at the prison. Instead of nooses and gas, lethal injections now do the killing. Florence won national notoriety in the summer of 2014 when the double murderer Joseph R. Wood III, shot up with a drug cocktail at the state prison, lay gasping for nearly two hours before he finally died.

Today, Florence is even more of a prison town than Eloy. No fewer than nine hulking penal institutions cluster along Highway 79 on the east side of town, their mammoth size and ungainly proportions making a stark contrast to the charming old houses in the historic district downtown. A guard standing lonely watch one dreary night outside an ICE-run detention center told me wearily, "There are more prisoners than free men in this town." It's true: Florence's prisoners outnumber its free residents, by a lot. The town officially counts eleven thousand people living in its houses and apartments, and sixteen thousand more behind bars.

There's a reason for this ratio. "The prison industry benefits Florence with jobs for its citizens even when times are difficult," Christine Reid and coauthors wrote in a history of the town.[1] On the one hundredth anniversary of the state prison, Tom Rankin, a former mayor, declared that even in a bad economy, "one of the last things that's going to shut down is your penal institutions. We're very stable in that way."[2]

Rankin and Reid weren't referring only to prisons that lock up murderers and thieves. Since the 1990s, Florence has also had an appetite for the economic benefits of immigration detention. Some fifteen hundred immigrant detainees are confined in four different prisons in Florence, doing their bit to help the feds meet the bed mandate, injecting money into the town, and providing jobs for the descendants of miners and ranchers and cowboys. The detention centers—one operated by ICE, two by the Corrections Corporation of America, and one by Pinal County (until 2014)—share the desolate prison highway with the state penitentiaries.

The four Florence detention centers, varying dramatically in their compliance with ICE standards and in their treatment of detainees and families, mirror the crazy quilt of detainee prisons around the country. The nation has more than 250 detainee prisons, operated variously by private for-profits, local governments, and ICE itself, making up what one writer called "a ramshackle network of private and public lockups, prone to abuses and lacking legally enforceable standards."[3] ICE owns and runs only a handful of these jails, leaving the rest to private for-profits and small county jails eager for extra cash, but it touts its own ICE-run Florence Service Processing Center (FSPC) as a model facility. In stark contrast to Eloy and Florence's other detention centers, ICE's FSPC has a family-friendly visiting policy that allows loved ones to visit seven days a week, between noon and 7:00 p.m. weekdays, and between 8:00 a.m. and 7:00 p.m. weekends and holidays. It has a library inside, and a soccer field and basketball court outside. Detainees say even the food is good. On an evening when I stopped by, two men—a Nigerian waiting for his asylum petition to go through and a Oaxacan fighting his deportation—cheerfully agreed that their Chinese dinner had been delicious. It's not home, but at least it's not Eloy.

The enterprising CCA, the same for-profit outfit that runs Eloy, owns and operates Florence's Central Arizona Detention Center (CADC) and the Florence Correctional Center (FCC). These two are run along Eloy's more punitive model, and they drastically limit visiting hours, even more than Eloy does. FCC allows family and friends to visit only on Fridays and Saturdays, during the limited hours of 8:00 a.m. to 9:00 a.m. and 11:00 a.m. to 2:30 p.m. CADC is even more restrictive: visitors are permitted only on Mondays and Wednesdays in the early morning, from 7:00 a.m. to 9:00 a.m., and they must sign in by 6:30 a.m. or they're turned away. The strict penal mentality is bolstered by the fact that both prisons double as lockups for criminal convicts, taking in state prisoners sent by California and Vermont. The FCC has one more lucrative sideline. It jails Operation Streamline convicts, the immigrants who daily flow out of the fast-track mass hearings in Tucson. Some sixty migrants each weekday plead guilty in federal court to the crime of reentry into the country; they leave with a jail sentence, with deportation to follow.

The fourth, and most feared, of the Florence detention centers was the Pinal County Jail. Like the two CCA operations, Pinal incarcerated both prisoners and detainees. The immigrants were held under such harsh conditions that Detention Watch named the place one of the ten worst detention centers in the country. It was at Pinal that I met a Brazilian detainee named Marco Antonio Galdino.

The first time I saw Marco, he was just a grainy image on a tiny video screen. He was somewhere inside the Pinal County Jail, and I was in a visitors' room, squinting at the screen, trying to make out his features. As best as I could tell, he was plump and round, in his late forties. I had to hold an old-fashioned phone receiver to my ear to hear his voice, but the phone was as clunky and out-of-date as the screen.

It was difficult to make out what he was saying, a problem compounded by his eccentric English, which was inflected by the Spanish he'd grown accustomed to in the United States and the Portuguese he grew up with. It didn't help that I was in a room that was noisy and hardly private; a woman a few chairs down sobbed as she spoke to her on-screen loved one. "Are you sure you're OK?" she asked through her tears. "Don't worry about the kids."

Marco was composed, or making an effort to be. "I try to keep busy every day," he told me. "There's nothing to do here, no activities. But I have books for reading." And he was writing. He'd been keeping a prison journal that over the years had added up to more than twenty-four hundred pages in twenty-two volumes. And he'd also been writing books, all unpublished. His third, now underway, was a "comic book about living in Salt Lake City," he said. He was bad at drawing the cartoons, but he was enjoying turning his previous life as an undocumented gay Mormon Brazilian in the Mormon capital into fiction. Tentative title: *My Days as a Sorcerer*.

Escaping into his book's humorous fantasy world helped take his mind off his circumstances. Marco had been in the Pinal County Jail for two years, and in immigration detention more than six, the longest time served of any detainee I'd ever met. It was December 15, 2011, Christmas was just ten days away, and he mournfully pointed out that "this will be my seventh Christmas in detention."

He had been jailed since October 1, 2005. He was picked up in Salt Lake City, where he'd been living freely for ten years, and eventually sent 723 miles away to Florence. It was a common-enough practice in the patchwork ICE system to ship detainees to faraway states, and Marco knew no one in the little Arizona town. Since he'd arrived, he'd been making the rounds through the town's gallery of detention centers, starting out at the best, the ICE-run Florence Services Processing Center, then cycling downward through the circles of detention hell. He'd been at one of the CCA prisons before descending to the worst that Florence had: the Pinal County Jail.

Pinal started out as a simple county jail, serving as a drunk lockup, a pretrial holding tank for criminal suspects ineligible for bail, and a jail for convicts serving short-term sentences. Like other jails for short-timers, it didn't have activities or programs, aside from some Bible-study classes and legal-orientation programs. Convicted criminals with longer sentences were incarcerated in one of the state prisons, where there was at least a pretense of rehabilitation: the state pen had training programs, classes, and outdoor exercise. Arizona even ran a prisoners' retail outlet store in town, where people on the outside could buy inmate-made metal and wood crafts fabricated in the prison shops.

Pinal had nothing like those workshops, and it didn't change its nothing-to-do protocol even after it went into the immigration-detention biz in 2005. The jail had opened in 1995, and the county leaders soon saw how much its CCA neighbors were profiting from the federal bed dollars. They decided to lasso in some of that detention money for Pinal as well. After that the jail had 1,540 beds, 915 for criminal convicts and suspects, and 625—well more than a third—contracted out to ICE for immigrants fighting deportation. Eventually the county supervisors started complaining that their profits were too low and demanded a higher per diem from ICE. But when the beds were full, Pinal raked in an estimated $36,000 a day from the feds, adding up to about $13 million a year.[4]

The immigrants at Pinal courtesy of ICE were supposed to be in civil, not criminal, detention, and not subjected to punishment. Yet they endured the same—and sometimes worse—conditions than the criminal suspects and convicts housed at Pinal. Plus, the immigrant detainees typically stayed longer than the others. And though ICE freely sent detainees there, Pinal County Jail was operating under long-out-of-date ICE standards, from way back in 2000.

In a November 2012 letter to President Obama, Detention Watch Network and more than two hundred other legal, religious, and social service organizations called for the termination of ICE contracts with all the detention centers on the ten-worst list. (Many of the other offenders were also county jails.) Immigrants at Pinal were plagued by a host of woes, the letter said, including "food on dirty trays, worms found in food, bugs and worms found in the faucets, receiving dirty laundry, and being overcrowded with ten other men in one cell and only one toilet."[5]

In a separate report, Detention Watch also complained

of verbally abusive guards who too often put inmates on lockdown, meted out discipline for minor offenses, and threatened to harm their immigration cases by reporting infractions to the court. Detainees all over Florence knew how bad Pinal was: "Guards commonly threaten them with transfer to PCJ if they file grievances, complain, or make requests that are deemed unreasonable by guards."[6]

The bug-infested bathrooms and harsh guards aside, the "non-contact" visits were one of the most onerous aspects of Pinal. Families of long-detained immigrants sometimes traveled hundreds of miles to visit their loved ones, only to see them as no more than a blurry image on a video screen. They were denied even a single touch; fathers were unable to pat a child's head, wives unable to kiss their husbands. All four of the other detention centers in Arizona allowed families to visit in person, to be physically together with their imprisoned loved one. Pinal alone denied this comfort.

The jail did have an outdoor recreation yard, but it was reserved strictly for the criminal suspects. As for the immigrant detainees, "we never go outside," Marco said. They didn't even have a walled, ceilingless room like the one that marginally brightened Mariana's days at Estrella. Instead, they had a so-called exercise room outfitted with basketball hoops; its only connection to the outdoors was a single open-air window high up on the wall, without glass, covered by a metal grate. Sunlight filtered through the grate for only a brief period every day, and the prisoners politely took turns standing in the single beam of light.

Confined day in and day out to cramped quarters that veered between overheated and freezing, Marco went outside only when he was driven the short distance to court. The lack of outdoor time was a clear violation of ICE standards.

Pinal's daily schedule was strict, and boring. "I wake up at five," Marco said. "At six I have breakfast. Then I go back to the room and sleep till nine or ten." He could watch TV, or visit the small law library, before being locked up again for the night at eight or eight thirty. He'd been enduring this stultifying routine for two years.

Marco's troubles had started in São Paulo, where he was born in 1963. He was different from the other boys from the time he was a small child, he wrote in his asylum petition, and when the other kids teased him and called him a "fag," his father was so enraged that he beat Marco into unconsciousness. When he was a teen, his father punished him by sodomizing him with a sharp instrument that tore his flesh.

Marco fled his home at eighteen and moved in with a boyfriend, Andres. "One day, my father appeared at my apartment with some men," Marco wrote in the petition. "My dad pushed me, beat me, kicked, ransacked the apartment, broke furniture, and kidnapped me." He brought Marco forcibly back home, and locked him up for days in the basement. After that attack, Andres disappeared. Marco's father was associated with the security forces, and Marco feared that his father's men had taken Andres. Though police harassed and beat gays regularly, Marco went to the station to report him as a missing person. The cops laughed and said it was just another story of a gay man "looking for his husband." They shoved Marcos into a cell packed with twenty prisoners, and he was beaten and raped. He never saw Andres again, and he believed that his father had him killed.

Marco loved his family's Mormon faith, even though it opposes homosexuality. In 1990, his father forced him into a marriage with a woman from church. "I only entered this marriage because my father threatened to kill me if I did not," putting a gun into his mouth the day of the wedding, he wrote. The couple had two children. "I tried hard to live this life," Marco explained. "I could not, and my depression deepened."

Marco and his wife moved to the Mormon capital of Salt Lake City in 1996, traveling on six-month tourist visas. His wife returned to Brazil, and Marco remained, overstaying his visa, and began leading a gay life. When his wife back home found out, she told him he couldn't see the kids again and she informed his father, who threatened to kill his son if he returned to Brazil.

Marco found work easily: he was a line cook at the Marriott University Park Hotel in Salt Lake City, a data entry clerk at First American Title Insurance Agency, and a computer programmer working on his own. He was distraught about the children, and he began to self-medicate his worsening depression; eventually he was caught with an illegal drug and charged with possession. In 2005, a cop pulled him over for a traffic violation—he'd forgotten to use a turn signal—and the arrest triggered his deportation case. With the drug arrest on his record, he faced mandatory detention, and he had been incarcerated ever since.

It was not until he was in Florence that he realized he might have a case for asylum. "I did not know that one could get papers based on sexual orientation," he said. "I did not find that out until the Florence Project did a presentation of rights in my detention facility. I thought, at that time, that if I had to return to Brazil I would first kill myself than go back."

The Florence Immigrant and Refugee Rights Project operates out of a small office on the prison highway, dwarfed by the buildings that house its clients. The number of cases that come its way are overwhelming: with fifteen hundred detainees in Florence and another sixteen hundred in Eloy, the nonprofit's five lawyers can't possibly represent every immigrant who needs help. So they do the know-your-rights presentations and try to give the detainees enough information to represent themselves in court.

Relying on their advice, Marco put together a long asylum petition. He narrated his history of abuse and argued that if he were deported to Brazil, he would be killed. "My father would do it himself or ask the security forces to help him. The government would not protect me. . . . I am truly terrified of returning."

Despite the harrowing tale it told, Marco's petition was denied. One judge told him this was a family affair—a father tormenting his son—sad, perhaps, but it did not meet the legal standard of persecution of a particular class of people. Marco had a right to appeal, and his case went up the legal chain, from the immigration judge in Arizona, to the Board of Immigration Appeals in Virginia, to the US Court of Appeals for the Ninth Circuit. If he had accepted deportation, he'd have been out of Pinal quickly; continued detention was the price he paid to pursue his legal rights.

After he'd been incarcerated more than six years, he finally persuaded a local judge to let him out on bond while he awaited word on his appeal. But the judge set the bond at a hefty $10,000. Luckily for Marco, he'd come to the attention of Casa Mariposa, an immigrant support and advocacy group in Tucson, and its members began to raise money to get him out. It was a slow slog. Meantime, they exchanged letters with him to relieve his loneliness, visited regularly, and enlisted others, including me, to go see him. Marco soon began writing to me.

"Hoping that this letter finds you well together with your loving family," he wrote days after we met. "Thank you for finding time in your busy schedule to come visit me. I hope that you have a nice Merry Christmas." Another one, in lonely January: "How are you, I just sent this letter to say Hello." In March, he hesitantly asked for books in Spanish. I picked up a secondhand copy of Isabel Allende's *The House of the Spirits* and a mystery and shipped them off to the Pinal County Jail. All too soon, I got a letter back, a "notification of denied mail" stating that "items are denied based on safety and security concerns or content that may pose a threat to facility operations." Under no circumstances was I allowed to mail a book independently. Only full-price editions, from certain approved publishers, and shipped directly from the publishing house, were permitted. The authorities had confiscated the two books I'd sent, the note said, and filed them away with Marco's other possessions, to be given to him when and if he ever got out of detention.

Marco was beginning to despair. Just when he was about to give up, on a day that he prayed what he thought would be his last prayer to God, a donor he didn't know gave $5,000 to his bond fund.[7] Together with the money Casa Mariposa had already raised, it was enough to spring him from jail. It didn't mean his case was closed. He might lose his appeal and still be deported. It did mean that for now he was a free man, for the first time in six and a half years.

When he walked out of the Pinal County Jail, he raised his face up to the Arizona sun and gulped in great breaths of fresh air.

Two years and three months after Marco got out, ICE ended its contract with the Pinal County Jail.[8]

Jena, Louisiana, is a little town even smaller than Florence, deep in the pine forests of Central Louisiana. The mayor, Murphy McMillin, liked to boast that the surrounding countryside had some of the best fishing and hunting in the United States. In 2006, Jena had a brief moment in the national spotlight, when six black teens, arrested for beating a white classmate, were charged with attempted second-degree murder. "Free the Jena Six" became a rallying cry, and the national media descended. Most of the time, Jena was pretty quiet; the town slogan was "A Nice Place to Call Home."

Jena had just thirty-three hundred residents who called

the place home—sixty-seven hundred fewer than Florence —but the two towns had much in common. Jena was the seat of LaSalle Parish, as Florence was of Pinal County, and Jena was likewise proud of its historic downtown buildings, especially the Strand Theater. Jena had also thrown in its lot with the immigration detention industry. The LaSalle Economic Development District announced in 2006 it intended to pursue an immigration prison, and in 2007, the GEO Group, CCA's chief rival in the lucrative private prison business, won the contract. Mayor McMillin applauded the good-paying prison jobs, which would number as many as 224 when the detention center opened.[9] Construction crews felled great swaths of the piney woods on the northwest side of town to make way for a massive low-rise center, and the first ICE detainees began arriving in October 2007. Under contract to ICE, the new LaSalle Detention Facility had 1,160 beds.

In 2010, two young mothers from Tucson, improbably, filled two of them for forty-seven days.

The two women, Alma Hernandez Rodriguez and her sister Norma, had been picked up in Tucson and sent to Florence only briefly. Then, just as Marco was cycled down from Utah to Arizona, the sisters were shuffled out of Florence and shipped to rural Louisiana. They were transported halfway across the country, by bus, plane, and van, 1,289 miles from their hometown and their kids. On the Fourth of July, they landed in LaSalle.

Alma told me their story at her rundown apartment in heavily Mexican South Tucson on a sweltering day in June 2013; like Mariana's place in Phoenix, it was in the shadow of an elevated freeway, I-10. She was twenty-nine years old and great with child, expecting her fourth baby, a boy, in five weeks. Her little girl, Maritza, now four, was skittering around the tidy kitchen. The two boys, eleven-year-old Luis and seven-year-old Raymundo, were up the street at summer school at Mission Elementary, a Spanish-style building with curving white arches and a red tile roof. It was Alma's old school. She was only eight when she arrived in the United States, and she'd been in the neighborhood—and the country—long enough to send her children to the same school she'd attended as a child.

"I was born in Guadalajara, Jalisco, in 1984," she said in English. "My parents brought us here. I studied here. I see this as my home. I remember one or two years of school in Mexico, but it's so long ago it's like a dream. My memories start here."

Her father had worked as a butcher for years at Los Amigos Meat Market in Tucson; his boss tried to help him regularize his status, but nothing ever came of it. "We were never in trouble with Immigration," Alma said, "but Dad was scared to take us anywhere, to parks. We didn't understand. He knew Immigration was all over the place. Now I understand. He was protecting us. We were always home."

Alma never quite grasped her status until she met her future husband, Armando, at sixteen. "Armando didn't have papers either. He explained it to me." In the early 2000s, shortly after they met, Arizona began enacting punitive laws against immigrants, and the couple soon came to realize just how risky their undocumented status was. Eventually they would be harmed in every possible way by the new immigration crackdown: they would be riven apart by both detention and deportation, and after Armando was expelled he would make a dangerous trek across the desert to get back to his family.

Armando was arrested on Halloween 2008, when Maritza was a newborn. A landscaper who worked for himself, he was spending the afternoon dropping off business cards in a wealthy neighborhood near Sabino Canyon, a saguaro-studded federal recreation area in the foothills north of Tucson. A deputy from the Pima County Sheriff's Department saw him walking along and asked if he was illegal. "He said yes," Alma said. Armando had been deported before so he was sent to Mexico almost immediately.

"He was picked up on Friday afternoon and he was in Nogales by 2:00 or 3:00 a.m. Saturday."

Alma had no idea where he was. "I took the kids trick-or-treating," she said, and as the evening wore on, "I was thinking the worst, that he was in a car accident." Armando didn't know he could ask for a phone call. Fortunately, he had twenty dollars in his pocket and as soon as he was released in Mexico he called his wife. Alma quickly borrowed money from family and friends and sent it to him in Nogales via Western Union. His brother's wife, a US citizen, drove down to the border, just sixty miles from Tucson, and brought him clothes, shoes, and more money.

Within days, Armando had crossed the border and was headed north, walking the Arizona desert with a coyote. With a newborn baby girl, two little boys, and a wife at home, there was no way he was not coming back. To pay the coyote, Alma borrowed more money, $1,500, from the same family and friends. The whole time he was out in the wilderness, she worried. "My husband was gone a week. I was stressed, crying. My kids suffered. My son said, 'Man, I hate cops.'" When Armando straggled into Tucson, he was sunburned and his skin was scratched and pockmarked by cactus spines.

Armando had to work even harder after his deportation. Not only did he have to make up his lost wages, he had to pay back the well-wishers who had lent him money in his time of need. The family had to move in with Alma's parents to catch up financially. They were still struggling when Immigration struck again, a year and a half later.

In late June 2010, Alma and her sister, Norma, spent the day together with their kids, celebrating a nephew's birthday. They parted ways at the end of the afternoon, and Norma headed toward home with her three children. On the south-east side of town, a Pima County Sheriff's deputy pulled her over and asked for her driver's license. Norma had only a Mexican ID to show him, and the deputy called Border Patrol. Norma panicked and phoned Alma, and though she told her to stay home with her own kids, Alma hopped in her car to go help her only sister. When she arrived, Border Patrol questioned her too, and took both sisters into custody.

"We were like criminals," Alma recalled. "There were three Border Patrol cars. Three Pima County Sheriff's cars." Norma's terrified kids—ages six, five, and three—were taken to Border Patrol headquarters too. "They were crying. They were scared, asking, 'What's going to happen, Mommy?'"

One agent was lenient with the children but another barked at Norma, "You find somebody to pick them up. If they don't come in twenty minutes, we'll call CPS." A friend managed to arrive in time, and Norma signed a document allowing the woman to take the kids.

Alma and Norma slept on the floor that night at head-quarters. "There were twenty-five or thirty ladies in the little room," Alma said. "There was one toilet in the middle of the room. The room was freezing, sixty degrees. It was June twenty-ninth and I was wearing shorts and spaghetti straps. It was cold. They said it was because of the germs. It was like a refrigerator in there."

The Border Patrol's freezing holding tanks are legendary, so much so that immigrants have nicknamed them *helado-ras*—iceboxes—a bilingual pun that's a knock at ICE. The flimsy blankets that Alma and her sister got weren't much help; they were itchy and smelly. The food was poor and scanty: small hamburgers accompanied by milk.

When the agents came in the morning, Alma remem-bered, "One officer said, 'These bitches are cold.' I said, 'It's freezing there. What do you expect?' He watched his lan-guage from then on." Alma heard plenty of other agents also make insulting remarks to the women, assuming that they couldn't understand English. One officer told a Guatemalan woman, "'Why are you coming here to dirty my country?'" Alma recounted. "Only he used very bad words."

The women were piled onto a bus and taken north to the ICE processing center in Florence. After being in custody nearly twenty-four hours, they finally were allowed to call their worried families. It was a small comfort to their parents back in Tucson that the two women were together. "My sister and I were never separated, thank God," Alma said.

They had had little to eat at Border Patrol, but in Florence they had a decent dinner, meat stew and an apple. They were sent to bed in bunks in a large dorm with about one hundred women. At two or three in the morning, they were abruptly awakened. The guards handed them papers, and ordered them to sign: the documents declared that they were agreeing to a transfer to LA. Not yet knowing their destination, Alma assumed that the initials stood for Los Angeles.

Twenty-three women were marched onto a bus at 5:00 a.m. and began the long ride to Texas, eating breakfast en route. In El Paso, "they started chaining us up, handcuffs on wrists and ankles, chained to the waist," Alma said, shaking her head. The cuffs rubbed her bare skin raw. The women were taken to an airport; only after they boarded the flight, chained like criminals, did they learn their destination. "The ladies on the plane were very nice," Alma said. "They told us we were going to Louisiana."

Alma had started her period at Florence, and the staff there gave her a single tiny menstrual pad. She bled on the bus and was mortified to see the deep red stains soiling her shorts. On the plane, the flight attendants gave her some more pads, and she had to struggle to put one on, maneuvering in the small bathroom, with her body cuffed and chained. The humiliation put her over the edge.

"I cried," she said. "I broke down. My only crime is being here with no papers. I didn't kill nobody. I didn't do nothing. I always followed the law."

Their flight landed in Alexandria, Louisiana, and the guards who met it yelled at the women to hurry to a waiting shuttle bus. The forty-four-mile drive took them through the Kisatchie National Forest; its green trees and wetlands were a stark change from the dry desert the sisters called home. When they arrived at LaSalle on Independence Day, the guards took their chains off, one by one, and the women wearily lay down on the floor in still another cold room.

"It was the fourth day already," Alma said. "By then we knew each other. We lay close to each other so as not to be cold," nestling like spoons. "Everybody was hurting, tired, disappointed."

In the middle of the night they were awakened again. This time they were taken to a not-so-nice place they'd call home for weeks, a dorm with forty sets of bunk beds. LaSalle was set up more like Estrella than Eloy; most of the time the women were confined to one large multipurpose room. They ate at ten long dining tables not far from the bunks, and a bathroom with showers and toilets adjoined the big space. A caged outdoor room, ten feet by ten feet, served as their recreation space. "It had no roof and we could see the sky," Alma said. "We were allowed in it thirty minutes a day. We could see the sun." The women never argued because they had learned that the punishment was cancellation of their few minutes of yard time.

As at Eloy and Pinal County Jail, there was little to do. They got up early and spent the day playing board games, drawing, writing letters, or watching Spanish-language *telenovelas*. They could request time at the library, which had about a hundred books and a few computers for legal research. "If you were sick you had to send a request to the doctor or nurse," Alma said. "I got the flu three times—fever, coughing, cold. The room was so cold, but the water in the showers was practically boiling. For menstrual periods, they gave us one packet with five pads."

Alma had only four dollars with her when she was arrested, and her sister had twenty. The money went quickly to pay for shampoo and soap, and for ramen noodles and cookies to supplement the prison chow. Norma worked in the laundry, earning three dollars a night for a ten-hour shift, from 8:00 p.m. to 6:00 a.m. Their family deposited money into an account for them, and out of sixty dollars the sisters got just five fifteen-minute phone calls.

"Twice I talked to my husband," Alma said. "It was a horrible time for him. When I talked to the kids, we were all crying. My older son would say, 'Are you OK? I miss you.'" She missed the children desperately, and it broke her heart when little Raymundo started kindergarten "without me being there. I'm a twenty-four-hour mommy."

Norma and Alma's parents had hired a lawyer right away to represent them both, but the man "had a hard time finding us, we were transferred so many times. No one knew where we were. He finally found us on July fifth." After five weeks in detention, on August 12, they got a bond hearing, via video link, with a judge who was elsewhere. The lawyer, on the phone, argued successfully that the sisters should be released while they fought their deportation cases, given that neither woman had a criminal record, "we each had three US-citizen children, and we lived here all our lives."

The family paid the bonds in Tucson, at the ICE office. Norma had some money of her own to pay her $3,000 bond. Alma's was less, $2,500, but she didn't have it. Her father borrowed the money from his boss at the meat market to free her. "We got out on August nineteenth, my mom's birthday, at six p.m."

Now it was up to them to find their way home, at their own expense. Their father arranged for a cab to pick them up at the detention center and drive them back to Alexandria, a town that had both an airport and Greyhound bus station. A third woman who had just been freed went with them, and she paid $60 for a motel room for the three of them. The next day, via Walmart, their mother sent them some money to repay their friend and to buy bus tickets. The two sisters had to pay a pricey fare to get back to Tucson, $220 apiece. Detention had already cost their families plenty. Alma's husband, Armando, had had to stop working to take care of their three small children, ages eight, four, and two at the time. Then there was the cost of the bonds, and the $1,250 the lawyer charged for each sister. Alma's costs alone were close to $4,000.

Alma and Norma boarded the bus in the afternoon for a twenty-eight-hour journey home. They traveled through small towns all across Texas, transferred at Dallas to a bus that took them to El Paso, then on through New Mexico, and finally back to Tucson. They had been gone six weeks.

"Our family knew we were coming," Alma said.

Friends met them at Greyhound and took them to a joyous family celebration. "Everybody was at my house. It was the best. Maritza was two. She didn't recognize me. I got upset but I was so happy. I hugged my kids. My husband cried. Later he cried like a baby, with all he went through."

Alma worked to protect herself so she'd never be detained again. First she studied for her GED so she could get Deferred Action status (applicants must have completed high school or gotten the GED equivalent). Then, in the fall of 2012, ICE, using its option for prosecutorial discretion, closed her case.

"I'm totally legal now," she said, beaming. Like every Hispanic woman and man in Arizona, she still had SB 1070 to deal with. Under the law, cops can question people about their immigration status only if they have a "reasonable suspicion" that they're undocumented and only if they've stopped them for some other infraction. Police are not permitted to pull people over simply because they look like they might be immigrants or foreign nationals. That's not how the law worked in practice, Alma said.

"People with brown skin are targeted more now. Things have only gotten worse."

Armando was still undocumented, so Alma drove him—always—to his landscaping jobs and every other place he had to go. Her own legal status didn't protect her from police questioning. A few months before I met her, Alma had driven with all three of the kids to Food City, a southside supermarket that specializes in Mexican foods. She was in the parking lot, a mom about to go shopping with her children, when a cop pulled over.

"He asked me what I was doing there, and asked me for my ID. I gave him my driver's license. Then he said he was checking if I was doing drug trafficking," Alma recounted with disgust. "With the kids in the car."

From then on, every time Maritza saw a police officer she started screaming. "My kids are always with me," Alma said. "They're the ones taking it the worst. They're the future of the United States. We need all this to stop."

CHAPTER FIVE

Greyhound

Gracias a Dios que estamos afuera.
Thank God we're out of there.

—*María, detainee released from Eloy*

On the dark side of Tucson, on a chilly October night in 2011, the only light came from the Greyhound bus station. The depot was at the edge of downtown, out by the freeway, occupying a prefab hangar in a vast and shadowy parking lot. The city leaders had banished the station from a more convenient and safer site downtown, to make way for new glam restaurants and high-rise apartments. Poor travelers weren't high on anyone's agenda, and the city preferred to keep them hidden away. On this night, several dozen of them were gathered inside the makeshift station, awaiting their long-distance buses. It was the only kind of transportation they could afford.

October was early for this desert town to be so cold, and a kindly Franciscan friar, David Hoer, had already begun his usual winter rounds delivering hot chocolate to Tucson's outcasts. Fresh from visiting the homeless in a downtown park, he drove up to the station. He pulled a Styrofoam urn out of his trunk and hauled it inside. The room was chilly and sprawling, with overbright fluorescents glaring down on the people sitting in rows of chairs. Vending machines lined one wall, and a TV droned on another. Brother David walked around this harsh space in his brown robe and sandals, offering cups of steaming cocoa to surprised passengers: a Spanish-speaking family biding their time for the bus that would take them to Los Angeles and home; a black man waiting for a bus to New York that wouldn't arrive until midnight. The LA trip wasn't bad, just an overnight ride, but the journey to the Big Apple would take almost three days.

Around 9:00 p.m., an unmarked white van pulled up outside in the dark. More customers for Greyhound, six men and three women, disembarked into the desolate parking lot. Right away anyone could see that they were different from the other passengers. They had no jackets against the cold night, and they had no luggage, no bags of food, no supplies for the long bus trip ahead. They were carrying their few possessions in see-through plastic bags. And they were being dropped off by officers in uniform, wearing the insignia of ICE. One of the guards held out a friendly hand to one of the men. "Good luck, man," he said in English.

The passengers would need that luck, along with the friar's hot chocolate. They were newly liberated detainees. They'd just been released from Eloy, the private detention center that was as little noticed by Americans as that bus depot by the highway. They'd been sprung that afternoon by the immigration judge who presides daily at Eloy. After paying bonds of thousands of dollars—money scrounged up by their families—they'd been issued papers to travel legally. The judge was willing to set them free while they fought their deportation cases, but they weren't off the hook. They could still be deported. They had to report for hearings before another immigration judge in thirty days, in the far-flung US cities where they were now headed. Some of them were recent border crossers who were going to join family in the Bronx or Minneapolis for the first time, but many were going home, to towns where they'd lived for years: LA or Reno or Vienna, Virginia.

And there was a catch. The travelers not only had to find their own way home, they had to pay to get there. The feds felt no obligation to return them to the places where they'd been picked up, to homes hundreds or even thousands of miles away from this bus station. From ICE's point of view, it was a kindness to bring them to Tucson at all. The agency could have just set them free at the gates of the rural Eloy prison and let them fend for themselves.

The station would close just after midnight. It was already past nine, and the sleepy Tucson depot had only two buses still scheduled to go out—the 10:35 west to Los Angeles and the midnight bus to El Paso and points east. The immigrants had no phones, and most of them had no money; their only hope of getting out that night was to somehow track down a family member or friend who could get on the Internet fast enough to plunk down the $220 for a ticket to New York City, or the $200 to get to Minneapolis. Even if they managed to reach someone able to help, by this late hour the buses were often sold out. And once the depot locked down at the witching hour, the ticketless would be shown the door, and stranded in the dark. The station would not reopen until dawn.

On this evening, a few of the nine ex-detainees managed to score a ticket and a seat on the last bus west. María, a forty-something Mexican, was going home to her kids in LA, and she was jubilant. When it came time to board, she hugged the other women and waved to the men. Just before she went through the door to the bus bay, she turned and flashed a radiant smile at her marooned companions. At least they weren't in Eloy anymore, she said. "Gracias a Dios que estamos afuera," she said. *Thank God we're out of there.*

———

A few hours before this bittersweet drama played out at Greyhound, the members of Casa Mariposa—Butterfly House—sat down to dinner. The house was a century-old bungalow in Armory Park, a historic neighborhood just south of downtown's towers, near the railroad tracks. In the old days, back in the late nineteenth and early twentieth centuries, the railroad men had to obey the "one-mile rule," living close enough to the station to hear the whistle calling them to work. Casa Mariposa occupied one of the sprawling old boardinghouses where the railroaders used to live; like the other houses in the neighborhood, it had warrens of bedrooms along a central hallway and an old-fashioned screened-in sleeping porch in back. It was perfect for one of Mariposa's many missions: rescuing ex-detainees stranded at the bus station.

The group was faith-based, and its half-dozen live-in members included a Quaker, John Heid, who regularly appeared in the Tucson papers for his arrests protesting outside Raytheon, the giant arms manufacturer at the south end of town, and an Episcopal minister, Kate Bradsen. The members lived simply, and took on outside jobs (John was a house painter) to support themselves. Casa had started up after the numbers of immigrants confined in Arizona's detention centers began to skyrocket. As Marco Galdino had learned, a changing roster of live-in and outside volunteers regularly drove north up the highway to visit lonely detainees locked up in Florence or Eloy; they wrote letters to the prisoners and raised bond money to set them free.

The Casa folks made good use of the many rooms in the Armory Park house and not just for overnight bus travelers. Detainees with any hope of bonding out had to give the judge an address where they would live. Mariposa regularly welcomed these temporary visitors, sometimes housing them for months on end.

On this particular October evening, after a prayer circle

and over a meal of black beans and salad, they celebrated the arrival of their newest guest: a Mexican man who had just gotten out of detention. Ernesto needed a place to stay for the thirty days before his hearing at the Tucson federal courthouse. He stood up and profusely thanked the residents of Casa and its community volunteers. He promised to be a good guest and to faithfully keep his commitment to appear before the judge. Without their help—and God's—he said, he never would have gotten out of Eloy.

Yet Mariposa's most visible work was among the forlorn immigrants at the bus depot. Five nights a week, one or more of the volunteers would go to Greyhound, and when would-be passengers got stuck, as they often did, the Casa volunteers would bring them back to the house for a meal, a shower, and a bed for the night. Early in the morning, after a hot breakfast, they'd take them back to the station to make the next bus. In a pinch, the overnight guests could walk the one mile on their own two feet. But even the spacious Mariposa house often filled up, and the outside volunteers regularly brought overnight visitors to their own homes.

On this night, Marco Manzo was taking his weekly turn. He dropped by Casa Mariposa to pick up supplies, and I followed him as he set out into the dark night. At Greyhound, Marco and I first enjoyed a cup of Friar David's cocoa, and then fretted while we waited for the detainees. The later they arrived, the worse would be their chances of getting a seat on that night's buses. When they finally walked in after nine, they blinked in the harsh light and looked around in bewilderment. They were surprised to find a friendly young Tucson man there to greet them. "Bienvenidos," Marco said with a smile. *Welcome.*

Marco's first and most important order of business was to lend the new arrivals his cell phone.

"You can call your family," he explained, "and get them to buy you a bus ticket." They'd have to act fast to get a seat on the bus they wanted. There was no time to spare. Another Casa community volunteer had turned up to lend her cell phone, and I contributed mine to the cause as well. María called her kids in LA, exclaiming, "Hola," with a big grin on her face, and got her sister to make the arrangements for her ticket. An affable man from Phoenix did likewise. But there were some problems Marco and the phones could not readily solve.

Pilar, a twenty-two-year-old Ecuadoran woman, was the youngest of the group, and she stood a little apart from the others. While her *compañeros* smiled and joked about their new status as free men and women, Pilar was silent. She seemed jittery and fearful, and her eyes darted around anxiously as Marco approached. She was leery of this male stranger, but she was finally persuaded to use his phone to call her worried family in the Bronx. They wanted to buy her an airplane ticket, damn the expense, to get her safely to New York the next day. She'd already been through so much, and they didn't want her traveling cross-country alone, on a bus, for three days. But no matter how much money her relatives were willing to shell out, Pilar couldn't fly.

Marco patiently explained. A bureaucratic catch-22 prevented it. Pilar had documents from one federal agency— ICE—that allowed her to travel legally, but she didn't have the photo ID that another federal agency—TSA, the Transportation Security Administration—required to board a plane. More than once, Marco and other Casa volunteers had taken a traveler down to Tucson International Airport and explained the situation to the TSA supervisors. But each time, the ex-detainee was turned away. No official photo ID, no plane ride. Pilar's only option was the bus.

Marco had brought along an array of sturdy donated bags—cloth totes, backpacks, and even heavy-duty grocery bags with handles—to replace the flimsy bags the detainees had been discharged with. María happily grabbed a patterned grocery bag and dumped her travel papers inside it. Marco also had fresh water bottles and travel-friendly food: apples and crackers, and soups that could be heated up in the bus station microwaves. As I learned on subsequent visits, sometimes volunteers even brought along small blankets; winter and summer, the passengers had to brave the freezing AC of bus stations and buses alike. Other Casa workers thoughtfully printed out simple maps of the United States to hand out. The travelers were undertaking complicated journeys, interrupted by transfers and layovers—the trip to New York that Pilar would have to make involved no fewer than twenty-eight stops—and the maps helped them understand the vast distances.

As the midnight hour drew near on this October night, most of the remaining released detainees accepted Marco's offer to sleep in the old boardinghouse. Not Pilar. She might have been willing to use his cell phone, but she was afraid to go out in the dark, with a man she didn't know, to sleep in an unknown house. Marco understood, and he gave her one more option. The female volunteer would drive her to one of the inexpensive motels nearby on the freeway frontage road. Pilar didn't need to worry about the cost. Marco would pay with his own money for a room where she could safely spend the night.

"Unpredictable random release" is how one immigrant advocate described ICE's system of releasing vulnerable immigrants in a strange city at night. It was great that they were getting out of detention, Cindy Schlosser, the social services coordinator for the Florence Immigrant and Refugee Rights Project, told me, "but you're dumping them there at the bus station. We've had clients suddenly get released and we didn't know how to get in touch with them." And their families didn't always know how to find them either.

That's what happened on another busy night to the family of a freed man named Pablo. Pablo was actually happy to be at Tucson Greyhound: ICE had unintentionally delivered him to his hometown. He rushed to call his family, only to learn that they were up in Eloy, in the detention center parking lot, waiting for him to emerge from the jail. They had somehow gotten wind of his release and, overjoyed, drove all the way up to the prison to fetch him. ICE felt no obligation to inform families like this one about procedures, or to tell them where and when their loved ones would be dropped off. When Pablo told his family he was in Tucson, they did a fast U-turn at Eloy and sped south. Pablo joked about the mix-up, but he could afford to take it in stride. He knew he'd be seeing his family soon.

A man with him, Manuel, was in quite a different state. He hadn't made it onto the Los Angeles bus and he was so distraught that he was thinking about taking a cab all the way home to California. Pablo told him he could sleep at his family's home in Tucson, but Manuel was too upset to listen. Nor did he pay attention to the Mariposa volunteers who told him a cab would cost him hundreds of dollars. He was antsy and agitated, rushing to and fro in the station. Eventually he bolted for the door and ran out into the darkness.

Taxi drivers often circled around the station, hoping for a major fare among the disoriented and distressed. One driver told me that his best gig so far was taking a woman clear through to Sacramento. She wasn't able to get on the LA bus, and her husband was beside himself that, after her long lockup in Eloy, she was about to be stranded in Tucson overnight. He agreed to pay the driver $600 if he would bring her home to California, right now. The taxi driver looked after his own interests, to be sure, but he wasn't all bad; he regularly lent money to the immigrants to pay their bus fares. The families carefully took down his address over the phone, and not one, he told me, had ever failed to send him the money they owed. They were grateful for the help.

Over months of stopping by the station, I met immigrants from China, Ecuador, Guatemala, El Salvador, Iraq, and even Russia. Some were first-time border crossers, but plenty had lived in the United States for years. A stylish young California woman of Korean heritage had been picked up in southwest Arizona while driving with a friend to a wedding in Phoenix. The woman, Christina, was twenty-six, a college grad with a good job, and unbeknownst to her, undocumented. She'd grown up thinking she was an American citizen, and was shocked to be arrested by Border Patrol at a highway checkpoint. She was hauled up to Eloy and missed the wedding. The tearful bride came to visit her shortly after, stricken that her happy event had been the occasion for her old friend to be thrown into detention. Christina's family had hired a lawyer to get her bonded out, and now she was on her way home, with a deportation hearing still ahead of her.

Vivian, a Guatemalan woman, had lived in Vienna, Virginia, for eighteen years with her husband; they had two US-citizen children, a girl and a boy, now both in their teens. Vivian and her husband had had an application in for residency when her father fell ill with kidney disease. Legally, she was supposed to stay put until her case played out, but she had no choice but to return to Guatemala, she said. Her parents were divorced, her brothers were useless, and as the only daughter she was duty-bound to care for her father. She spent two years in Guatemala, tending him until his death. On her way back home, she'd been caught by Border Patrol in the Arizona desert. At Eloy, she wore a uniform; her own soiled clothes were returned to her only when she was released. Now, as we sat and talked in the bus station, she carefully picked cactus prickers out of the jacket she'd worn on her failed desert journey.

Vivian was looking at a three-day bus ride to DC, where

she'd face the judge. She'd been told already, she said, that her family emergency—a dying father—had not been *suficiente* as an excuse for leaving the country. She had no money for a lawyer. She was worried that she'd lose her case and be separated from her kids once again.

Thirty-year-old Eduardo Rodriguez, a Mexican national, had lived in the Golden State for years. Before the economy nose-dived he'd worked good jobs in construction in Bakersfield building houses, he told me proudly, speaking in excellent English. After the recession kicked in, "I started working for a guy who owns a bunch of houses. I do the maintenance and repair. I can do anything: tiling, plumbing, carpentry."

Things went south for Eduardo when he was caught driving without a license and was shipped 545 miles to Eloy. He'd been there several months. The detention center itself "wasn't so bad," he shrugged. What had hurt was the separation from his wife and his three little ones, including a newborn baby girl. He hated that he had missed her first few months. Eduardo was optimistic about his case though. The Eloy judge had bonded him out, and everyone else in his family, including his wife, was an American citizen.

Volunteer Margie King had been leaving messages for Eduardo's wife, and Margie's phone soon rang. It was Eduardo's wife calling back. "He's right here," Margie told her, "with a beautiful smile on his face." Husband and wife spoke happily, but he wouldn't get home as soon as he had hoped. There was no room for him on the late-night bus to Los Angeles. His wife bought him a seat on the morning bus for $115. It would take Eduardo seventeen hours—and a trip through twelve cities—to get back to Bakersfield and to the family that needed him.

On another hot summer night, the first to get off the ICE van was a strapping young man named Raúl, a six-footer with shoulder-length black hair. He was agitated as he strode into the terminal's glaring lights and looked around wildly.

"Where am I?" he cried out. When someone told him, he bellowed, "Tucson?! I'm from Reno. What am I doing here?"

Unlike that friendly agent in October, who'd offered a handshake and wishes of good luck to a passenger, the ICE officers who'd driven Raúl down from Eloy had maintained a strict silence. They'd told their passengers nothing. As tough a guy as Raúl seemed to be—he'd been picked up by Reno police after a scuffle in a bar and then turned over to ICE—he went into a panic. He'd never been in Tucson before and knew no one there. He had no money. He had no idea how to get home. And he lived 861 miles distant, in faraway Reno, at the western end of Nevada, past the Grand Canyon, past the Las Vegas desert, past Lake Tahoe even.

Margie stepped up and gently handed him her phone. He could try to get someone to buy him a ticket online, she explained, and if all else failed, Casa would lodge him for the night, feed him, and get him back to Greyhound on the morrow. Raúl was dumbfounded at the unexpected kindness of this stranger. He took her phone and quickly started punching in numbers. "I'm in a bad situation," he told one surprised friend after another. But none of his calls hit pay dirt. There was no way he could get out of Tucson that night. Margie stood by him, and once he took in that she and the others had no intention of abandoning him, he calmed down. At the end of the evening he contentedly went off with a volunteer to the Butterfly House.

I saw the nighttime routine at Casa Mariposa myself late one evening, after driving a trio who'd struck out at Greyhound. Two were young men in their late teens: Julio Cesar of Ecuador and José from El Salvador. The third, María Juana Guamán, a twenty-eight-year-old Ecuadoran, was going to Albany, New York, to reunite with the husband she had not seen in four years. She told me that after two long months of travel from Ecuador to Arizona, by bus, plane, and on foot, she had been caught in Tucson by the local police. Yet she was almost grateful for her three months in Eloy: behind bars, she had made a life-altering conversion from Catholicism to Protestantism. A fervent young Guatemalan evangelical had persuaded her that Catholicism, with its saints and angels, was idolatry. Now María Juana understood that "there is only one true living God," she explained, and she was radiant in the joy of her new faith.

Even so, she got scared when we arrived in Armory Park. A big man opened the door of the casa, and she recoiled. The only other guests were the two young men we had come with, and María Juana began shaking at the thought of being alone in a house of men.

I didn't recognize him at first, but the big man turned out to be Marco Galdino, the gay Brazilian detainee I'd last seen on a video screen in Florence. Unbeknownst to me, he'd bonded out of detention that spring and was now living at Casa Mariposa, still awaiting an answer on his asylum appeal. I was astonished to see him here and overjoyed to see him free.

Marco had taken on the job of tending the wayfarers who landed at the house almost every night. Now he turned his large frame toward the fearful María Juana. He took both her hands in his and looked into her eyes.

"I'm an immigrant, and I have suffered," he told her. "I would never harm you." She calmed visibly as he held her hands and smiled up at him. Now that Marco was free of Florence, his jovial personality had returned. He fetched the copy of *The House of the Spirits* I had sent him and said he was enjoying it immensely. He put the three overnight guests to work in the kitchen, and teased José and Julio Cesar unmercifully about their poor cooking skills. The two young men, novice cooks, laughed over their feeble attempts to scramble the eggs and mash the black beans; María Juana, by contrast, efficiently attacked the dirty dishes stacked in the sink and set about putting the kitchen to rights. All of them basked in the simple pleasure of these domestic tasks, long denied them at Eloy. They were exuberant by the time they sat down at the long table, gave thanks, and broke bread.

The number of released detainees escalated over the course of the busy summer of 2012, and Casa Mariposa was often overfull. The all-night Denny's on the frontage road near the bus station provided an alternative for stranded men. Eduardo, the family man from California, took advantage of the diner the night he missed the LA bus. He had befriended a young man from Ecuador who'd arrived in Tucson on the same ICE van. Giovanni Chuqui, twenty-three years old, was a fellow construction worker and also a father of three. He was a first-time crosser on his way to the Bronx, where his cousin had lined up a job for him. If he could get past the deportation judge, he planned to work for four years and then return home to his family laden with money.

Neither Giovanni nor Eduardo was getting out of Tucson that night, and they learned from a volunteer that five dollars would get them each a cup of coffee and an all-night seat at a Denny's table. Making jokes about the poor quality of the chow house's cuisine, they walked off on foot, with hopes of starting for home tomorrow.

Private houses were another option. Margie often put up people in the guesthouse in her yard in midtown Tucson, and got up at dawn the next day to bring them back to Greyhound. Sometimes there were so many immigrants at the station that they had to lodge in multiple houses. Marco Galdino became the bus station wrangler, directing the travelers to the volunteers' cars and persuading the timid to drive away with strangers. One crazy night when no fewer than twenty-three detainees were unable to board a bus, I was drafted to drive a carload to Margie's place. Marco directed eight women to pile into my station wagon. It was past midnight by the time we took off. As we pulled away from the station, the car weighed down by all the passengers, I joked that I was a coyote. The women all laughed heartily, but briefly. They were exhausted and they fell into a sad and anxious silence as we made our way through the nighttime streets.

Unexpectedly, Greyhound also reached out to help the marooned. If all else failed, the staff was willing to house stranded immigrant women in a tiny office for the night. One evening a pair of indigenous Mayans from Guatemala were candidates for bus station quarters. Mina Morales was from northern Guatemala, near the pyramids of Tikal; she was only in her late twenties but her face was lined and weary. She and her husband, Otber Rayes, had had a grueling journey north atop "La Bestia" (The Beast), the cargo train that carries so many migrants from the south of Mexico to the north. She pantomimed how she'd leaned against her husband, tucked between his legs, wrapped in his arms, to stay safe. They survived the train only to be caught in Arizona. At Eloy, they were permitted to see each other only once every eight days, for two hours. Now ICE had separated them altogether: Mina had been released, but Otber was still in detention. She was going to Atlanta alone to join her brother.

Mina was sitting on the bus station chairs sharing her woes with Ana Chilen Juarez, a woman from San Marcos in western Guatemala. Ana had been caught by Border Patrol just south of Tucson, and she'd been in Eloy three months. She was still disturbed by what had happened to a pregnant woman in her pod: the woman's husband had died in the heat out in the Tohono O'odham Nation west of Tucson. The woman spent her days at Eloy "llorando y llorando"—*crying and crying.*

Ana was also going east to reunite with family, but neither she nor Mina had made it onto the nighttime El Paso bus.

A Casa volunteer pleaded their case with the ticket-counter staffer: these two women had no place to go for the night. The sympathetic clerk called her boss and got permission to shelter them both in an office in the station.

The room opened onto an outside walkway, near where the buses roared in and out. It was tiny, about ten feet square, crammed with desks and chairs. The clerk showed Ana and Mina how they could sit back on the rolling chairs and put their feet up, but they were dubious, not to mention scared to stay there all night. Their host did her best to reassure them; at midnight, she said, "I'll lock the door with a key," she said, giving a demonstration. No one else would be able to get in, yet the two guests could open the door from the inside in case of emergency. At five in the morning, another employee—a woman—would come and unlock the door and they would have to leave. The two Guatemalans hesitantly agreed to the plan, tested out the chairs, and settled in.

The Greyhound buses themselves were squalid by the time they got to Tucson. I briefly boarded the LA-bound bus one night with a passenger, and it was crowded and messy and dank with the smell of sweat and urine. But the Tucson staff was unfailingly helpful to the ICE detainees. Many of the workers spoke Spanish and carefully explained the complicated routes to the passengers, marking up the paper tickets with a yellow highlighter to indicate the transfer points. If no Casa volunteers were at the station when immigrants arrived, Greyhound staff would call them; their phone numbers were taped to the counter.

Suddenly, at the end of the summer, the detainees stopped coming. After several nights of waiting in vain for the van, the Casa Mariposa volunteers learned that ICE had switched its ferry operations to the Phoenix Greyhound bus station. In many ways, that was an improvement: Phoenix is a much bigger city, with more bus routes, and the station had the virtue of staying open all night. But it was way out by the airport, even more isolated than the Tucson depot, and its staffers lacked the compassion of their Tucson colleagues. "They say, if you don't have a ticket by a certain time, you can't stay all night," one activist told me, and they'd mumble insults from behind the counter, saying, "We've got illegals hanging out."

With no immigrants to greet nightly at the Tucson station, Casa Mariposa reoriented its work, concentrating on housing people who were seeking asylum. At one point the members hosted a family of seven from Honduras, and at another time a gay Honduran man named Estrella who'd fled persecution at the hands of the army. A Guatemalan, César Lorenti Castillo, stayed for months at Casa after being released from Florence. He had shown the judge government documents showing that four of his family members had been slaughtered in the wake of Guatemala's bloody civil war: his son Gerber in 1997, his brother Mario in 2000, his nephew Julio in 2007, and his great-nephew Angel in 2001.[1]

The Casa Mariposa folks moved out of gentrifying Armory Park when a donor bought them a house in the working-class Mexican neighborhood of Menlo Park. The new place had plenty of room, in a main house in front and a guesthouse out back. And it was still within walking distance of the bus station. Which turned out to be a good thing: in the fall of 2013, Greyhound called once again, when a tidal wave of Guatemalan women and children began washing up all along the southwest border.[2]

In the middle of a cold night that December, a flock of five Guatemalan women and ten children—including three nursing babies in arms—stood outside in the Greyhound parking lot. The station had closed at 12:00 a.m. and wouldn't reopen until dawn. The Casa Mariposa volunteers had come by earlier in the evening and offered them lodging for the night, but the Guatemalans declined. The women were wary of the strangers. They had just endured two days in the Border Patrol holding tank in Tucson, and they were still shaken by how badly they had been treated.

After Greyhound workers shooed them outside at midnight, the women didn't know where to go or what to do. Then one of them spotted a convenience store in the distance; its neon sign a beacon that cast light into the darkness. The moms herded the tired kids over the bus depot's vast parking lot, then across four lanes of Congress Street, mercifully deserted at this hour. Finally they got to what they hoped would be their refuge: an all-night Circle K hard by the elevated interstate.

The store's clerks were used to travelers walking over from Greyhound to stretch their legs and buy chips or burritos. But the worker on the graveyard shift was dumbfounded to see this troupe of infants, toddlers, and mothers in the middle of the night. Luckily, Casa Mariposa had left some phone numbers at the store, for just such an emergency as this. The man dialed up and reached the genial Marco Galdino. The new house was less than a mile away, and Marco and another volunteer arrived within minutes. After Marco gave them the same spiel that had charmed María Juana, the women realized they had only two options: stand outside Circle K all night or go with this voluble stranger. They opted for the hot meals and warm beds of the Casa.

I met up with them the next evening, a Monday, at the bus station. By then, after a good sleep and with full bellies for the first time in days, they were almost cheerful. The kids who could walk were scampering around. The families were waiting for the bus to El Paso and points east. Lucía, the friendliest woman, had a mouthful of gold teeth and an energetic seven-month-old son; he alternated nursing heartily at her breast and trying to crawl away on the floor. She laughed each time she had to retrieve him. The mother of six sat apart from the others, minding her kids. She looked strained, and no wonder: she had a three-month-old bound to her chest in a shawl, and five highly mobile offspring ranging in age from two to eight. The eight-year-old, a serious young girl, clasped the two toddlers by the hand; the two other children were by turns tamed and bored by the TV on the wall.

All of the families had three days of travel ahead of them—the six-kid family of seven was on the way to West Palm Beach, Florida—but their journey had already been long. They were indigenous Maya from Guatemala's poverty-stricken western highlands, from the departments of San Marcos and Huehuetenango, along Mexico's southern border. They knew some Spanish but they mostly spoke Mam, Lucía told me, one of Guatemala's twenty-one Mayan languages. The women had paid a bargain price of $2,500 apiece to a coyote to get them all the way from Central America to the United States. He provided them with false papers to travel through Mexico, but once they arrived in the Arizona desert they were quickly caught by Border Patrol. The coyote, Lucía said, simply turned around and ran back to Mexico.

They'd spent the wintry weekend in the Border Patrol *carcel*. December was always Arizona's coldest month, yet the agents had kept the holding cells frigid. "It was very cold," one woman, Jimena, told me, as her companions nodded. "The Border Patrol took away our sweaters and jackets, and didn't return them until we left. We had no blankets. We slept on the floor." Migrants often reported that food was scant on weekends at Border Patrol, and the only nourishment offered this group was juice and crackers. There was no milk, even for the babies and toddlers.

Dozens of Guatemalan women and babies were suddenly being caught every day all across the borderlands, a prelude to the hundreds—including unaccompanied minors—who would overwhelm border authorities in Texas each day in the late spring and early summer of 2014. Immigration workers in Tucson that winter believed that coyotes in Guatemala were spinning the news of possible immigration reform in the United States into a false promise to women: they told potential clients that the new law would allow migrant women and their children to stay legally. The window of opportunity was small, they were warned, and they had to act fast. But the talk was just that: these groups of vulnerable travelers were arrested by the Border Patrol. ICE did release them, under supervision, but they still faced deportation hearings. The coyotes were right in one respect: traveling with small children gave the women an advantage. Eloy and the other detention centers had no interest in going into the childcare business. The families were sent directly to the Border Patrol's Tucson Sector headquarters, released after a few days, and given orders to report to an immigration judge in the cities they were trying to reach. The agents dropped them off at the Tucson bus station, and they were free, just like the released detainees, to travel to their families across America.

The large number of these women and small children—and their needs—quickly overwhelmed local volunteers. The Casa Mariposa volunteers were going to the bus station every night, and were being called at odd hours by Greyhound staff. Over that one weekend, when the Circle K group was locked up inside the icy jail, Casa had been inundated with twenty overnight guests, all of them women and small children. On Monday night, Mariposa volunteer Laurie Melrood gave the resident members a break by bringing some new arrivals to her own home. After I bid farewell to Lucía and the others at the bus station, I went to Laurie's house to meet her guests, Blanca and her five-year-old son, Brian, both of them luxuriating in the heat and comfort of her cozy home.

Blanca was also from the western highlands of Guatemala, from San Marcos. As she and Brian ate a hearty meal of black bean soup and tortillas—a menu designed to tempt the palate of the most homesick Guatemalan—Blanca still was rattled by her recent misadventures in the desert. She had paid $6,000 to a coyote in Guatemala for passage for both her and her son. Laurie asked if the smuggler had warned them that they might be caught by the Border Patrol. Not really, she said. His main concern had been to caution them that they were not to reveal his identity if they were arrested.

Blanca's group had taken the route through Altar, Sonora, and into the Arizona desert west of Sasabe. Like the other Guatemalans, she was surprised at how cold an Arizona December could be. They were in the desert a night and a day, and she was terrified by the nighttime howling of the coyotes, the animal variety, that is. She even saw them, she said, her eyes widening, a pack with big animals in the front and little ones in the back. "They'll eat people," she insisted, "if they get hungry enough."

After the sleepless night in the cold and among the howls, Blanca and Brian kept going. Brian was a smiley kid who didn't seem the least upset by all that had happened. When *la migra* turned up, he recounted, he and his mom started running. Then the officers pulled out their *pistolas*, he said, aiming his finger like a gun. He grinned at the tale, as excited as if he'd just seen the scene in a movie—or been in one. It was true, Blanca said, the agents shouted and pointed their guns at the fleeing migrants, men, women, and children alike. *Gracias a Dios*, she said, they didn't shoot.

At the Border Patrol holding tank, Blanca and Brian nearly froze. Blanca was indignant that the agents had confiscated not only her own coat and sweater, but her son's warm winter jacket as well. She and the boy slept on the floor in jeans and T-shirts with only aluminum space blankets to cover them. She wrapped her arms around herself as she spoke, still trying to erase the memory of the bitter prison temperatures. "It was so cold," she said.

At least they'd been fed better than the Circle K group.

Blanca and Brian got small burritos to eat when they'd arrived late on Sunday, and early on Monday, before they were discharged, they were given tiny *hamburguesas*. At Laurie's, they had seconds of everything, and asked for fried eggs as well. Even Brian washed his supper down with a piping hot cup of coffee.

They'd sleep well this night in Laurie's comfy guest bed, under plenty of blankets. Early the next morning, they'd take the 7:00 a.m. bus, bound for Baltimore. Blanca's brother was expecting them. Brian had always had an American name and it would go well with the new American life they envisioned. His mother was still searching for one. "What's the American name for Blanca?" she asked me. I was nonplussed. "We don't have one," I said, at least not yet. "We just have Blanca."

Their travails would be worth it if everything turned out right, Blanca said. She was surprised when I asked her why she had come. The answer seemed obvious to her. "I came here to work," she said, "and for a better future for my son."

PART TWO

Deportation

CHAPTER SIX

Woman Without a Country

I was so crazy the day I was deported. I can hardly remember it. They took me from my home.

—*Elena Santiago, deported mother*

One block from the looming border wall, in the gritty border town of Nogales, Sonora, customers in the lunchtime crowd at Leo's Café were reveling in a holiday atmosphere. It was September 12, 2012, just four days before Mexico's Día de la Independencia, and the place was gaily decorated with plastic bunting in patriotic red, white, and green. Mexican flags sprouted everywhere, sticking up in vases of colorful paper flowers, poking out of a wreath by the cash register.

Husbands and wives, grandmothers and grandfathers, little kids in tow, were getting the celebration started early over plates of carne asada in the middle of the workday. One adoring *abuelita* carried her baby granddaughter over to see the birds in a big cage on the floor. The baby's eyes popped at the sight of three bright yellow *pájaros* fluttering inside.

Elena Santiago[1] seemed to be the only one at Leo's in low spirits. She looked down at her slice of birthday cake and smiled wanly. It wasn't much, but that little sliver of chocolate with pink icing on top was just about the best thing that had happened to her lately.

Her American friends Laurie Melrood and Blake Gentry, immigrant advocates from Tucson, were trying to cheer her up with a hearty lunch. Her fortieth birthday had been a few days before, and Blake had conspired with the mustachioed waiter to deliver the cake to the table. Blake had even ducked out into the crowded noontime streets of Nogales to buy candles for the surprise fiesta.

The waiter lit all six candles, and Elena leaned in to blow out the flames. Unbeknownst to her, they were trick *velas*— each time she blew a candle out it flickered right back on. She attacked the candles playfully, pulled them out of the cake, and doused them in a glass of water with a laugh.

The moment of levity was brief. A first grader at a nearby table ventured away from her parents to peek at the fluttering birds. The little girl was wearing her school uniform, a navy-blue jumper, and her black hair was pulled into a thick braid that trailed down her back. She bent down to look inside the cage and then grinned, showing the gap where her front teeth should have been.

"Pájaros!" she called to her parents. *Birds!*

Elena looked over at the happy child and her beaming parents, then turned away. Tears filled her eyes. She had two kids of her own, a boy, fifteen-year-old Luis, and little Joy Camila, just two. They were up in Phoenix, out of her reach, wrenched away from her the day ICE descended on her home and hauled her away. She hadn't seen either of the children in almost a year, since the day she was deported from the United States and dumped down here over the border in Mexico.

"It was on the third of November 2011," Elena said in Spanish, slumping a little at the table at Leo's. "ICE came to my house. They didn't come inside."

It was a school day and Elena was up early, as usual, in her rental house in Glendale, a suburb of Phoenix, getting her family ready for the day. She had her job at a store to get to, Luis would be going off to high school, and little Camila would tag along with her mom to work. Among the million morning tasks she faced as a single working mom, she had to feed the pets. The family had a whole menagerie of animals, "two dogs, two cats, two turtles," she said proudly. "I bought them for my kids. I had a big yard."

When she went out back to tend to them, she heard odd noises coming from out in front of the house. She came back in, and when Luis had his backpack on and Camila was zipped into her jacket, Elena opened the front door and saw what she most feared. A platoon of Immigration and Customs Enforcement agents, armed and ominous, were gathered outside. A fleet of law enforcement vehicles idled in the road.

"They closed the street, like I was a criminal," she said, trembling at the memory. "There were a lot of cars, a lot of agents."

Elena was terrified but she buckled her toddler into her car seat and shooed her son into the car. At the moment she started to get behind the wheel, an agent called out her name on a megaphone, broadcasting it full blast for all the neighbors to hear.

"Elena Santiago," he bellowed. "Elena Santiago."

The officers came over and handcuffed her in full sight of the kids, marched her over to one of their SUVs, and locked her into the back. Seeing their mother in the hands of the police, both kids started wailing.

"The police turned on their car radio so I couldn't hear the children," Elena said.

Inside the ICE SUV, over the din of the radio blaring and the kids screaming, the officers started asking questions. "Are you pregnant? Sick? Taking medicine?" Then they came to the most fateful: "Who are you going to leave the kids with?"

Elena had no one who could help her. Her mother was dead. The kids' fathers were out of the picture. She had only one real friend, a woman who was in no position to take in Luis and Camila. So the agents called Arizona's Child Protective Services, the agency that takes abused, neglected, and abandoned children and puts them into foster care.

In short order, a CPS woman arrived and leaned into the window. "Do you want to sign the children over to us?" she asked.

"I said, 'Yes. *Temporarily*,'" Elena recounted.

Armed with the document that Elena signed, the CPS worker turned to the kids. Luis always an attentive big brother, cradled the screaming Camila in his arms and climbed into the CPS van. In that anguished moment of seeing her kids taken from her, Elena suddenly remembered the family pets.

"I said to one of the agents, 'What about my dogs? My dogs are going to die.'"

The agent, she said, turned to her and sneered, "Who cares about the dogs?"

Elena trembled as she remembered his casual cruelty. "It was all for my kids," she said of the animals. Ten months later, she had no idea what had become of the dogs and cats and turtles, not to mention the family's furniture and electronics and clothes and car.

The family, divided into two vehicles, went their separate ways, the children to CPS, their mother to ICE. Elena watched out the window of the ICE SUV as the kids' van disappeared into the distance. She hadn't even been allowed to say good-bye.

At the ICE lockup, two officers tried to talk her into voluntarily signing an order of deportation. She knew better than to agree to be deported across the international line, far from her kids, and she refused, again and again.

"I kept saying, 'I'm not going to sign.'" *No voy a firmar.*

Frustrated, the agents took matters into their own hands. Literally. They grabbed her arms, she said. One man pulled her left arm behind her back, and the other grabbed her right. "That other guy put my finger in the ink and forced me," she said, demonstrating how the agent coerced her into making a fingerprint on the paper—the equivalent of a signature.

"They made me *firmar*," Elena said in Spanglish, the borderlands mix of English and Spanish. *They made me sign.*

Now the agents, and the US government, had everything they needed to deport Elena from the country where she'd lived since she was a young teen, and away from the country where she'd given birth to her two children, both of them US citizens.

"En horas," Elena said—within hours—ICE put her on a bus headed for the Mexican border. Three hours and 180 miles later, she walked south over the line with other deportees, past the dusty canyons separating Nogales, Arizona, from Nogales, Sonora, past the border wall, into Mexico, a country where she had not set foot in twenty-seven years.

She would get no news of her children for a month.

"I've lived in Phoenix my whole life," Elena told me on another visit that difficult fall. I'd come back to Nogales with Laurie Melrood to accompany Elena on a frustrating round of visits to Mexican government offices. Elena was trying to get a copy of her Mexican birth certificate. She had no papers at all: no Mexican identification, no US driver's license (though she'd had one once), no passport from either country. She had nothing to prove she was who she said she was, and she was beginning to feel like a woman without a country.

We'd met up with her that morning near the border wall, on a pedestrian walkway lined with dentists' offices that served a mostly American clientele. I'd asked Elena how she was doing. She shrugged sadly and said, "So-so." Now we were back at Leo's, feasting on baked potatoes smothered in carne asada, Elena's favorite *plato* on the menu.

Elena was plump, with pale brown skin, light brown hair, and constant worry in her face. She'd been born in Mexico in 1972, in the sprawling metropolis of Mexico City, or D.F. (pronounced Day Effay, in Spanish), short for Distrito Federal. She didn't remember much about it.

"I came to the United States when I was almost thirteen years old," she said, traveling north with her mother around 1985. They settled in Buckeye, a sleepy town about thirty-five miles west of Phoenix, with spectacular views of the White Tank Mountains. Now a rapidly growing bedroom community, in the mid-1980s Buckeye was still largely agricultural, a vast flatlands watered by canals.

"I started working when I got here," Elena said. "At the age of thirteen, I was picking in the fields." She and her mother got up at four in the morning to pick potatoes, carrots, melons, and onions, earning, as Elena remembered it, sixty cents for every two large containers they filled with veggies.

She didn't go to school, but school truant officers and immigration agents didn't bother much with field hands in those days. "I never had any problem with Immigration," she said. "I was lucky."

When she grew up, Elena left the farms and went to Phoenix, using the fake name of Bianca Vega to work at a long string of jobs. At a restaurant where she cut up fruit and vegetables, the elderly Chinese owner took a fatherly interest in her. Elena could read and write a little in Spanish, thanks to some lessons from her mother, but the man was scandalized by her lack of education.

"He thought I was like a wild animal," she said fondly. "But he liked me. He taught me to read and write English." She was a grown woman, but she got herself a backpack and used it to carry all her lessons to work each day, just like a schoolgirl. They'd sit together at one of the restaurant tables, their books spread out, poring over English stories. The man couldn't see well, so Elena learned to write in a large, looping script.

She had grown up without a father, and she loved the attention. "He was very important to me," she said.

Elena was blessed by her two children but not by their fathers. She met the man who would become Luis's dad when she was in her midtwenties. He was a violent man, and she fled his beatings. When Luis was born Elena didn't give the baby his father's last name, in hopes the man wouldn't find them. He continued to harass her by phone and eventually he located them. A few years later, in 2001, two armed men broke into Elena's house and attacked her; she believed that Luis's dad had sent them.

Elena's mother was still alive then and Luis was just a toddler; the men tied up the child and his grandmother and locked them in another room. Then one man raped her and threatened to kill her if she told the police. The attack left her reeling. After they left, she managed to pull herself together and with the help of a friend she did report the crime.

Camila's dad wasn't much better. By the time Elena's immigration woes started, in November 2010, the year after Camila was born, he'd already taken off.

Elena came to the attention of the authorities after a dispute with a landlord. The landlord called the cops. When they arrived they checked the records and discovered that Elena had accumulated unpaid traffic tickets amounting to $850. "I was in jail for twelve days," she said. Notified by the police, ICE officers picked her up when she finished serving her time. Deportation proceedings were begun, but Elena was allowed to go home to await her hearing. The agents gave her strict instructions to report to their office regularly.

Though she conscientiously kept those appointments, something went wrong in August 2011. A court hearing was set for August 25, but Elena didn't show. She said she never got the notice. The next time she went in for her regular appointment, she learned that she was in deep trouble: the judge had ordered her deported. An ICE agent slapped an ankle bracelet on her and warned her to get a lawyer. She tried, but the one attorney she talked to wanted $5,000, money she didn't have. Not knowing what else to do, she went about her business, taking care of the kids, going to work, until the morning ICE turned up on her doorstep.

Elena's story is not rare: she is just one of thousands of deported parents who have been torn away from their children in the United States.

"Children and families are being separated," says Laurie Melrood, an independent social worker in Tucson who spent an untold number of unpaid hours advocating for Elena. "It's more common than the public knows."

ICE's figures show that from July 2010 to September 2012—the period during which Elena was expelled from the country—the United States deported some 204,816 parents who left behind children who were US citizens.[2]

If the number of deported parents is high, the number of children left essentially parentless is staggering. Between 1998 and 2013, researchers estimate that some 660,000 US-citizen children lost a parent to deportation. The numbers of these kids have increased steadily each year, spurred by the ramp-up of deportations in the early 2010s. Many of the women and men deported in this push had lived in the United States for years, and were more likely to have children born in this country. In 2012 alone, the year after Elena was exiled to Nogales, 152,426 children, all of them American citizens, were separated from a mother or father by deportation.[3]

These are only the children ICE knows about. Experts believe that undocumented children don't always make it into the statistics. The tallies "only reflect people reporting that they have US[-citizen] children," says Victoria Kline, MSW, a social worker based in Mexico. "We don't really know how many undocumented children" are left behind. Parents nabbed by ICE may not tell officers they even have children, documented or not, for fear that the state will take their kids away from a loving aunt or grandmother or friend now caring for them. And if that aunt or grandmother or friend is undocumented, parents worry that these people too will be picked up by ICE.

Thousands of deportees' kids end up in foster care. Journalist Seth Freed Wessler found, in a landmark 2011 study, that some 5,100 children of deportees were in foster care, being raised by strangers.[4]

In Arizona, anecdotal evidence shows that hundreds of kids of deportees are being held in foster care on any given day, Laurie told me. Ironically, at the same time that Arizona's CPS was taking custody of kids with perfectly capable parents like Elena, the agency was being investigated by the state for its failure to monitor more than six thousand troubled families on its rolls. Many of their children had been abused or neglected; a few ended up dead.[5]

When the children of detainees and deportees are put into foster care, they get caught between two giant bureaucracies—the state Child Protective Services agencies and the federal Immigration and Customs Enforcement—that work at cross-purposes. Parents and children are "formally separated," Laurie said, and communication is difficult if not impossible. Detained parents are faulted for failing to appear for CPS custody hearings. Deported parents, trapped on the far side of the border wall, are considered to have abandoned their children.

And while immigration cases often proceed at a glacial pace, the state CPS agencies are under strict federal timelines to move foster-child cases along swiftly. Judges have some discretion, but if children under three—like Camila at the time of Elena's deportation—are not reunited with the parent within six months, the state can move to sever parental rights and put the child up for adoption.

"We don't know how many children of deportees are adopted out," Victoria Kline says; CPS agencies don't separate those statistics out. But anecdotal evidence shows that it happens. Yolanda's attorney, Nina Rabin, had at least one deported client who lost her parental rights to her children.

This was the threat facing Elena. She had never before been accused of being a bad mother, but Arizona was building a case to sever her parental rights. CPS argued that Elena knew that she likely would be deported, yet she had failed to plan for the care of her kids. That made her a criminal.

"CPS considered it neglect," Laurie said. And if neglect was bad, actual deportation was even worse. Dumped over the border into Nogales, Elena was now an even more objectionable mother because she was unavailable to take care of her children.

As Victoria put it, in the eyes of CPS, "deportation equals abandonment."

In Nogales, Elena found herself in a shifting community of deportees, all of them suddenly stranded in a confusing town that few of them knew. Elena was used to Phoenix, a wide-open city sprawling out over the flat desert between the mountains, its millions of residents, Elena included, routinely negotiating its boulevards by car. Nogales was completely different. A teeming hill town of about 212,000, Nogales was jammed with pedestrians, street vendors, and cars jockeying for position on narrow, bumpy streets. Taxis honked and music spilled out of the stores. Hemmed in on the north by the border wall, the town climbed up and down crazily steep hills.

Some 55,000 deportees are marched across the line into Nogales most years. In 2011, when Elena was deported, 54,977 *deportados* flooded the town, the equivalent of a quarter of the city's population.[6]

They had become a familiar sight in town. The border crossers who'd been caught in Arizona by the Border Patrol and quickly returned were still dusty from the desert, their *mochilas*—backpacks—strapped to their backs. The detainees who'd been in Eloy or Florence lugged all their worldly goods in the clear plastic bags issued by ICE. Elena didn't even have that much. She had only the clothes on her back. Like many of her fellow deportees she had lived in the United States for years and was traumatized by the abrupt separation from her family. She was desperate to return North.

Elena stuck close to the border, near a soup kitchen and the migrant shelters. Typically the guests had to leave these refuges at first light. Winter and summer, the displaced men and women spent dreary days in the elements, idling outside offices, roaming the streets. They sat on benches outside the office of Grupos Beta, the Mexican border force whose mission is to help migrants. Or they took naps in the cemetery, sleeping behind gravestones to escape the scrutiny of the local police.

Elena found her way to the shelter at the bus station Transportes Fronterizos, right by the border wall, and stayed for a month and a half. It was a rough, bare-bones affair in a shabby set of buildings, but it provided the wayfarers with a bed or maybe a mattress on the floor. In theory, those who stayed there were supposed to have bus tickets, but the rules were loosely applied.

The men slept in a crumbling trailer outfitted with bunk beds and the women on double beds and floor mats in an upstairs room reached by a set of rickety stairs. Temperatures in Nogales drop down to the twenties at night in winter, when Elena was there, and the shelter's showers were outdoors, open to the sky. Fenced in by wooden panels painted white, the splintery stalls had the unlikely look of a seaside bathhouse.

Elena was afraid in the crowded city. Twice, she told me later, men had tried to drag her into their cars. The Sinaloa drug cartel controlled the region; known by migrants as *la mafia*, the *narcotraficantes* had expanded into the lucrative human smuggling trade. The *federales*—armed Mexican soldiers—were in town too. When we were at the birthday lunch at Leo's, we saw a truckload of helmeted soldiers bouncing down the rough street, their rifles propped up, aimed at the sky.

It's hard to know what might have happened to Elena if she hadn't encountered some journalists from Los Angeles. They were in town interviewing deportees, and told her about No More Deaths, a human rights group out of Tucson that helps deportees in Nogales and migrants in the desert. The volunteers ran a telephone ministry outdoors at Grupos Beta and at another shelter, Albergue San Juan Bosco, proffering cell phones to deportees to phone home. A month into her time in Nogales, Elena went to the volunteers for help.

One of them was Hannah Hafter, an indefatigable activist who seemed always to be wherever deportees were. Elena told Hannah that she hadn't talked to her kids in a month and didn't even know where they were. The only number she had was for CPS, and she hadn't been able to connect to a live person when she called on a borrowed phone.

Hannah got in touch with Laurie, and Laurie quickly worked her contacts at CPS. Within days, she found out the whereabouts—and phone numbers—of Luis and Camila. Luis was in a group home in Glendale, and Camila was living with foster parents in a suburban town way east of Phoenix. When Hannah got the numbers, she handed Elena a phone, and for the first time in a long and painful month,

Elena was able to speak with her children. Hannah reported later that when Elena heard Camila's high-pitched voice say "Mamá?" she "just cried and cried and cried. It was like you could see this darkness lift off of her."[7]

No More Deaths gave Elena some clothes, helped set her up in an apartment, and kicked in for a phone and cell service. Once she had that phone, Elena called Luis and Camila almost every day. Before long, she even landed a couple of jobs, working first at a series of taco shops, then at a beauty salon, doing nails and learning the art of hair coloring. Her boss, Angel, became her literal angel in Nogales: he was a compassionate gay man who was appalled that she had lost her children. He did what he could to help her.

Luis, a minor at fifteen, was in the custody of CPS yet legally old enough to chart his own course. He could have gone to Mexico to be with Elena but he decided, with his mother's blessing, to stay in the country of his birth and get an education.

School wasn't going all that well though. Luis had been forced to transfer to a new high school, making for one more disruption in his life. And he was getting into scrapes at his group home. There'd been a scuffle with another boy and the two were brought before a juvenile judge. Luis was just plain angry. Angry that his home had been broken up, his family splintered, his mother deported.

He was furious at the separation from his beloved little sister. By law, CPS was supposed to arrange for visits between the siblings, but for six months after the bust-up of their family, none took place. At one of his regular hearings before a child-welfare judge, Luis complained. The judge sharply reprimanded the CPS caseworkers and ordered them to bring the kids together, pronto.

Finally, they began to have visits. Luis didn't like the

changes wrought by his sister's caregiver. "He says he doesn't like the yellow shoes they bought her," Elena told me, giving a quick smile.

Elena felt the same way.

"Camila's OK, but she's very skinny," she said disapprovingly. "She only wants to eat chicken nuggets and apple pie." At least the foster mom, a fifty-something grandmother, gave her juice instead of the soda she wanted. Worse, Elena worried that Camila was forgetting her own mother. Camila was just three, and Elena wanted her back. With Laurie's help, Elena got a laundry list of tasks from CPS she had to perform to prove that she could take care of Camila in Mexico. She had to get counseling, undergo a psychological evaluation, and submit to regular—and expensive—"drug drops," peeing into a cup to prove that she was drug-free. These tasks were required of all parents, documented or not, who were trying to get their kids back from CPS and foster care—even if, like Elena, they had never used drugs or harmed their children. Angel gave Elena time off for her appointments and sometimes even drove her.

Laurie checked out orders from CPS and DIF—Desarrollo Integral de la Familia—its Mexican counterpart, trying to make the documentations flow smoothly between the two agencies, no small task. After DIF did a home study of her bare-bones apartment, Elena was ordered to buy a refrigerator; with a price tag of sixty-nine dollars, the dorm-size fridge made a huge dent in her budget. The mandated visits to a therapist for counseling cost Elena thirty dollars a pop; the therapist advised Elena, absurdly, to get a social life. Hannah took Elena to the movies to help her comply; Laurie told Elena "to report that she and I went to Leo's restaurant." On her own initiative, Laurie sent report after report to the family court in Phoenix, documenting Elena's activities and even including snapshots, trying to impress upon the judge that this deportee was a real person, with a real life.

While Elena was working the Camila-in-Nogales angle, a lawyer in Phoenix was tackling the bring-Elena-back-home angle. Laurie and Hannah had persuaded a forceful immigration attorney to take on Elena's case pro bono. The lawyer dived down into Elena's complicated history and came back up with shocking news.

Elena was a victim of a crime in the United States—the gang rape and beating that had been duly reported to police years before—and as such she was eligible for a U visa through the Violence Against Women Act. She had a right under the law to be in the United States.

She had been deported anyway.

Four months after her fortieth birthday party—and fourteen months after she last saw her children—Elena had a morning telephone appointment with the family court in Phoenix. The judge would be hearing arguments, pro and con, on whether Arizona should sever Elena's parental rights to Camila. As a deportee Elena was not allowed to be physically present. Strangers who had never met her would debate her fate, and she would not be allowed to speak.

"Elena has met all the requirements she knew of," Laurie said that morning, as she and I drove down to Nogales to witness the phone call. Despite Elena's manifest efforts to rebuild a life that ICE had nearly destroyed, CPS still wanted the state to take Camila away from her permanently.

Laurie sighed. "Elena has had a bum life," she said. But she was a good mother. She still called both kids regularly, even though Camila no longer seemed to know her. "And the children visit each other. It's a testament to the mother's will that the family has maintained some unity."

It was a bitterly cold January day, and Elena was going to take the call in an unheated room at Repatriación Humana, the Mexican government office serving returned migrants and deportees. She was wrapped up against the chill in a camouflage jacket over a thick sweater. She brought along a yellow legal pad and pen, prepared to take notes.

Promptly at 9:30 a.m., the phone rang. The court was on the line. Besides the judge, there were four people present. A lawyer from the state attorney general's office and a CPS caseworker would argue for severance, and an attorney representing Camila's interests and Elena's family law attorney, provided by the state, would take Elena's side.

The phone connection was poor, and the call cut out once. The speakers were heard only tinnily through speakerphone, discussing the home study, the therapy, and the drug tests Elena had easily passed. An interpreter translated into Spanish, and Elena rapidly wrote down everything that was said, using the lovely handwriting her Chinese mentor had taught her.

Then began a cascade of critical comments. Elena heard for the first time that her Mexican therapist had concluded that Elena had a "negative pathology." As she scrawled those damning words on her yellow legal pad, tears rolled down her face.

A silence followed, then a sympathetic voice was heard. It was Elena's attorney.

"The mother has done nothing wrong," the lawyer said. "It's not that the mother doesn't want the baby."

The judge cleared her throat and spoke up. Though Elena had been instructed by CPS to work with DIF, the judge made the surprising declaration that she had no way to evaluate anything the Mexican social workers said, good or bad. She called for another meeting, closed to Elena, where both sides could present their cases once again. The CPS attorney would draw up papers for severance.

It looked bad. Laurie had counseled Elena to remain calm during the hearing, but when the strangers in Phoenix hung up, Elena began to sob.

——

Fifteen days later, Elena got another call. It was a complete turnaround. The judge had ruled in Elena's favor. Camila was coming back to her, the very next day.

No one who cared about Elena could quite believe it. January 24, 2013, dawned as another brisk winter day, cold enough that the Santa Rita Mountains between Tucson and Nogales were capped with snow. Elena called Laurie early in the morning. She had already talked to Luis by phone, Elena reported, and he had been told by CPS to expect a farewell visit from Camila. Laurie took that as a positive sign.

I joined Laurie and her husband, Blake, for the trip south, but first we stopped at a Tucson supermarket to buy a cake— white icing with pink flowers—and balloons. None of the store's balloons seemed right. They offered birthday wishes, congrats on a new baby, but nothing to celebrate the re-union of a mother and child after a government-engineered separation. Then Laurie spotted some early-bird Valentine's balloons. They were red, heart-shaped, and printed with the simple words *Te quiero*. I love you.

In Mexico, we found Elena near the Repatriación office. She was worried. "I have heard nothing from CPS," she fretted. *Nada.* But someone from the Mexican Consulate had called her to report that Camila was en route. She would arrive in the consul's car no later than 11:00 a.m.

To keep up Elena's spirits—and to pass the time—we went to an outdoor breakfast place in a nearby alley. A man cooking in the hole-in-the-wall kitchen delivered scrambled eggs with bacon and tortillas. Elena rejected his Mexican-brewed coffee and went instead for an all-American Coke, her favorite drink.

Elena called Luis, again, for comfort. "I talk to him every day," she explained. "Sometimes we spend three hours just chatting." When she got him on the line, the first thing she said was, "Have you eaten? What did you eat?" Then, "I love you, *hijo*." But he had worrisome news. Camila had not been brought to him for the promised good-bye visit.

It was 11:45. Breakfast was over, and there was no sign of Camila. Elena was on edge. We returned to Repatriación to wait. As Elena sat nervously on a bench, a fresh line of returned migrants walked by. She eyed them sympathetically. "I was so crazy the day I was deported," she said. "I can hardly remember it. They took me from my home."

Twelve thirty-five and still no Camila. Elena fell silent. Then a Protección officer appeared. "We've been in touch with the van," he said gently in Spanish. "It's coming."

Elena tried to smile but couldn't. "I've been waiting fourteen months," she told him.

Minutes later, a gleaming white van rolled up. A young woman, a consular officer, climbed out, reached in, and carefully lifted out a sleeping little girl. She hoisted her onto her hip, then stepped up to Elena and handed her her child.

Elena took Camila in her arms and cradled her and murmured to her in the few English words she still knew. "How are you, Camila?" she said through her tears. The little girl was sleepy and quiet and nestled into her mother's embrace.

A few months later, Hannah Hafter spoke at a public hearing of the Arizona Civil Rights Advisory Board, a state panel that was looking into the impact of SB 1070. Without giving their names, Hannah described what had happened to Elena and Camila.

"It crosses the line into cruel and unusual punishment when loving parents lose their children," she said. "By the time this mother and child were reunited fourteen months later, they no longer spoke the same language."

Camila had forgotten her Spanish, and Elena had never been able to speak much English. Camila mixed the two idioms at first, but she rapidly became fluent once again in her first language, the Spanish she heard all around her.

Less easily repaired was Camila's bond with her mother. The cracks began to show even on the joyous day of their reunion.

Elena's supporters had gathered at Leo's to celebrate. Her new *Nogalense* friends arrived bearing gifts. The consul staff carried in all the American goods Camila's foster parents had showered on her, and piled them up on the floor: a car seat, a pink plastic bicycle, stuffed animals, stacks of clothes. Laurie's balloons floated above the table and the friendly Leo's waiter, who'd seen Elena at her saddest, laid the table with the restaurant's best dishes. The pink and white cake from Tucson had a place of honor.

For Camila, ripping open one present after another, it was like a birthday and Christmas rolled into one. She stood on a chair, eating french fries and chattering in English, reveling in the attention of a tableful of adults who delighted in her every move.

Yet Camila seemed to have no clear idea of who these people were. In a quiet moment, she told me about her dog, her brother, and her grandma. But she wasn't talking about the dog left behind on the day of the raid, or Luis, or Elena's mom. She was talking about her new life in Apache Junction, where she'd grown attached to the foster family's pet, to a little boy who was also being fostered, and to her foster mother, whom she'd called Grandma.

The months ahead were rough. Elena's great supporter, her guardian Angel, moved on. Elena had to fret about childcare when she was working. Camila missed Grandma and called her often. Twice Elena gave the woman permission to come down to Nogales to visit, and both times Camila erupted in tantrums and tears.

In December, almost a year after mother and child resumed their life together, I tagged along with Laurie on another trip to Nogales. We met up with Elena and Camila at Lupita Taquería, a restaurant up the hill, a mile from the border. Elena didn't want to go to Leo's anymore, a reminder, perhaps, of her worst times, and she seemed to be spooked by the border wall. Camila was a beautiful child, with black hair and brown eyes, and she was rambunctious. She jumped out of her chair repeatedly and skipped around the restaurant, more than once heading for the door.

Elena was tired and frayed, a single working mom with a host of worries. After lunch, when Camila rolled in a patch of dust and dirtied her dress, Elena scolded her.

Camila stood up and put her hands on her hips. "You can't tell me what to do," she declared in Spanish. "You're not my mother. I'm going home."

The little girl was behaving like a typical four-year-old, trying out defiance, but her angry words betrayed the confusion that had scrambled her young life. The deportation of her mother would have long and lingering effects.

One piece of good news had come in October from the immigration attorney. Elena's U visa had been approved. She could return to the United States and live with both her children as a family. There was only one catch: she had to come up with a Mexican passport.

That was no small matter. In more than a year of trying, Elena had made little progress on getting an approved birth certificate, a prerequisite for the passport. She knew very little about her early life, other than that she was from Mexico City, a city of nearly nine million people, millions of them as poor and unnoticed as she was. Her mother was dead. She had no relatives that she knew of. And she had no ID.

Armed with scanty information, she had been making her way mostly uselessly through a labyrinth of local, state, and federal offices in Nogales talking to magistrates, notaries, clerks. Nearly every office required a payment up front. In the United States, staffers in the Mexican Consulate in

Tucson had made a stab at tracking down the birth certificate from afar, at Laurie's behest. They didn't ask for money, but they came up as empty-handed as their colleagues across the line.

The day of the dirty-dress incident, Elena and Laurie were following up on what had seemed like a promising development on the Mexican side. One magistrate, for a fee, had obligingly created a birth certificate, but it didn't pass muster. A second one he created for a second fee seemed acceptable, and Elena had submitted it to the local passport office, Secretaría de Relaciones Exteriores.

Now she was ready to fill out the passport application. After lunch, Laurie, Elena, and I went to the office, dragging along a squirming Camila. The haughty clerk at the counter informed Elena that the birth certificate had been lost. We rushed out and got another copy, for another fee, and rushed back. This time the clerk put up a new and different obstacle. The certificate had to be notarized and authorized by a judge.

On a downtown street, we found a notary Elena had used before; he could do the job, he said, for an additional forty dollars. Elena muttered about *una mordida*—a bribe—as Laurie handed over two crisp twenties from her own pocket. It would be a month and a half before the notary got back to Elena with the birth certificate, now all gussied up with seals and signatures.

Elena delivered this splendid document to the passport office and was told to come back later for an interview. In March 2014, at that meeting, Elena was told that her mother (now deceased) would have to appear in person to validate her daughter's claims. Oh, and Elena needed to provide her elementary school records. Both demands were impossible. Now it was Laurie's turn to mutter *mordida;* she was sure the workers were trying to get cash out of Elena.

Attorney Judy Flanagan told Laurie that the birth certificate impasse was threatening to derail the VAWA visa. It had to be used within a year. If Elena didn't get a passport by October 2014, she could lose her chance to get back into the United States.

"Elena's case is boilerplate for everything wrong that can occur when a child is in CPS and a parent is deported," Laurie told me. In being deported from the United States, and marginalized by Mexico, "Elena really did lose her identity. She is a stateless person."

As of September 2014, Elena was still waiting, biding her time in Nogales, manicuring nails and chasing after Camila. She had not seen her son, Luis, in almost three years.

CHAPTER SEVEN

In the City of the Deported

The biggest change is we see many women who
have already lived in the United States. They don't
want to stay in Mexico, leaving their children in
the United States. They are absolutely, positively
going to cross back.

—*Sister María Engracia Robles,*
director of a women's shelter in Nogales, Sonora

On a beastly hot June day, Jesús Arturo Madrid Rosas stood
near the DeConcini Port of Entry, keeping a close eye on the
street that somewhere on its downward slope transformed
itself from Grand Avenue, Nogales, Arizona, into Avenida
Adolfo López Mateos, Nogales, Sonora. The two nations
jostled up against each other here at the crowded crossing, and armed guards—American and Mexican—prowled
around just steps away from each other. Jesús was on the
lookout for *deportados*. He was an officer for Mexico's federal
Repatriación Humana, and it was his job to welcome home
his compatriots, deported Mexicans who were being uncer-
emoniously pitched back to their native land.

He never knew quite when the exiles would be arriving.

They turned up at all times of day and night, whether they were first-time border crossers freshly plucked from the desert or Mexicans who'd lived so long in the United States they could barely remember the land of their birth. On this day, a large group of deportees had arrived by the dawn's earliest light, and now, at midmorning, he figured the Border Patrol would soon deliver more. But he'd been on the job long enough to know that the agents didn't always stick to their own rules.

"They're supposed to send children, women, and the sick before six p.m.," he said. "But they arrive at all hours. Maybe five times a month these groups arrive in the middle of the night."

The wee-hour drop-offs were particularly problematic for the women. Nogales's red-light district was just a block to the east, and hustlers, pimps, extortionists, and drug dealers lurked in the *calles*. Even by day, the deportees were easily preyed upon.

"There are coyotes," Jesús said, "those trying to trick them with phone calls. It's dangerous." The scammers routinely tried to get the phone numbers of the deportees' families to extort money out of them. And *narcotraficantes* were always looking to turn would-be migrants into mules who would haul marijuana through Arizona's treacherous back canyons. The deportees used to be shuffled through the safer Mariposa Port of Entry on the quiet west side of town, but the Americans had been rebuilding it for some years. It would be better for the deportees when it was finished. For now, in 2013, it was Jesús's job to spot the newcomers at the chaotic downtown crossing and guide them to safety.

An unmarked white US van soon pulled to a halt in the no-man's-land between the two nations. Two women and two men climbed out, still dusty from the desert, their backpacks in their arms. They trudged wearily down a fenced metal walkway back to Mexico and stepped across the line.

"Bienvenidos," Jesús greeted them. *Welcome.*

Ever since the turn of the century, after the United States sealed off safer urban crossings in El Paso and San Diego, would-be migrants had flocked to deadly Arizona. And given the dramatic uptick in immigration and border enforcement, that meant that every year, Nogales got thousands of destitute returnees who'd been caught by Border Patrol or ICE and sent back over the international line. The flood of strangers had become a permanent feature of life in Nogales, and the Mexican government had finally been forced to act.

"We provide a lot of support to the deportees," Jesús told me in Spanish. "We've been doing this since 2008."

Before then, deportees mostly had to shift for themselves, finding their own way through a maze of programs run by charitable groups and the local government. When the Mexican feds got involved, Repatriación Humana not only partnered with the local groups already helping, it set up a formal receiving center right on the border and offered services of its own. The agency had a nurse on the premises; the month before, in May 2013, the clinic had treated no fewer than 584 returnees. Most had suffered from dehydration or blisters inflicted by the Arizona desert; one patient, in serious condition, had been taken by ambulance to the hospital.

Repatriación offered the displaced half-price tickets home and issued deportee IDs that entitled the newcomers to services. For eight days, they could eat hot meals at the *comedor,* an eatery run by the Catholic Kino Border Initiative, and for three nights, they could bunk down in Albergue San Juan Bosco, a private shelter up in the hills. Grupos Beta, the federal agency charged with helping migrants, would drive them where they needed to go, and provide a place to hang out during the day. Kino was invited to operate a medical clinic in the Beta office, and No More Deaths added a telephone ministry, the service that set in motion Elena Santiago's reunion with her little girl.

The needs were great, Jesús said somberly, and the plight of the repatriated was under worldwide scrutiny. Criticism had flared over violations of migrant human rights on both sides of the border. "The eyes of the world are upon us."

Gatekeeping was one of Jesús's most important jobs. He had to make sure none of the newly returned were minors traveling alone—if they were they'd go straight to DIF, the Mexican social services agency. If he suspected they were Central Americans masquerading as Mexicans, then back to Arizona they'd go. It would be up to Uncle Sam to deal with them.

Jesús was satisfied with the answers of the four who had just arrived. Three were from Mexico's poverty-stricken south; two, a married couple, were from Oaxaca, and the other woman was from Guerrero. All three had the dark skin and small stature of the nation's *indígenas*. The other man had just been returned home: Nogales, Sonora, was his birthplace.

They were all young. Both women were just eighteen, the husband was twenty-three, and the oldest, the Nogalense, was a venerable twenty-nine. None of them had made it far into *la Tierra Prometida*, the Promised Land. They'd been captured by the Border Patrol after a short desert trek *al Norte*, funneled through the agency's jail, and dropped back over the border.

The temperature was a sizzling 98 degrees and each of them gladly accepted a bottle of water. They declined an invitation to visit the clinic's nurse, but they had no choice about watching a video about the dangers of the desert crossing. It was mandatory for all returnees. The movie was like the "scared straight" films shown to American high school students to deter them from using drugs. The narrator shouted in Spanish, "This could be you!" while a montage of frightening images passed across the screen: a blinding sun, a burning desert, a venomous rattler. Worst of all were the pictures of dying border crossers lying prone in the hot sands, their faces bloated, lips cracked, water bottles lying empty and useless nearby.

The four migrants sat stone-faced; any of them could easily have met the fate of the video's border crossers. Arizona was in the grip of a deadly heat wave that would keep the temperatures simmering at 100 degrees or more for an unprecedented thirty-nine days straight, and claim the lives of thirty-five migrants.[1] No one in the office knew it yet, but the skeletons of two border crossers had been pulled out of the dirt that very day, one just seven miles away. Those bones had been found northeast of Nogales, Arizona, a stone's throw from the Kino Springs Country Club, where an irrigated golf course glittered emerald green, like an Irish mirage in the desiccated landscape.

The four travelers had survived that heat but they were exhausted. The Mexican government stood ready to help, Jesús advised them, and wished them well. Led by an officer, the quartet shuffled off to a government van, and climbed aboard. They were off to Grupos Beta, where they could take a shower, arrange cut-rate bus tickets back to Guerrero and Oaxaca, and reassure their worried families by phoning home.

No More Deaths volunteers had been patrolling the Arizona desert since 2004, trying to save migrants from dying. And for years they'd run an aid station for deportees in Nogales, Sonora. But in 2010 the volunteers had switched from dispensing burritos to offering phones. They'd discovered that a growing number of deportees had lived in America for many years. Their most pressing need was to call their families, in Mexico, yes, but also in cities all over the United States.

"They're anxious to speak to their family," volunteer Dorothy Chao told me. "I've seen people cry. It's their first contact with their family saying, 'I'm alive.'"

I found Fernanda standing patiently in line at the telephone ministry, in the same gravel yard where Elena had first heard her children's voices after her deportation. A thirty-seven-year-old fruit picker who'd grown up in the Pacific Northwest, Fernanda had to telephone two countries to reach her divided family: her mom and kids were in Washington State and her husband was back in Morelia. Fernanda's childhood in the United States had been more third world than modern American; instead of going to school, she had picked apples and peaches for American tables. She had three US-citizen children; she'd gone back to Mexico only after her husband was picked up in a traffic stop and deported. Now she regretted leaving. She was trying to get back to her kids, but so far she'd been caught twice in the Arizona desert. Like so many other long-term undocumented residents in the United States, she was learning that the crossing was far more difficult than it had been when she was a child. Now she was in a near-panic in Nogales, terrified that she wouldn't see her children again. It helped to talk to them by phone.

Gregorio Rivera Sanchez, a forty-seven-year-old who worked construction in Chicago, was limping around on crutches, awaiting his turn at the phones. He had a menstrual pad stuck inside the plastic Crocs sandals he was wearing, to cushion the monster blister on the bottom of his foot. Worse, his knee was banged up from a fall in the hills west of Green Valley, thirty miles south of Tucson. And there were angry bruises all over his back.

Gregorio had first come to the United States from Mexico twenty-five years ago. And until now he'd always been able to get back easily for visits. This last time, he'd gone back to Acapulco for a year to live with his wife and be a father to their two kids. When the money ran out, he'd gone north again, bound for Chi-town. This time the crossing was harrowing. He saw a human skull in the Arizona desert, and by the fourth night of trekking up and down steep hills, he'd developed a debilitating blister. On the fifth, he fell in the darkness and tumbled twelve feet down the slope. His leg was too badly banged up for him to continue the hike—he learned later he'd torn tendons in his knee—and the group left him behind.

The Border Patrol found him two days later. One agent ordered him to get up, he said, and when Gregorio couldn't, the agent angrily kicked the injured knee. Then other *migra* handcuffed him and threw him into their truck, hurting his back. The Border Patrol held him for three days, and the only real medical care agents dispensed was a pair of crutches, he said. Gregorio used them to walk back over the line when he was deported.

"I'm coming home," he told his wife when he finally got the phone. He didn't tell her about the injuries, not yet. He didn't want her to know that he wouldn't be able to work for a long time. Not that it mattered. There was no work in Guerrero anyway.

The travelers couldn't use any of the migrant services for long; even the phones were supposed to be reserved for the new arrivals. If deportees were still in Nogales after their three allotted days at the *albergue*, they could seek refuge in a series of shelters that spiraled down in quality. There was the Transportes Fronterizos bus station and its crumbling dorm, where Elena bunked for weeks. Then there was La Roca, a cinder-block hilltop aerie right by the border wall.

That one was run by an evangelical couple who were generous but penniless, and the deportees they welcomed slept on floors and used buckets of water to bathe.[2]

Deported men who had run out of options sometimes slept in the graveyard; an even lower circle of Nogales's deportee hell was Tirabichi, the foul-smelling town dump. Male exiles occasionally joined the poorest of the town's poor there, squatting in shacks slapped together from trash. For women, rock-bottom was prostitution. One young woman deported from Tucson was so terrified of the pimps trying to reel her in that she ran north through the port of entry. She was charged with felony reentry and ended up in Eloy.[3]

Women did have one shelter option that was closed to men. The Catholic Kino Border Initiative ran Casa Nazaret, reserved exclusively for women—and their children—who had been badly traumatized. It was housed in a couple of walkup apartments on the fourth floor of a shabby mini high-rise on the west side of town. On this wretched June day, when I visited with a group of American social workers, the building was baking in the heat; it was so hot its cinder block walls were warm to the touch. But the Missionary Sisters of the Eucharist who ran the place had made it homey; flower-decorated posters celebrating women's strength hung on the walls, and gauzy peach curtains drifted across the open windows, blocking the worst of the sun.

"We try to make this a family space," said Sister María Engracia Robles, the Mexican nun who presided over the casa. Sister Engracia—her name means "full of grace"—was tiny and tough, and immensely compassionate.

"The women usually stay about eight days," she continued, speaking in Spanish; they were allowed to linger until they felt safe again. The house had been named for the biblical childhood home of Jesus, Nazareth, where the Holy Family had lived together in peace and harmony. The residents were encouraged to cook and eat together to reestablish a feeling of normalcy, and they could call their families on the house phone. They could also get legal help. Casa Nazaret had contacts with a US immigration attorney who offered discounted services. And if the deported women had children in the United States, the nuns could help them write letters assigning guardianship to a loving family member or friend, to keep the kids from being farmed out to foster care, as Camila and Luis had been.

In 2012, the year before, 302 women, border crossers and deportees alike, had found refuge at Casa Nazaret. "The danger of violence is higher these days," Sister Engracia said. "On this side the cartels are exploitive. On the other side, the *migra*. The walls are higher. We're seeing many more broken bones."

The shelter's youngest resident that day was Adira, a twenty-one-year-old rape victim from Oaxaca who had arrived two days before "in great crisis," Sister said. Adira looked very young, with freckles sprinkled across her broad face. Her eyes were wide with terror. She wept without ceasing as she spoke to our group, but her story just poured out of her. At home, she'd been raped repeatedly. "It was horrible," she said. "I wanted to leave all that and be as far away from Oaxaca as possible." She signed on with a coyote in Sonora and crossed north into the Tohono O'odham reservation. Stretching seventy-five miles along the line between Arizona and Sonora, the rez was remote, hot, and little populated. For years it had been the deadliest of migrant corridors in the Southwest. Adira had the bad luck to hike it during the record-breaking heat wave.

"During the day the heat was horrible," she said. "The stones were very hot." The migrants soon ran out of water; some started bleeding from the nose, and Adira believed one of them died. She herself began to convulse. She lost track of time and started hallucinating. "In the desert the hills talked to me," she said. "I was delirious."

Someone set a fire to attract the Border Patrol, and at last "a helicopter came for us. I lost consciousness and I woke up in a hospital." She was hooked up to an IV, and she found red marks on her chest, where an EMT had used a defibrillator to restart her heart. She had been very close to death.

Two other women staying with the nuns had also been hauled out of the burning desert, but their backstories were different. María Dolmos and Norma were mothers, older than Adira, and both were reeling from the separation from their children. "The biggest change is we see many women who have already lived in the United States," Sister Engracia pointed out. "They don't want to stay in Mexico, leaving their children in the United States." Despite the dangers, "they are absolutely, positively going to cross back into the US."

Norma had two sons, an eleven-year-old American citizen and a fourteen-year-old Mexican citizen. She was a factory worker who'd lived with her husband and the kids in the Bronx ever since the older boy was one year old. She and her older son had gone to visit her grandmother in Mexico City. When it was time to go back home to New York, they lined up a coyote in Altar, a Sonoran town sixty miles south of the border. The man lied, telling them that the walk through the desert would take just three hours.

"We had to walk a frightening distance," Norma said. "We only had food for two days. We had no water. Someone was going to bring water to us. It was so hot." The nights were cold even during the heat wave, and Norma wrapped her son in a plastic bag to keep him warm. Finally, after three days and three nights, she couldn't walk another step. Her son begged her, "Mom, keep walking." But she couldn't continue and the Border Patrol found them. In short order they were repatriated to Nogales.

Norma had since found a way to get her son back over the border—she wouldn't say how—and now he was in the

Bronx with his dad and brother. In anxious phone calls, the family urged her to cross the desert again: it was the only way they could be together. "They want me to go," she said, starting to cry. "I don't know what to do. I'm afraid the coyotes will deceive me again. I don't think that I can try it again. It was terrifying."

María Dolmos had the opposite problem: her home was in Florida and her children were in Querétaro, in central Mexico. Six years before, María and her husband had left their kids with her parents; the children were tiny then, just four, two, and one. María took time off from her job in a restaurant to go back to see them from time to time; until now she'd always found her way home to Florida relatively easily. "The last time, I went through a barbed-wire fence in Nogales and walked a few minutes," María said, before getting picked up by her ride.

That was then. This was 2013. The border had been fortified, the walls were higher and longer, the number of Border Patrol agents had multiplied, and immigrants had to walk farther afield to get through. But María's daughter desperately wanted her in Querétaro for her First Communion. The girl was ten now, and she felt abandoned. "My daughter said to me, 'Are you going to come home now, or wait until I graduate from university?'" María couldn't repeat her daughter's angry words without breaking into tears. "When kids are little, they don't understand. But when they're older, you can't deceive them. Parents are supposed to be there."

So back to Querétaro she went. At the First Communion, she saw her young daughter splendidly arrayed in white and receiving the Body of Christ for the first time. On her way back to Florida, she'd had the misfortune to arrive in Arizona just as the May heat turned the Sonoran Desert into a cauldron. She'd paid the coyote half his fee upfront: $1,750, with the second half to be paid on delivery in Phoenix. The group slipped across the border in the dead of night. "It's sad in the desert," she said. *Triste.* "The days are hot, and the nights are cold."

The coyote had promised a hike of five days, but on the fifth day they were still out in the wilderness and out of water. "I couldn't walk anymore," María said. "The coyote got mad. He treated me badly; he pulled my hair. He grabbed my hand and pulled me." She fell, hurting her leg and hip; now she could only hobble along. Two days later, she and seven others gave up; they staggered out to a road and flagged down the Border Patrol.

"I lost half the money," she said. "But it's better to get caught than to die."

She had been recuperating at Casa Nazaret for three weeks. "I thank God and the nuns that I am alive," she said. Now she was agonizing over what to do next. She could go back to her kids in Querétaro. Or she could risk her life again to return to her husband and the job in the United States that paid to keep those kids alive.

"If God's willing, I'll try again," she said. "But not in the desert. Crossing is completely different now. It's much harder. Coyotes were more human back then. Now they don't have a heart."

Around the corner from Casa Nazaret was the comedor, the eatery for border crossers and deportees. It was in another tumbledown building, this one of stucco, on a deserted street close to the Mariposa Port of Entry. The steep stairs leading up to the doorway were so uneven that even the nimblest of migrants—let alone the walking wounded who frequented it—had to grip the railing to keep from tipping over. Workers had tried to brighten the place up, covering its peeling walls with Rivera–style murals of campesinos laboring in the fields or crossing the desert. A painting of a migrant Last Supper presided over the dining room.

The comedor had been started up by a local Catholic parish, Cristo Rey, years ago, when migrants first began surging into Nogales. In 2009, the dining hall was folded into the new Catholic Kino Border Initiative, a cross-border partnership named for a padre who roamed this land before there even was a border. The consortium included the Jesuits and the dioceses of Tucson and Hermosillo, but it was the Missionary Sisters of the Eucharist, operators of Casa Nazaret, who commanded the comedor.

With the help of a changing flotilla of volunteers, the nuns cooked up vast quantities of food in a tiny kitchen. They fed border crossers and deportees hot meals twice a day, seven days a week, three hundred sixty-five days a year. The eatery was strictly limited to people in transit—Kino couldn't afford to feed all the poor of Nogales—and the travelers could eat there for no more than eight days. In 2012 the comedor counted some fifty-eight thousand meals served. The Kino group also paid a social worker to help diners with special needs, and volunteers dispensed donated clothing after the meals.

I'd been to the comedor many times. I'd seen it jammed with as many as eighty-five diners, a full twenty-five of them women, along with four young children. Other times it was mostly men. On one of my visits, a Belgian film crew was there, hoping to interview some of the sad folks at table; another time, a PBS team was on hand. The comedor was a place where human misery was always easy to find.

On the blistering June day that the women of the Casa wept, two men limped into the nearly empty dining room. They were tardy for the 4:00 p.m. meal, and no wonder. Daniel Toral Moreno had lost most of his left leg; he was staggering along on his one good leg with the help of a pair of crutches. His buddy, Orbelín Salazar Valencia, still had both his legs, but one was encased in a cast from knee to foot. Orbelín was on crutches too, but as the more able-bodied of the pair, he shouldered two backpacks, Daniel's and his own.

Cutting through the afternoon's heavy heat, Mexican music blared on the loudspeaker, a tenor singing happily in Spanish to a chorus of horns and violins. Maybe it was the effect of the beach music, but Daniel was remarkably calm for a fisherman who'd just lost a limb. Now thirty-two years old, he had grown up by the sea in lush Veracruz, a moist and mountainous state that cascades down to the Gulf of Mexico. He used to travel 150 miles clear across Mexico to the Pacific to go shrimping out of the port of Salina Cruz in Oaxaca. "I'd go for one month on the boat," he said, "hauling in the shrimp." He smiled. "It was nothing but the sea and the sky."

In between stints on the water, he'd return to Veracruz, but the murderous drug wars had changed the beautiful old colonial town, and not for the better. Criminal cartels had taken root. "Los Zetas are in Veracruz now," he said. "People are hanging from telephone poles." In the fall of 2011, thirty-five people were tortured and slaughtered, their nude bodies dumped in a public roadway. Authorities blamed the murders on a turf war between the Zetas and an upstart cartel, New Generation. Then thirty-two people more were butchered, then four more.[4]

The following year, Daniel fled the violence, with plans to follow a Veracruzano neighbor who had gone to Tucson. Landlocked Tucson was no place for a fisherman, but it had the advantage of being just sixty miles from the border. He had to make the trip on the cheap, and he would walk the desert without a coyote.

"I had five hundred pesos all together," he said, the equivalent of thirty-eight dollars. He paid for a bus to Mexico City, then he climbed atop a cargo train—the dreaded La

Bestia—with the idea of riding it straight through to No-gales. Dangerous as that rooftop was, it was free. Daniel was one of many migrants on board, bracing themselves against the wind and the weather, clinging to whatever they could to keep from falling off.

He managed to hang on for more than a thousand miles, all the way to Benjamín Hill (given the Spanish pronuncia-tion of Ben-ha-meen Heel), a sleepy ranching and railroad town shy of Nogales by a hundred miles. Then he was at-tacked. "Criminals were chasing me and assaulted me," he said. "They took fifty pesos and my clothes." Worse, much worse, he lost his balance in the scuffle and tumbled down from the boxcar roof to the tracks below. The train's wheels sliced his leg off in an instant, and La Bestia just kept rolling along.

Alone in the dark, Daniel dragged himself to a road. A passerby called the cops, and they sped him to the big-city hospital in Hermosillo, the capital of Sonora. He underwent emergency surgery, and after twenty days recuperating he caught a bus to Nogales. He'd learned that a charity there provided free prostheses. Now he was biding his time in "No-gie," awaiting his new leg, pondering his future. It didn't look likely that he'd ever get to America, and only time would tell whether he could ever return to the sea.

Orbelín, thirty-seven, also had been pushed out of his home—Chiapas, Veracruz's neighbor to the southeast—but not by anything so brutal as the drug wars. It was econom-ics that took his livelihood away. He had worked in *maíz*, cultivating corn in the fields around the capital city of Tuxtla Gutiérrez, but the cheap Iowa corn flowing into Mexico post-NAFTA undercut the price of his Chiapan corn. Once the trade agreement was in place, Mexico went from a corn-producing to a corn-importing nation. Orbelín was one of the casualties.

"No gané mucho allá," he lamented. *I didn't earn much.*

He was separated from his wife, but he had two boys, ages eight and nine, and their school fees were high. His brother was in LA, and he decided to join him up there to scrape out a better living. On his first try, he broke his leg in the Arizona desert—he didn't want to say how—and he wouldn't be going anywhere for a while. But he was confident his body would heal, and he would cross over again and look for a job. What kind of work did he have in mind? He was puzzled by the question. "Lo que sea," he said. *Whatever there is.*

By the next time I visited the comedor, on a blessedly crisp October morning, Kino had had to expand its services. The Mexican government, under the new administration of President Enrique Peña Nieto, was less willing to collaborate with do-gooding foreigners; the telephone ministry and the medical clinic had been banished from Grupos Beta. The phone volunteers moved their operation to the comedor; after meals, diners could call home. The new medical clinic was spottier. Father Sean Carroll, director of Kino, was plotting to buy a bigger building that would accommodate all the travelers' needs, from a shelter to a larger dining room to a full-size medical clinic. For now, from time to time a volunteer doctor or nurse would convert a corner of the cramped comedor into an examining room.

At the October breakfast I counted just thirty-seven seated at the three long tables, only a handful of them women, and none of them children. They were mostly young men, with a few middle-aged men tossed in here and there, all of them dressed in worse-for-the-wear jeans and T-shirts. The volunteers scurried around handing out plates of food, and the diners politely passed them down the tables to their *compañeros.* The menu varied depending on what the nuns could rustle up, and that day it was pinto beans and rice, fresh zucchini and tomatoes, and hunks of white bread. To wash it all down there was coffee and *jamaica*, a popular Mexican drink made from rose hips. Before they could dig in, one of the nuns, Sister Diana, stood at the far end of the packed room and began to pray aloud.

"I give thanks that we are alive," Sister said in Spanish. In this crowd, gratitude for "being alive" was not just a prayer convention. Some of her listeners had risked their lives in the desert—or on the journey through Mexico—and others were revving up to strike out soon into the wilderness. "Lean on each other in the *camino*," Sister advised them. "Immigrants, you live in the hearts of each of us."

The breakfasters mostly bowed their heads as she spoke, and many made the sign of the cross. But one man was too distracted to pray. His left foot was in a cast, and he held it in his lap, grimacing in pain. His neighbor explained later that the man was a deaf-mute; he could neither speak nor hear. He had traveled the desert anyway, and he'd fallen and hurt himself while running away from the Border Patrol.

Another nun took to the floor to deliver warnings about what the newcomers would encounter in Nogales. Still swathed in the yellow apron she'd donned for kitchen duty, she bellowed over the din of the clacking plates. She cautioned the breakfasters about the same things that worried Jesús over at Repatriación: the coyotes who would worm their phone numbers out of them and the narcos who would entice them to work as mules.

There was no banter as the guests dived into the meal. They mostly ate without speaking, quietly pondering their own woes.

A man named Jorge was squeezed in at the far end of the table, right under a mural painting of a man holding a child in Arizona's Sonoran Desert. He was thirty years old, and originally from Honduras. Before he got picked up by the authorities, he told me, he had lived in North Carolina for nine years. He was married, and he and his wife had two children, an eight-year-old son and a seven-year-old daughter, both of them born in the United States. He had had a good job in Durham, as a welder. Then, one morning in 2011, the police showed up. Jorge was arrested and turned over to the feds, cycled through the system, and speedily deported back to his homeland.

The first time he left Honduras he had been a young man of twenty-one, and he'd gone north because "there was no work and no money," he said. Now, the nation was still desperately poor, but it was dangerous as well, overrun by gangs and government death squads. But the poverty and crime weren't the main reasons Jorge had left Honduras again. This time he'd come because he desperately wanted to be back with his family in North Carolina. He talked to them on the phone sometimes, but he hadn't seen them in two years, a long time in the life of a child, or a marriage. He had been a good provider, and he agonized that not only was he absent from their lives, he was failing to support them financially.

"My family needs money," he said simply.

He had already tried twice to get back to them. Both times, he had crossed the border with a group led by a coyote, and both times he'd been quickly caught. Now, the third time around, he wouldn't make the same mistake. He'd go solo, one lone man, practically invisible, hardly a blip on the Border Patrol radar. "I'm going to cross again, by myself," he declared.

His seatmates were alarmed. The man across from him was a native Mexican who had recently been deported from his longtime home in Tucson; he knew the dangers of the Arizona desert. "Ten cuidado," he said, frowning. *Take care.* Everyone knew about the desert's heat and the lack of water. But there were other perils Jorge might not have heard of, and the man ticked them off: narcos, rattlers, scorpions, bobcats. Another man chimed in that he had been kidnapped by smugglers when he was crossing, and his family had been forced to pay $4,500 for his release.

Jorge was unmoved. He didn't care about the risks. He was going to get back to his kids and his wife, no matter what.

Jorge reminded me of Gustavo Sanchez Perez, whose deportation from Phoenix is recounted in this book's introduction. Gustavo, another young father, had been in Arizona since the age of eight and deported at twenty-five.[5] I had met him at the comedor in 2011, when it was beginning to become apparent how many of the deportees in Nogales had lived in America for years. There were still plenty of first-timers pushed north by poverty or violence, but out of three diners who talked with me that day, two considered the United States their home; they had deep roots in their communities and children who were American citizens.

Gustavo's tablemate that day was Francisco Vasquez. Francisco was about forty and his kids were nearly grown, but he longed for them just as much as Gustavo missed his toddlers. "I have three children," he said proudly. "They're twenty-one, eighteen, and thirteen." Not only were they US citizens; his wife was too. They were all in the Northwest. Years ago Francisco had traded one O for another, moving from his native Obregón to Oregon. He had been harvesting fruit for years, on farms near Portland.

"I picked cherries and apples," he said. "It was a lot of work and a lot of fruit." *Mucho trabajo y mucha fruta.* The pay wasn't bad. He didn't quite understand what the difficulty was, he said with a smile. Americans wanted fruit, and he was happy to pick it.

He had been going to see about a job when he got arrested. Now, he was sixteen hundred miles away from his family. They couldn't even help him by wiring money: he had no identification. It was a common enough complaint. *La migra*, he said indignantly, "has my papers, my ID, all my cards. These are very important to me. All they said was, 'Go to Mexico!'"

A fresh-faced young Honduran listened with interest to these tales from the two hardened immigration veterans. Just twenty-two years old, he was about to embark on his first attempt to breach the border. He had his own American dream: he hoped to make balcony railings with his cousin in New Jersey.

It was July, and hot, and he knew he would need lots of water. But he was going north with four other young green-horns, all from Honduras, and they didn't plan to pay a guide who knew the terrain. "We're going to cross near Sonoyta," he said, just west of the desolate Tohono O'odham Reservation, where so many migrants have died, and where, I learned later, forty-one bodies were found that month. Nevertheless, he felt sure that he would make it through, "with the help of God."

CHAPTER EIGHT

Albergue Evening

The mafia has people on mountaintops
with walkie-talkies. It's really organized.

—*Ciro Antonio Solana, deportee who tried
to cross the border a second time*

Nogales was hopping early on a Saturday evening in April.
People were strolling the springtime streets, cruising in cars,
sitting in the tiny church plaza downtown near the border
wall. Taxis were trawling for partygoers. Neon signs were
starting to glow pink and purple on the bars, competing with
the day's fading light. Somewhere a norteño band played, its
polka rhythms bouncing out into the *avenidas*. Los Noga-
lenses were anticipating fun times.

South of downtown, the mood was different. A Grupos
Beta driver steered a big passenger van through the crowds,
driving it up the hilly road that hugged the railroad tracks.
After a bumpy mile and a half, he changed gears and turned
into a tangle of steep streets twisted like mountain switchbacks. He pulled to a stop on the sloping roadway and
jammed on the emergency brake.

Up here on the hilltop, the views of the distant peaks
and city lights were beautiful, but the van's passengers didn't

pay much attention to the scenery. The dozen travelers who dragged themselves out onto the sidewalk had none of the cheer of the Saturday-night revelers downtown. They were deportees adrift, seeking shelter and food. They trudged silently to the door of Albergue San Juan Bosco and hauled themselves up its high steps.

Inside, the soft twilight on the mountains gave way to harsh fluorescence. The dining hall that the travelers entered was shrilly lit by overhead lights, and the place was institutional and shabby. Still, the shelter workers had made an effort to make it welcoming. All was in readiness for a meal. Three long tables had been arranged end to end down the center of the narrow room, creating one long dining surface ringed by twenty-two metal folding chairs. Behind a kitchen counter, three enormous cooking pots sat on top of a commercial stove. The burners had been turned off and the aroma of the evening's stew wafted out into the room.

The walls were painted a soothing tangerine, and a hospitable sign greeted the newcomers: "Albergue para Migrantes, San Juan Bosco." Dedicated to a nineteenth-century Italian saint famed for rescuing street kids, the shelter was a refuge for the displaced and the sorrowful. It gave the detained and the deported a home away from home for a few nights. But the sadness of the visitors, as piercing as those fluorescent lights, hung heavily over the place.

When it came time for the pork stew to be served, the room was quiet. First the women and then the men moved silently forward in the dinner queue. Many labored as they moved along the line. Two women rolled along in wheelchairs; one of them had casts on both legs. When the men took their turn, more than a few walked with difficulty. One very tall man was limping, shuffling along on feet swathed in bandages. His counterpart, an unusually short man, winced with every step. A forty-something, older than the average visitor, dragged his aching feet.

The low mood seemed to spread to the workers. Normally the shelter's caring volunteers managed to nudge up the spirits of the sad souls who'd come in for a meal and a bed. Tonight even they seemed downcast. María Díaz Rodriguez, the cook, and her daughter, Adriana—longtime Phoenix residents who would themselves be detained in Eloy in the months ahead—had worked hard to rustle up that tasty-smelling meal. And they were pleased to see their pal Bob Kee, a Tucsonan who came to San Juan every Saturday night, bearing gifts of coffee and sugar for the kitchen, and clothes for the deportees. Even so, María and Adriana were shaken by the high number of bad injuries their guests had sustained in the desert—one of the wheelchair women had broken bones jumping down from the border wall—and some horrific tales they'd heard earlier in the week.

Ana, a thirty-year-old woman who had just been released after two months in Eloy, had come to the albergue a few nights before. She had been crossing the Arizona desert in a group with her eight-year-old son, she'd told them, when a howling pack of coyotes descended upon them. The migrants had climbed frantically into the small desert trees. But the animals had gotten ahold of the boy, she claimed, and tore his flesh apart and ran off with his remains. The Border Patrol arrested the group a short time later, and Ana was too afraid of the agents to tell them what had happened.

Coyote attacks on humans are rare, fatal attacks even rarer, and María had no way of verifying the woman's account. But Ana's terror had been genuine, María said. "It was dreadful," and now Ana wanted nothing more to do with "the other side"—*el otro lado*. She was skittish and fearful, and spent only one night at the shelter. She went south the next day, hurrying pell-mell away from the horror.

A man at the albergue had wept as he told Adriana that he had been forced to watch as his wife, son, and daughter all got raped in the desert by the *polleros*—the "chicken wranglers"—the lowest-ranking guides on the migrant smuggling chain.

"What is the world coming to?" Adriana asked glumly.

It was Bob who finally helped break the spell of sadness. María beamed when he presented her with a gift of her favorite chocolates from the States, where she'd lived for twenty years. And he and fellow volunteers from the Tucson Samaritans, a group that searches the desert looking for border crossers in distress, loaded up a table with donated used clothes and toiletries. The forty-year-old deportee with the aching feet looked up with interest. He reached for a pair of gently worn running shoes that were up for grabs. He pulled off his own sneakers—riddled with holes from his desert journey—and with a big smile tied the new ones right on.

An unaccountably chipper young fellow in the chow line was thrilled to see the visiting Americans. The man was toting all his possessions in a clear plastic bag—a sure sign that he'd recently been lodged at Eloy, courtesy of the Corrections Corporation of America. He wanted to practice his newfound language skills.

"I learned English during two months at CCA," he said brightly. Then he joked around with the visitors. "Thank you, sir! Thank you, sir!" he said repeatedly. "Thank you."

In the dim light of the albergue chapel, Araceli, a thirty-seven-year-old native of Guerrero, was sitting in a wheelchair. The chapel had a makeshift altar loaded with candles and plastic flowers. Sometimes Father Sean Carroll would come up from the Kino comedor to say Mass, but most evenings it was quiet, and dejected immigrants like Araceli could be found there, taking respite in the stillness. Just days before, Araceli had broken both her legs, in three different places, and she was in terrible pain.

I had come up to the shelter as Bob's guest, and Araceli

consented to tell me what had happened. As she spoke she often wiped away tears, and her husband, Sergio, hovered over her anxiously.

"We came here to work," Araceli said in Spanish, smiling ruefully. The couple had gone to Denver six years before, leaving their home in Guerrero, a poor state on Mexico's southwest coast. The three oldest of their five boys were born there in the Mile High City. "I never had trouble with *la migra* or with jobs," Araceli said; she'd always been able to find work in restaurants or in hotels. Cleaning hotel rooms, she sighed, was "pesado y pagó mal." Hard and poorly paid. "You get used to it."

She and Sergio missed their families, and after a half dozen years, they went back with the kids to visit the grandparents. There was never any question of staying permanently. Guerrero is famous for the tourist mecca of Acapulco, but elsewhere there was little work. By some estimates more than a quarter of the state's population had migrated to the United States.

Eventually, Araceli and Sergio joined the northbound throngs once more. Their plan was to get resettled in Denver and then send for the kids. The couple made it safely to Sonora, but they trekked three long days through the Mexican desert before they even crossed into Arizona. They were already worn out when they entered near Sasabe, thirty-seven miles west of Nogales. The desert there is treacherous, hilly, and laced with rocks and roots, and they'd gone only a short way when Araceli took a bad fall.

"I slipped between two rocks," she said. "I fractured two legs—one near the ankle in my right foot, two bones in the left leg. I couldn't take another step."

It was early morning and the first rays of light gave them away. Border Patrol agents spotted their group and pounced. Some migrants escaped, but Araceli was lying on the ground, unable to run, her husband by her side. When *la migra* saw how badly she was injured, they were very nice, she said. *Muy amable.*

"They helped us and treated us well," she said. One agent fastened temporary protective coverings on her shattered legs. Then "six Border Patrol carried me, for two hours," Araceli said. "My husband walked in front." In a little procession of international cooperation, the Mexican husband marched ahead and reached for the brush and the mesquite, pushing the branches aside to make way for the American agents carrying his wife.

After they arrived at the road, though, Araceli and Sergio were split apart and driven to Tucson in separate vehicles. She was taken to the University of Arizona Medical Center, he to Border Patrol headquarters. The hospital doctors and nurses were gentle with Araceli, speaking to her through an interpreter on the phone. They X-rayed her legs, put them in casts, advised her to see a doctor when she got home—and discharged her to the Border Patrol.

Now she too was driven to the Border Patrol lockup. Araceli asked where her husband was, but the jail is run strictly along gender lines, and she wasn't allowed to be with him. Both got a little food—cold fries, small burgers, juice, and crackers.

Araceli was parked for the night in a wheelchair near the agents' computer workstation, and Sergio lay on the floor in a cold cell nearby. He had only a Mylar blanket for cover. It was so cold "we couldn't sleep," she said. And with fresh breaks in three bones, she was in agony.

The hospital docs had given her painkillers, and the station agents commandeered them, as Border Patrol rules require. But the agents refused to give her any, despite a policy that permits detainees to take American-prescribed meds under supervision. Eventually, her pain was so acute that she wept and cried out. It was only then, after many hours, that the agents relented and gave her her pills.

In the morning, things looked up. Araceli got special treatment because of the severity of her injuries. Instead of being loaded onto a bus with the other returnees for the trip to the border, she and Sergio got a private ride in a comfortable agency SUV. The compassion of the Border Patrol agent who drove them almost made up for the cruelty of his colleagues.

"He treated us well," she said. "He was a very good person." *Muy buena gente.* She paused. "There are some very nice North Americans, and some who aren't."

Alerted by the Border Patrol to the arrival of a badly injured woman, a representative of the Mexican consul greeted Araceli at the border. He gave her a wheelchair to keep, and the Mexican Red Cross whisked her off to the hospital in Nogales, Sonora. The doctors hooked her up to an IV for rehydration, and gave her more painkillers before releasing her to the shelter.

Four days later, when I met her at San Juan Bosco, she was suffering. "It still hurts," she said, beginning to cry. "I can't make my foot comfortable."

On Monday, in two days, she and her husband were to be flown back to Guerrero, their tickets paid for by the Mexican government. She couldn't imagine how she would manage on the trip: her doctors had instructed her not to walk, at all, for another ten days. Her biggest fear was for her family's future. "There's no work in Guerrero," she said, weeping, "but we won't try again" to cross. Sergio's family had a piece of land, *una tierra*, in the countryside, but it was hard to wrest a living out of its soil. Still, they would try. And the family would be together. Their children were in Mexico, not trapped *al otro lado*, like the children of so many other deportees.

At least she had survived, Araceli said. "I give thanks to God that I'm alive."

———

Albergue San Juan Bosco housed men, women, and children in its two dorms, on bunk beds and on mattresses on the floor. Adriana Díaz, the young Dreamer biding her time, pondering how to get home to Phoenix, volunteered to show me around. Down a narrow corridor, behind a door marked *Damas*—Ladies—were two small rooms crammed with ten sets of bunk beds. The beds were squeezed into almost every inch of floor space, providing a place for twenty women and girls to sleep. Plaid Mexican blankets colored purple and red—the cheap acrylic kind seen in every Nogales market—were draped over the mattresses. Off the rear bedroom was a lone bathroom, supplied with a single toilet, sink, and shower. Later in the evening, I saw a long line of women patiently waiting their turn to get in.

"So far I've counted twelve women tonight," Adriana said around eight o'clock, but that didn't mean more wouldn't be coming later. The Juan Bosco workers didn't get much sleep. Resident volunteers like Adriana and María and the two male staffers were often awakened during the wee hours by the arrival of still another Grupos Beta vanload. The weary deportees could come any time of the day or night, depending on when the Americans dropped them off at the border. And whenever they arrived, the workers got up to greet them.

Usually more men than women showed up, Adriana said. The men's dormitory was much larger than the women's and its bathroom had three showers. In the single big bedroom, there were ten triple bunks, giving thirty men a place to sleep. Eight standard double bunks yielded berths for sixteen more. And stacked up against one wall were dozens of foam mattresses to handle overloads. Those extra mats got used, often.

Bob told me that he had seen as many as 135 men and women on a single Saturday night; 66 got the official bunk beds and the rest sprawled on foam slabs on the floor.

"I've been to the other shelters in Nogales," Bob said. "This one is best."

The albergue had been operating since 1982. Juan Francisco and Gilda Loureiro, a married couple who owned a shoe store in Nogales, opened it after they discovered migrants shivering at night in the church plaza. The couple paid for much of it out of their own pockets—Juan Francisco even built the bunk bed frames—while constantly hitting up local business owners for donations. Bob said the Loureiros kept scrupulous records of all donations, including every pound of coffee and sugar he brought along from Tucson. In recent years, with deportees overwhelming Nogales, they'd begun to get some Mexican government funding.

I visited in April 2013; that January San Juan Bosco had marked its thirty-first year of welcoming the desperate seven days a week, three hundred sixty-five days a year. At an anniversary party, the Loureiros estimated that they had served up to a million people.[1]

Even with all the help, the volunteer labor, the government funding, and the private donations, the Loureiros couldn't afford to house each of their guests for very long. Travelers were officially allowed to stay at Juan Bosco just three nights. The hard reality was that deportees had to decide quickly what to do next. Still, Juan Francisco and Gilda—known affectionately as Doña Gilda—were always granting extensions for special circumstances: for people badly injured, like Araceli, for women traveling alone, for families with children. When I met María and Adriana in April 2013, they had already been at the shelter for five months. In exchange for room and board they worked, cooking and cleaning, helping new arrivals get settled, and lending a compassionate ear to the migrants.

"Francisco and Doña Gilda are very kind people," María said warmly.

One rule was firm. The wounded and the sick could rest all day at the shelter, but able-bodied residents had to leave. Grupos Beta drivers returned early each morning to take them downtown to the comedor for breakfast. They could return to the comedor for the late-afternoon supper, but in the hours in between it was up to them to figure out how to pass the time. They were like the homeless in any city, wandering the streets, drifting from one place to another. Many lingered on the benches outside the Grupos Beta offices. At least it was safe there.

By the evening, when they were back up on the hill at San Juan, the temporary residents gathered in the chapel, relieved to be in one spot after a peripatetic day. Sometimes a No More Deaths volunteer would stop by with phones for the deportees to call their families. One time I saw the unflagging Hannah Hafter with a phone in each hand. She stood by the altar and in her impeccable Spanish invited anyone who cared to, to step right up.

A mother and grown son who'd lived for eighteen years in Las Vegas had been doing the shelter scramble for six days, getting up early at the albergue and spending the day out in the open. They were grateful to have been allowed to stay at the shelter so long—once again Francisco and Doña Gilda had made an exception—but now they were plotting their next move.

"I've contacted a couple of coyotes," Ciro Antonio Solana, the twenty-three-year-old son, told me. He and his mother, forty-seven-year-old Antonia Alvarez Martinez, spoke to me as they sat in the crowded chapel. It was a different Saturday night and the shelter was once again full. The pair had recently been caught crossing into Arizona, Ciro said. Now "we're going to try California or Texas."

Antonia and Ciro were part of a preacher family. For years, the clan had run an evangelical church—Iglesia Cristiana Ebenezer—in Sin City, giving praise to the Lord not far from the haunts of Vegas's gamblers and drinkers and prostitutes.

"My mom and dad are both pastors," Ciro said. "I'm a singer. We started that congregation. We bought the instruments. Once we were deported, there were no pastors and no musicians."

Ciro had lived in the States since he was three or four, and he spoke a fluent and colloquial English. He had been born in Morelos, a small state just south of Mexico City. "My dad used to leave for a couple of months every year, to go work in the United States," he explained. "My mom got tired of that. She said, 'Either stay here or we all go.'"

So north they went. It was the early 1990s, and "it wasn't that hard then. We crossed at Tijuana and we just walked two hours."

The family had six children, the youngest a little girl, now ten, who was born in the United States. They never had much money, and as a teen Ciro dropped out of high school to work at a restaurant and bring his wages home.

The Solanas made an effort to regularize their status; they hired a lawyer who advertised his immigration practice on TV. The "lawyer," they belatedly discovered, was no more than a notary public—a notary who charged very high fees. They'd paid him thousands of dollars, only to be given an order of deportation by an immigration judge two years ago.

Desperate to earn some of the money back, they disobeyed the order to report to ICE, figuring they'd first get in some work time—and stockpile some wages. When they failed to show up as instructed, "ICE came to the house in Nevada," Antonia said in Spanish, interrupting her son. "ICE came to the door."

The ICE officers rounded up Mom, Dad, and three of the grown kids. One adult daughter was allowed to stay in Las Vegas and care for the youngest, a daughter, then eight, who was the family's one American citizen. ("We were separated for a year," Antonia said.) A son who lived on his own in another apartment eluded ICE's grasp.

The five Solanos who were arrested were held briefly at a detention center. They knew that families are often divided up when they're deported, and "we asked them not to separate us," Ciro said. "They kept us about ten hours and deported us to Tamaulipas, all five together."

Tamaulipas is a dangerous state in northeast Mexico, just south of Texas. The Solanas were dropped off in 2011, the year that 193 passengers were pulled from public buses there and butchered by the Zetas cartel; the year before, the same cartel had slaughtered 72 northbound migrants and buried them in a mass grave. The family had to travel through this perilous territory. But their luck held; they rode safely by bus to Mexico City and then to Morelos, the Mexican hometown they hadn't seen in years.

They arrived penniless and in debt. Deportees often forfeit all that they've accumulated in the United States, but the Solano son still in Vegas sold their cars and TVs and sent them the proceeds. And the bereft congregation of Iglesia Cristiana Ebenezer took up a collection and lent $2,000 to help their deported pastors build a house in Morelos. It was modest by any measure.

"We have water and power but no windows, just wood, and laminate for a roof," Ciro said. The substandard dwelling was bad; worse was the family's crushing debt. "It kills us to know we owe money."

The Solanos had become a divided family: the two daughters spared by ICE were still in the United States, and so was the son. And Antonia said, "I have my mother in the United

States. She doesn't have papers. She lives in Las Vegas with one of my sisters."

A year into the separation, the daughters who'd been left behind rejoined the family in Mexico, but money worries cut the reunion short. The Solanos decided that Ciro, Antonia, and one of his adult sisters, Anita, would return to the United States. "We're trying to get back to working and pay the debt," Ciro explained. Economists call this phenomenon debt migration: deportees are in such bad financial straits when they get back to their home countries that their only recourse is to return to the United States.

Antonia had struck a Faustian bargain when it came to her family. She could once again care for her elderly mother in Vegas, but she'd be a half continent away from her youngest child. Antonia had no idea when she would see the little girl or the rest of her family again.

And at this moment she was stuck in Nogales. It wasn't looking too likely that she'd see her mother anytime soon.

So far, the Solano trio's odyssey through the world of smugglers and criminal gangs in Nogales had been a disaster. The Sinaloa cartel controls Nogales and the surrounding countryside; its chief, the notorious Joaquín "El Chapo" Guzmán, would be arrested in February 2014, nearly a year after the Solanos dealt with the cartel's local gangsters.[2]

Luckily for the Solanos, when they were in Nogales, El Chapo was still in charge and the cartel was peaceful, after a fashion. *La mafia*, as Ciro called it, was concentrating not on killing but on making money by smuggling migrants and drugs. Ciro, Antonia, and Anita had flown from Mexico City to Hermosillo, the capital of Sonora, and then taken a cab north the three hours to Nogales. They'd arrived three weeks before I met Ciro and Antonia at the shelter.

They'd contacted a coyote whose number they'd been given back in Morelos, and the smuggler parked them at his uncle's house for a week. "The guide was getting in touch with his people," Ciro explained. "The uncle was a Christian too. He was a great guy. We only had to pay him for food while we were staying at his house."

When all was in readiness, the coyote took the Solanos to a hotel and handed them over to a second smuggler. That man instructed them "to take the taxi that will come," Ciro said. "It was all set up." Antonia and Anita were ordered into the taxi, and Ciro was told to climb aboard a separate SUV. He was nervous about being separated from his family members, but after twenty minutes the vehicles converged on a single house.

The three Solanos were put into a room already jammed with thirteen or fourteen other would-be migrants and told to keep quiet. Every traveler was ordered to hand over four hundred pesos, about thirty dollars, for food and water for the desert trek. In the middle of the night, the journey began.

"We left at one or two in the morning," Ciro recounted. "The SUV drove us in two batches. We were crammed in. We couldn't see."

They drove about forty minutes west of Nogales to remote country where the steel-pole border wall ends. Out there the massive barrier gives way to barbed wire that's easily breached.

More migrants arrived during the night and in the end there were nineteen souls hoping to make it to the other side. They spent the night in a ditch near the line. The whole scene was eerie, "weird," Ciro said: in the darkness he could see both coyotes and *migra*, each standing guard, each watching out for the other.

"We saw the Border Patrol. And we saw the mafia. They have people on mountaintops with walkie-talkies. It's really organized." So organized that the mafia demanded payment from the migrants for passing through the land they controlled. The three Solanos had to pay "$300, $100 per person," just for the mafia fee. Beyond this little piece of travel extortion, the migrants had to pay $1,500 to $2,000 for the trip up into Arizona.

Once the group had snaked through the barbed wire along the border, a coyote led them into Arizona's Tumacacori Highlands, rough country that's both mountain and desert. It was cold at night when they started out, around 40 degrees, but the temperature shot up to 80 by afternoon. They walked fourteen or fifteen hours straight, and by nightfall Anita began to falter. "She got tired and we had to carry her," Ciro said.

Something spooked the guides and they ordered the migrants to drop to their hands and knees and crawl through the brush; Anita tore up her knee on the rocks. But that maneuver did them no good. They had been detected, and suddenly Border Patrol was everywhere. The migrants scattered. Three got away, disappearing into the darkness. So did the two guides, Ciro said disgustedly. They ran away "like little rabbits." He thought he himself might have had a shot at escaping, but he didn't even try. "I couldn't leave my sister and mother."

Back in Mexico after a one-day stay at the Border Patrol station in Nogales, Arizona, Anita got medical treatment for her scraped-up knees at the Grupos Beta clinic. She was traumatized and refused to cross again. Distraught by the terror she'd felt in the desert, she took the Mexican government's offer of a cut-rate bus ticket home and left for Morelos as soon as she could.

Ciro and Antonia intended to soldier on. He was worried how his mom would fare on a second attempt, but what else could they do?

"We have to try again," he said, going east to the Texas border or west to California to cross once more *al Norte*.

That trip would cost them another $4,500 apiece. Antonia was listening intently to her son. "Dios nos ayuda," she said. *God help us.*

Saturday after Saturday, Bob Kee heard about *la mafia* and *la migra*, about broken bones and families split apart. He came to the albergue not just to deliver food and clothes, but to listen. "These folks are going through who knows what," he told me. "Often they like to talk. They have horrendous stories."

Bob was a dental technician in Tucson who spent his week negotiating between patients with bad teeth and the labs that were making them new ones. Luckily, his job called for him to immerse himself in dental dilemmas only four days a week, Monday through Thursday. On Fridays he rested.

On his full-throttle Saturdays, he was away from home from dawn till midnight. He'd get up very early and turn his car south from Tucson, driving an hour down I-19. The road cut through the Santa Cruz Valley, paralleling the dried-up riverbed and skirting the Santa Ritas. Centuries ago this was a Spanish trail; and after the Spaniards departed in 1821 and before the Americans got it in 1854, this land was Mexico.

Just nine miles north of Nogales and the border, Bob steered onto Ruby Road. An old mining track, the road threads through spectacular country, past a ghost town, the remains of a mining camp, and even a couple of rare Arizona lakes. Bob would rumble along Ruby west a ways, then park and set out on foot into the Tumacacori. The landscape matches the spikey sound of Tumacacori's name; it's filled with prickly cacti and rocky trails and treacherous hills. One of its peaks rises up more than six thousand feet, so high that there's a different ecosystem up there, thick with live oak trees and sycamores instead of desert scrub.

Bob was hyper-fit. He had a barrel chest and swelling biceps, and he easily managed the rough wilderness trails and steep switchbacks. He loved the hike, but that wasn't the main reason he lit out to Tumacacori each and every week. He was a Samaritan, and in his monster backpack he hauled life-saving food and water. Many migrants had died out here in these remote Sky Islands, tripped up by winter's cold or summer's heat; Bob had five times found the bones of the dead.

All of them had perished after a four- or five-day journey from the border "on the third mountain range you have to travel. It's such an exhausting journey," Bob said. He hiked to keep more people from dying. He patrolled canyons and valleys and hills, trekking the trails that led down to the border. Each week Bob walked miles in and miles out, leaving water bottles and granola bars and pop-top cans of tuna along the active pathways. He had a strict policy of never going alone; a rotating crew of two or three fellow Samaritans from Tucson took turns hiking with him. Scott Nicholson, a volunteer community worker in Nogales, Sonora, sometimes came north across the line to go with Bob. Occasionally, they'd trek south to the border from Ruby Road, hiking to Walker Canyon in the Parajitos. The wooded canyon lay in both nations, with an active trail that led straight from Mexico into the States. It was somewhere out here that the Solanos had crossed over.

Bob didn't always see the travelers, but he nearly always spotted evidence that they were there. "The water we left the week before will have been taken," he said. "Or their backpacks are there, left behind." On his longest hike ever, a couple of miles past Walker Canyon, Bob had found plenty of backpacks and empty water bottles on the ground. In the distance, through the trees, he spotted five migrants hurrying north.

Sometimes, he'd come face to face with border crossers.

Once, "we ran into five guys in Walker Canyon," he told me. "They saw our Los Samaritanos T-shirts." Reassured by the group's green cross printed on the cloth, the men came out from their hiding places and into the open.

They were lost; they'd been wandering in the wilderness for eight days. "I don't know where they got their water," Bob said. "They all had clean water," but they had no food and gladly accepted what Bob had to offer. These walkers had become so confused deep in the Tumacacori that "they never went north at all," Bob said. Instead, by mistake, they'd been hiking laterally west to east, paralleling the border. Now they were ready to give up and go back to Mexico. Bob judged that they still had a difficult hike ahead. But these guys were still going strong, he said. "Four of them were pretty young, but one was about forty. They sat down with us for fifteen minutes. Then, like deer, they took off up the side of a hill. Amazing."

Bob had also gone down to Sonora to see Walker Canyon from the Mexican side; he hoped to get a better idea of what the albergue folks faced when they crossed to the north. He traveled with Grupos Beta; the officers drove about nine miles west of Nogales, sticking close to the international line. "After four or five miles, the wall ends," Bob said. "Then there's just barbed wire fence." A few small ranches hug the border in this back country, but beyond those, "there's nothing. Just trails." They got out of the van and followed a trail a few miles to Walker. He learned that it takes migrants two days to walk from Nogales to the canyon, and by then, "they're already starting to deplete their supplies. They may have run into the cartel" and been relieved of their money, or worse, their water and food.

A homemade shrine to the Virgin of Guadalupe nestled at the mouth of the canyon. Candles in glass vases imprinted with her image were set into the desert brush, and prayer cards were scattered around. Once, Bob and Scott saw a group of migrants stopping to pray in this holy place. One by one the men stepped forward, lit the candles, and begged la Virgen to help them cross the perilous desert ahead.

Even after his longest hikes, Bob didn't call it a day when he got back to his car in the late afternoon. Instead, he turned south from Ruby Road for the border. He still had work to do. San Juan Bosco called.

On the Saturday I talked with Araceli, I met up first with Bob and Scott at the McDonald's in Nogales, Arizona, just a block north of the line. Bob was in high spirits, charged up by the pleasures of spending the day in the outdoors. His backpack was empty now, its water bottles and granola bars and cans of tuna left behind in the Tumacacori. He opened up his car trunk and replenished the pack with albergue goods: coffee, sugar, rice, jeans and shoes, shampoo and soap—and chocolate for María. Scott was driving me the two miles up to the albergue, but Bob declined the offer of a ride. He heaved his heavy pack onto his back, and he stepped across the border into Mexico. Joining the Saturday-evening throngs, he hiked up the steep Sonoran slope to the shelter, through the twinkling lights, bringing his good spirits to the deportees on the hill.

PART THREE

Resistance

CHAPTER NINE

Showdown on Tenth Avenue

If this is how the Border Patrol treats old white people on a street in the city, imagine how they treat migrants in the desert where no one can see.

—Kathryn Ferguson, border activist

Agustín Reyes Sepulveda climbed into the van for his second shift of the day. It was early on a fall evening, October 8, 2013. He and his buddy, Arturo Robles, had already worked that morning, but they had another job ahead of them that night. They were going to Tucson's southwest side, out past San Xavier del Bac, the old Spanish mission. Instead of spending the evening with their families, they'd be installing a walk-in freezer at an old folks' home.

Agustín had been working this job a dozen years or more, outfitting industrial kitchens in institutions of all stripes. He'd been a single parent to his son Ramón, now thirteen, for eight or nine years, ever since the boy's mother had been deported to their native Mexico. "I am the parent who raised him, from Head Start to now," he told me during an interview the following week. "He's an eighth grader. He's a good kid, he gets good grades, he's very focused."

Agustín had a new woman in his life, Rosita, and she and

her kids lived with him and Ramón; the kitchen job helped support them all. Agustín liked the work, and he was good at it. He owned his own tools, and he'd stashed them in the back of the company van along with the materials he and Arturo would need for that night's construction.

Both men lived south of downtown, in the Mexican barrios where Spanish was more common than English. Agustín had been born in the copper-mining town of Cananea, Sonora, and he'd learned only a little English in his seventeen years in the United States. "It's difficult," he said, shrugging. On this work night, he drove north out of the neighborhood, Arturo riding shotgun. They glided past the barrio front yards adorned with shrines to the Virgin and paper flowers and potted plants, and on past Fourth Avenue's restaurant row, where Mi Nidito and Rigo's served up Mexican favorites from nopalitos to carne asada.

At about a quarter to seven, they turned west from Fourth onto Twenty-Second Street, a major thoroughfare that gave them a straight shot to Interstate 19. They had enough time, but only just, to get to the nursing home at the appointed hour of seven o'clock. "The main thing," Agustín told me, "is to be on time."

Ahead to the west they could see A Mountain, its dark peak outlined against the sunset's fading orange and pink. Then Agustín noticed something else: the flashing lights of a cop car in his rearview mirror.

Minutes later Dorothy Chao turned onto Twenty-Second from the opposite direction. She was on her way to the weekly Samaritans meeting at nearby Southside Presbyterian Church, the hub of the local immigrant-rights movement. Chao was sixty-five, a retired nurse who kept busy with the No More Deaths telephone ministry in Nogales; she also hiked out into the wilderness one day a week—like Bob

Kee—with fellow Samaritans, looking for migrants to help. But her outback treks and phone work had come abruptly to a halt that spring. She'd been diagnosed with breast cancer in February and had undergone a double mastectomy in April.

Dorothy still looked frail. She was thin and small, and she never went out without a kerchief—universal cancer signifier—covering her bald head. She was glad to be going to the Sams meeting, to see her hiking buds, to get back into the swing. As she turned off Twenty-Second and steered south down Tenth Avenue, she saw something troubling: a Tucson Police Department cruiser pulling over a white van around the corner from the church.

Once Agustín slowed to a halt, the officer peered in the driver's window. "The cop never said why he stopped us," Agustín said. "He just asked for ID"—from both driver and passenger. Under SB 1070, Arizona's anti-immigrant law, a cop can't just stop people because he or she suspects they're undocumented; the stop has to be triggered by a separate potential infraction. The officer was with TPD, the Tucson Police Department; a Mexican American named Fabian Valdez, he spoke to the two men in English. He skipped the explanation of what violation had caught his attention and went straight into a request for Agustín's driver's license and Arturo's ID. Neither man had a license to show him. Valdez wrote in his report that he asked Arturo for ID for "officer safety reasons to know who I was speaking to." Arturo didn't know that as a passenger he was not legally required to answer the officer's questions, but he did answer. And the fact that neither man had a license was a tip-off to the cop: undocumented immigrants can't get driver's licenses in Arizona. It gave him potential grounds for the "reasonable suspicion" required by SB 1070 to investigate the men's legal status.

Valdez called for backup; a Spanish-speaking officer,

David Fritsch, arrived and ordered the pair out of the car. Fritsch told them to sit down on the curb and asked them more questions, but as Valdez noted, at that point the suspects "refused to speak further." Three times in his report Valdez referred to the men's language skills: they spoke Spanish and understood very little English. But it was the men's lack of ID, their "nervous behavior and unwillingness to talk" that could indicate they were "possibly in the country illegally," he wrote in his police report. He called Border Patrol.

Agustín had his cell phone with him and quickly dialed Rosita. When she heard the bad news, she worked her phone as fast as she could, setting in motion the phone tree for Corazón de Tucson, a grassroots immigrant-protection league. As it happened, the Corazón members were meeting at that exact moment, and Rosita reached a small tribe of them in a single call. They were at Thirty-Third and Ninth, not far away, planning a *pachanga*—party—for Día de los Muertos, the upcoming Mexican holiday Day of the Dead. Within minutes, they converged at Tenth Avenue.

Raúl Alcaraz Ochoa had already arrived. An activist with the Southside Worker Center inside Southside Presbyterian Church, he was across the street working *his* cell phone, alerting members of the Protection Network Coalition, an umbrella organization of immigrant groups.

Around the corner at the church, just as Dorothy and the other Samaritans were arriving, Leslie Carlson was leaving. She'd attended the weekly meeting of the End Streamline Coalition, which aimed to put a stop to the mass hearings of immigrants held daily in federal court in Tucson.

"When I was walking out of the church, someone I knew from the community was running up to the church," Leslie told me the next week. The woman quickly explained that some men were in a fix with the cops out front. Leslie alerted the Reverend John Fife, a Streamline Coalition member and retired pastor who'd led the church for thirty-five years. Tall, lean, straight-spined, and outspoken, John had the air of a prophet and nearly always spoke in biblical cadences. He'd had his own run-ins with the law: in 1986 he was indicted along with other members of the Sanctuary Movement for harboring asylum seekers from Central America. Now he rushed out to Tenth Avenue with Leslie and the neighborhood woman.

John marched over to ask Valdez why he'd made the stop. The cop refused to say and ordered him back across the street. Moments later, Sergeant Baron Carson, Valdez's supervisor, drove up in still another cruiser; he told the pastor Valdez had stopped Agustín because the light over the van's license plate was burned out. "In good police practice: cops should say 'fix it' and walk away," John said the next day. "This was a simple traffic stop for an unlighted license. Most of us would have simply been ticketed."

Agustín had raised the officer's suspicions that he was undocumented, the supervisor went on. As a furious Fife recounted later, "The cop said to me, 'He doesn't speak English and he doesn't have a driver's license.' That's racial profiling"—which SB 1070 specifically forbids—"and it's happened again and again in our community." Carson's written report doesn't include what he told the pastor, but he did note that the two prisoners spoke to a passerby in Spanish.

John tried another tack, arguing with Carson about the amount of time police were allowed to detain the men. Under the Supreme Court ruling that put limits on SB 1070, cops can't hold a person longer than it takes to conduct their own police business. "You can't detain him longer than it takes to write the ticket," John told the cop. Then, in John's telling, "The officer grinned at me and said, 'Yes, I can, because I'm going to search the vehicle.'" And, the officer added, the Border Patrol had already been called, at 7:09 p.m.

There's no mention of the search in Carson's report, but Fritsch wrote that "once Sergeant Carson arrived on scene, he requested that I proceed with the inventory of the vehicle." The police began rifling through the tools, construction materials, and even the bag lunches Agustín and Arturo had stashed in the back of the van. Agustín's boss, Yvette Duran, manager of A-United Restaurant Equipment, was summoned, and the police allowed her to take the company equipment out of the van before it was towed away. Under Arizona law, vehicles had to be impounded for thirty days if the driver was found to be without a license.

Fourteen minutes after the cop made the call, a Border Patrol SUV rolled down Tenth. The agent parked in a narrow alley lined by palo verdes, the prickly state tree of Arizona. His first order of business was to step through the swelling crowd and take command of the two prisoners. "He made us put our hands on their truck," Arturo said the next week. "He asked my name and nationality." The agent hurt Arturo's wrists when he cuffed him, but otherwise "he behaved well." His hands restrained behind his back, Arturo couldn't climb easily into the high SUV, and the agent hoisted him aboard. Agustín, also handcuffed, followed. Ensconced in the vehicle, looking out on the gathering of people, the two had a front-row seat for the tumult that was about to erupt.

Raúl Alcaraz Ochoa's voice rang out above the din. "Let's go across the street and join hands around the Border Patrol truck!" he shouted. Earlier that year Raúl had crawled under a Border Patrol vehicle to stop the arrest and possible deportation of a father of six who was cuffed inside. He'd been arrested himself and become something of a local hero, and now many in the crowd responded readily to his call. Leslie was one of them.

"There were about nine or ten people," she recalled. "We joined hands and began chanting, '*Sí, se puede.*'" Yes, we can.

"And '*Ni una más.*'" "Not one more," the slogan of the anti-deportation movement.

Leslie broke ranks briefly to run back to the church to invite the Samaritans to join the circle. A gray-haired bunch who ranged in age from their fifties to their seventies, the Samaritans didn't hesitate. "We took off," Dorothy told me later. "When we got there, some No More Deaths people and maybe Corazón de Tucson were already there. We joined them, holding hands. We just grabbed on."

Inside the SUV, Agustín marveled at the response. "There were about a hundred people out there. On every side there were people. Some were circling the truck. Then more came and they made a double circle. Then more Border Patrol arrived."

And more police. Samaritan Michael Hyatt, a sixty-six-year-old photographer, eventually counted twenty-eight vehicles, belonging to both the cops and Border Patrol. The Border Patrol agents "were all decked out with guns and vests," Dorothy said. "They were all running around."

Michael estimated that twenty-five protesters clasped hands and stood in two rings around Agustín and Arturo. "The first circle had about fifteen people," Michael said. "I joined the second circle. On my right was a little girl, about ten, and then her eight-year-old sister and then their dad. Barclay Goldsmith"—a seventy-six-year-old theater director—"was on my left. We were holding hands."

It was dark by now, the street lit mostly by the flashing of the lights on the battalion of law enforcement vehicles. The people holding hands were singing "No Nos Moveran"—the Spanish version of the old protest song "We Shall Not Be Moved," and chanting "*Ni una más.*"

"I was prepared to be arrested," Leslie said. "I didn't want to be. But it's not OK with us, that people are being abducted from the community, for things like a license light." Dorothy was nervous. "I remember thinking, 'My goodness, I might be arrested.' I have a fear of arrest. But I was mainly just thinking, 'We're all in this together. Community gives people courage.'"

John Fife was in the circle too and he knew the civil disobedience drill. "I expected to hear the Tucson police make an announcement through the bullhorn, saying, 'You're in violation of the law. If you don't leave, you'll be arrested.'"

That never happened. Instead of taking control of an incident on the streets of Tucson, the Tucson Police Department ceded power to the US Border Patrol.

Some thirty minutes into the standoff, the Border Patrol agents made their move. A phalanx of officers broke into the lines of hand-holders, shoving their way into the rings of old people, young adults, and children. They gave no advance warning.

"There was no announcement until they barreled into the crowd," Michael said. "The agent in the lead said, 'We're coming through. If any of you touch us, you'll be charged with a federal crime.'"

Despite the police sirens and the chanting, the chaos and the darkness, the agent did not use a bullhorn. Like many of the other protesters, Barclay heard no announcement, and neither did Leslie. Even if they had, there was no time to react and retreat. The agents were already in their midst.

"They formed a triangle in the street, like a pyramid," Dorothy said. "One person was in front, then two people," then two or three more.

"They were very aggressive," Michael said. "About four or five Border Patrol yanked people. The Border Patrol was lunging into the crowd. At the inner circle it got rough. They pushed and shoved. There was a lot of shouting going on.

People were protesting being manhandled. I saw them pulling people apart."

Leslie recounted that the agents "were roughly pushing and shoving us away from the Border Patrol truck. One guy pushed me repeatedly. Shove. Shove. Shove. And I'm not very big. Some people were pushed to the ground."

One of them was Dorothy Chao.

"They busted the line in front of us," Dorothy said. "I was pushed to the left. I realized I was going down." As she tumbled, she had a fleeting realization of how dangerous it would be to be underfoot in a mob of terrified protesters and booted Border Patrol officers. "I was afraid of being trampled," she said. "Then I was on the ground."

Her belongings scattered. Dorothy crawled around in the dirt, frantically searching for her purse, her sweater, her meeting notes. While she was on her knees, one of the agents snatched her kerchief off her hairless head. "It was definitely done on purpose," she said. "It was the first time I was exposed publicly. I was bald. I don't remember any compassion." Officers yelled at her to get up. "The Border Patrol were pulling on my shirt, pulling it away from my body."

Arturo watched in horror from the SUV. "I don't know who it was," he said, "but two Border Patrol dragged a woman."

Samaritan Sandra Anderson saw it too. She didn't know Dorothy, but she later described seeing "a woman with cancer, wearing a kerchief on her head. A Border Patrol agent knocked her down and pulled off her kerchief. He grabbed her T-shirt and yanked her up by the shirt, and said, 'Stand up!'"

After three or four minutes, when Dorothy finally managed to get back on her feet, she shouted at the agent. "You're picking on a cancer patient. Shame on you." The man replied: "I'm just doing my job."

Dr. Norma Price was the next to hit the dirt. All of five feet four and 114 pounds, Norma was seventy-one, a retired physician who regularly cared for migrants in the desert and deportees in Nogales. "I saw at least five or six Border Patrol agents moving in toward the vehicle," she said. "I don't know how many people touched me. It was so fast. I was looking in the face of one. I think he must have grabbed my arm, and I fell to the ground." Norma was wearing a sleeveless dress, and as she went down, she fell against a palo verde tree; its prickers dug into her right arm, scratching her skin from shoulder to hand and tearing her right leg. The arm, she said, "bled quite a bit."

Next, white-haired Barclay Goldsmith nearly toppled onto Norma. As he described in an account he wrote shortly after that night, "I am seventy-six and not always steady on my feet, so I broke hand grip with Michael Hyatt. I was walking away from the group towards the street and a border patrolman shoved me aside quite strongly. I almost stumbled and fell. I corrected my balance and again began to walk towards the street away from the bus and the ensuing chaos with protesters, police, and border patrol when again I was pushed aside and almost fell on top of Dr. Norma Price, who had been pushed to the ground, I believe." Luckily for them both, Barclay was able to right himself.

Cuffed and caged inside the SUV, Agustín and Arturo could only watch helplessly. "I saw the Border Patrol pushing people and knocking them down," Agustín said. "I saw Rosita and the kids. I was worried, naturally. I was scared. But I was grateful for the support of the people.

"There were sirens and lights, police all over. It was really something to see, like being in a movie. There were cops blocking the street. And cars of people who came to support us."

Finally, with the circles broken and demonstrators forcibly pushed away, the Border Patrol agent hopped into the vehicle, switched on the engine, and started backing up. A roar went up from the crowd. A young man had thrown his body behind the back tires to stop the vehicle from taking Agustín and Arturo away.

"I shouted, 'There's a guy on the ground,'" Michael said. Two TPD officers rushed in, grabbed the man, and carried him off.

The coast clear, the Border Patrol agent revved into gear, then sped all the way to headquarters. "He was driving fifty to sixty miles an hour down Twenty-Second Street in a forty-five-mile-per-hour zone, through the construction," Arturo said. "He was angry after all that had happened."

Samaritan Kathryn Ferguson had hiked the desert for years, helping migrants in distress and collecting their stories of Border Patrol abuse. She was there for the protests and, as she saw it, the violence of the Border Patrol agents that night in Tucson was a window onto their behavior elsewhere.[1]

"If this is how the Border Patrol treats old white people on a street in the city," she said, "imagine how they treat migrants in the desert where no one can see."

After Arturo and Agustín were dispatched from the scene, the protesters lingered in the street. They were angry and still vocal, but "we probably would have dispersed at that point," Leslie said.

Instead of allowing the situation to wind down, a Border Patrol agent provoked another confrontation when he arrested Rosa Leal, a woman from the neighborhood. "I was standing far away, down the block, away from the scene of the circle protest," Rosa testified at a special meeting the Tucson City Council held the next month, in November. The agent demanded her papers; she showed him her Arizona driver's license to no avail. "He said, 'If you don't show me any other document, you will be arrested,'" Rosa said. "Then he started pulling me and put me in the Border Patrol truck."

A cry went out. "Raúl called, 'They took someone else,'" Leslie told me. "I was completely incredulous. In the middle of a protest?"

Furious, the protesters surged south on Tenth and once again surrounded a Border Patrol vehicle, this one containing Rosa, and once again began chanting. Mari Galup, a University of Arizona grad student and naturalized American citizen, joined the circle. "Border Patrol started pushing," she told the city council. "I got grabbed by several hands, by several agents. They lifted me and dropped me. I landed on the ground." Then she too was arrested and loaded into the truck with Rosa.

This time around, the Tucson police sprang into action. Two officers pulled out pepper-spray canisters and took aim at the faces of the protesters. One of the people hit was Kathryn Ferguson.

"I had never been pepper-sprayed before," Kathryn said. "I threw water on my face—it was like a match to oil." Water, it turns out, is the worst thing to put on pepper spray. "It reacts. I couldn't see." Two young protesters, Leilani Clark and Cesar Lopez, also took a direct hit, and they sat on a curb wailing in pain.

Even those not in the direct line of fire suffered ill effects. "I didn't get it right in the face but I choked," Leslie said. "It made my eyes burn." The spray also drifted in Michael's direction. "I could feel a burning sensation," he said. "I could see. The minute I felt it, smelled it, I turned around and walked away. My eyes burned for four or five days."

Another TPD cop fired hard pepperballs out of a weapon that terrified people. "I saw an officer with a gun disguised to look like a semiautomatic rifle," Leslie said. "I didn't think it was live ammunition—I would not expect a police officer in the United States or Tucson to fire live ammunition at a crowd. But we were in the dark, at night, and he was shooting right at us. We thought it might be rubber bullets."

Testifying before the city council meeting, Monica Velasco, a Corazón member, said that she and her three children were running to escape the pepper spray when her daughter saw the cop with the weapon. "She started screaming, 'The officer is taking out his gun!' He pointed it and started shooting." The frightened family ran behind a car and crouched down below the line of fire.

Norma Price, having lately done battle with a palo verde, was enlisted to treat the injured. She drove to a nearby Circle K and picked up milk, balm for the burning sensation delivered by the pepper spray. The Tucson Fire Department also roared onto the scene; the department paramedics, colleagues of the police who'd sprayed the protesters, knelt down in the street and quietly cared for the afflicted. People began to disburse, and the battalions of law enforcement officers' vehicles drifted away. It was ten o'clock by the time Norma got home, and at long last bandaged her own wounds. Dorothy, now safely back at her house with the belongings she'd retrieved from the street, found a Border Patrol boot print on a page of her daybook.

The next day the city was in an uproar, and there were dueling press conferences at Southside Presbyterian Church and police headquarters. The Border Patrol, invoking the recently imposed federal-government shutdown, kept mum; agents had not been furloughed, but press officers were.

Young Ramón, Agustín's thirteen-year-old son, tearfully spoke to a mass of reporters at the church. "I'm suffering because my father has been taken," he said. "He has been my mother and my father since I was little. We have never been separated before. Please give him back." Arturo's wife, Lucy

Robles, told the crowd, "We have three US-citizen children, ages sixteen, nine, and five. ¡Ya basta!" Enough already. "We need to live our lives. We want our children safe."

An enraged Raúl Alcaraz Ochoa declared that "Ramón is evidence that these policies of separating family members must stop. Two workers and fathers were taken in a minor traffic incident.... Border Patrol used police brutality practices against nonviolent protesters. They were hitting and pushing women and the elderly."

John Fife likewise railed against both the police and the Border Patrol. "In the midst of a peaceful community protest, the violence was solely on the part of the BP agents and TPD officers," he said. "It was a violation of their responsibility and training, without any attempt to defuse the situation. Twenty Border Patrol agents attacked the citizens in the crowd, throwing women, youngsters, and the elderly onto the ground and into trees. TPD officers watched and did nothing as the Border Patrol attacked peaceably assembled citizens."

Over at police headquarters, Tucson Police Chief Roberto Villaseñor declared that it was the protesters who had turned violent and attacked officers. "The Border Patrol brought in twelve agents to remove the people surrounding the vehicle," he said. "The crowd was becoming physically aggressive. They were blocking the roadway, refusing to abide by orders.... People started grabbing and pushing an officer." His cops, he said, had had no choice but to use the pepper spray to subdue the protesters.

The chief insisted that the officers had aimed the spray at protesters' feet, not their faces. His words were belied the next morning, when the *Arizona Daily Star* ran a page 1 photo of an officer shooting directly into the faces of protesters, including Leilani Clark and Kathryn Ferguson.[2] Likewise, though he had said that an evening news video showed protesters attacking the officers, the tape showed the opposite: Border Patrol agents shoving elderly citizens.[3]

Villaseñor dismissed the allegation that racial profiling had played a part in the original stop, saying that the arresting cop himself was Hispanic. He blamed the fracas on the requirements of SB 1070. He had never supported the law, he said, in part because it "causes a confrontation between the community and the police." Yet he and his officers were duty bound to enforce it. The arresting officer had followed the law correctly, the chief said; Valdez had had "a reasonable suspicion that they [the men] were in the country illegally. Border Patrol determined that they are in the country illegally. That's a validation of the officer."

The melée took place just thirteen months after SB 1070 went into effect, in September 2012, and it reopened the angry debate about just what the law demanded of officers. According to its proponents, SB 1070 *required* local officers to investigate if they had reasonable suspicion about a person's immigration status. Yet some law enforcement agencies, including the Pima County Sheriff's Office, maintained that their officers had discretion to pursue—or not pursue—an immigration investigation during a police stop. They could use their own judgment to decide whether following up would take them away from their regular police duties.

UA law professor Andy Silverman told the Tucson City Council—and Villaseñor—at the November meeting that officer discretion was written right into the law. Section 2B, he pointed out, reads: "A reasonable attempt shall be made when practicable to determine the immigration status of the person." Those key words "when practicable" gave a cop— and the city—plenty of latitude.

Villaseñor disagreed. The city would be sued, he warned, if he and his officers failed to enforce SB 1070 to the letter of the law—and that meant that his cops were required to pur sue their reasonable suspicions when someone like Agustín came across their radar.

Notwithstanding Valdez and Carson's preoccupation with the Spanish spoken by the suspects, Villaseñor insisted that the Reyes-Robles affair had nothing to do with race. SB 1070 specifically forbids racial profiling, but its critics argue that profiling is an inevitable consequence of the law. A 2014 investigation by the *Arizona Daily Star* of SB 1070 stops conducted by the Tucson police found that the "largest cluster of checks was along Twenty-Second Street between Interstate 10 and South Park Avenue," a neighborhood with a high Latino population—and the exact location where an officer flagged down Agustín and Arturo. The police chief responded that these stats reflected not racial bias but the high drug and alcohol activity in nearby Santa Rita Park.[4]

The study backed up claims by neighbors in the Mexican blocks around Southside Presbyterian and its day-labor center that the police presence was constant, and police stops of local people all too frequent. Officers, they charged, were lying in wait, hoping to find a pretext—such as a burned-out bulb over a license plate—for stopping immigrant drivers. In the end, though Villaseñor told the city his actions were saving the city from lawsuits, the conduct of his police officers the night of October 8 got Tucson into legal trouble. In April 2014, six months after the Tenth Avenue showdown, the ACLU filed a legal claim against TPD. The claim—a prelude to a possible lawsuit—charged that Agustín and Arturo's constitutional rights had been violated, particularly their Fourth Amendment protection against unreasonable search and seizure. Attorneys were demanding $250,000 for each man.

In the aftermath, even the two agencies involved in the October 8 altercation—TPD and the Border Patrol—disagreed over who had had jurisdiction that night. "When Border Patrol arrived, we turned over custody of the individuals to them," TPD spokesman Sergeant Christopher Widner said. "They were in command. In a normal scene, we give the individuals to the Border Patrol and say, 'Have a nice day.' In this scene, we assisted them with security."

Andy Adamé of the Border Patrol took the opposite position. He maintained that local agencies like TPD retain control of their own streets during any operation. "We take the role of backup; it's not our job to take up civil disobedience. We provide assistance to the local group."

Andy declined comment on the allegations of Border Patrol violence, saying that the individuals at the protest had a right to file complaints if they believed they were mistreated. He added, "We receive extensive training for dealing with civil disobedience, and officers get riot training." But the Border Patrol's assault on American citizens in a city sixty-four miles away from the border took place at a time when the agency's treatment of citizens and noncitizens alike was coming increasingly under fire.

The federal ramp-up of border enforcement—and the dramatic growth of the Border Patrol—had put not only more migrants but more American citizens in contact with the agents. The nationwide roll call of agents rapidly swelled in the years after 9/11. It more than doubled in a little over a dozen years; the 9,212 officers working in the year 2000 rose to 21,391 on duty in 2013. The Tucson Sector, which took in most of the Arizona border, was the most heavily patrolled in the nation.

In 2013 the sector had a not-so-small army of 4,135 agents who had become highly visible in the southern part of the state. Besides standing watch over the border, driving the back roads, and hiking the desert in search of migrants, the troops now roamed parts of Tucson as well. At highway checkpoints that they operated miles from the border, they stopped every single driver on the road. Residents wearied of the mandatory stops and agent interrogations they faced each time they drove up I-19 or Highway 90 near Tombstone or out on Arivaca Road.

People living in rural Arivaca couldn't go anywhere outside their small town without passing through one of three checkpoints. They complained of repeated harassment by agents and of intrusive—and unlawful—questions that violated their civil liberties.

Fed up, a group of Arivacans determined to monitor the monitors and in December 2013 set up citizen patrols to keep watch over the checkpoint at Amado. One Arivaca activist videotaped an encounter she had with agents at the Amado stop; after she questioned an agent's demand to see her ID, she was pulled roughly from her car.[5]

The Border Patrol's use of deadly force against migrants and Mexicans across the border in their own country had also been under scrutiny for years. More Americans began paying attention when the death toll began to rise: agents killed forty-two people between 2005 and 2013.[6] An independent law enforcement review—commissioned by US Customs and Border Protection itself—slammed agents for their behavior in sixty-seven cases where they fired their weapons. Nineteen of the incidents—occurring in the short period between January 2010 and October 2012—had turned deadly.

Leaked to the *Los Angeles Times* in February 2014, the report said that some officers had stood in the path of fleeing cars in order to justify shooting the occupants. Agents cited rock throwing by migrants as a justification for shootings, claiming they feared for their lives. The report found otherwise: the investigators concluded that some agents had shot and killed rock throwers principally out of frustration. And even in cases where a victim died, the follow-up investigations were found to be lax.[7]

The death of José Antonio Elena Rodriguez, one of the

cases in the thick report, fell into that pattern. On the evening of October 12, 2012, the sixteen-year-old Nogales, Sonora, teen was shot to death by a barrage of bullets aimed through the border wall. After he died on the sidewalk in Mexico, the Border Patrol acknowledged that the boy had been killed by one of their agents, as yet unidentified. The shooter, they said, had been in danger—from rocks thrown over the wall from the Mexican side. The claim was improbable; the agent shot from high above the site where José Antonio collapsed and died. They were standing on a steep hill twenty feet above the boy, and they were behind the protective bars of the border wall, which rose another eighteen feet above the hill.

The tragic death of a young Mexican boy on Mexican soil, at the hands of US agents, became a cause célèbre in the borderlands. The FBI took control of the investigation but it dragged on; two years after the fatal shooting even the names of the officers had not been released. Araceli Rodriguez, José Antonio's mother, finally sued the United States government in July 2014, contending that "the U.S. Border Patrol agents who killed my son in a senseless act of violence are still out there and they need to be brought to justice."[8]

The glacial pace of the José Antonio investigation was typical. In May 2014, the nonprofit American Immigration Council found that complaints of agent abuse were often ignored or dismissed. The council examined 809 allegations of abuse, ranging from kicking and stomping to sexual fondling. The accusations had been lodged against agents on the southwest border between January 2009 and January 2012. Out of 809 complaints—a small sampling out of an unknown total—a mere 13 led to discipline against the accused agents. In this baker's dozen of cases, the punishment most often meted out was counseling.[9]

In the outrage that followed that revelation, James F. Tomsheck was removed as US Customs and Border Protection's chief of internal affairs. A few months later, Tomsheck lambasted his own agency, telling Andrew Becker of the Center for Investigative Reporting that of twenty-eight recent deaths at the hands of Border Patrol, perhaps seven were "highly suspect." He accused agents of trying to cover up their misdeeds in these questionable deaths and Border Patrol leaders of trying to "make a case to justify the shooting versus doing a genuine, appropriate review of the information and the facts at hand."[10]

After many years of treating migrants in the desert and in Nogales, Sonora, Dr. Norma Price said, "I wouldn't be surprised by anything the Border Patrol does."Too many migrants and deportees she'd taken care of had been "roughed up" by agents, she said, "and their medical problems neglected. The way they talk to them is disrespectful." Among the patients she'd treated after their release from Border Patrol, she'd seen a man with an unattended broken ankle, multiple people with "horrendous blisters," and a twelve-year-old girl with a worrisome injury to her eye. The girl's mother had "pleaded with Border Patrol to get her daughter medical help, but nothing happened."

PBS cameras recorded Border Patrol agents slashing water bottles left out in the desert for migrants in crisis, and No More Deaths did a massive documentation of migrant complaints of abuse. *A Culture of Cruelty: Abuse and Impunity in Short-Term U.S. Border Patrol Custody*, released in 2011 by No More Deaths, surveyed 12,895 migrants who'd been returned to Mexico. Ten percent reported physical abuse, and 86 percent of those with emergency medical needs said they were deported without receiving the care they needed. Conducting interviews in the three border cities in Sonora, Nogales, Naco, and Agua Prieta, the surveyors also heard all the usual complaints of immigrants held in Border Patrol holding pens: extreme cold, poor sanitation, overcrowding, and inadequate food.[11]

Agustín and Arturo's brief tour through the Tucson Sector Border Patrol headquarters bore out what the immigrant-abuse study had documented. They were held overnight that October Tuesday in a cold room with fifty men who had to lie on the floor to sleep. Only one of the room's three toilets was working, and the broken sinks were filled with water, Agustín said. A five-gallon dispenser had dirty water in it; when the water ran out, the men drank from a hose. The dinners Agustín and Arturo had packed were still in the back of the van, somewhere; at the holding pen they each got a pack of crackers with cheese or peanut butter, plus juice. Early Wednesday morning, they had a bean burrito for breakfast, Agustín said. "The agent told us, 'There's no juice, so don't even ask me.'"

They were glad to be put on a bus for Eloy just after dawn: it was heated, and they could warm up after their sleepless night in the freezing *heladera*. Sixteen other detainees, nine of them bound for Florence, were on the bus with them, including their fellow Tucsonan and arrestee Rosa Leal. Mari Galup, the American citizen who'd also been arrested at the protest, had been released. Border Patrol, realizing they had no business detaining an American citizen, randomly dropped her off the next morning at a Circle K miles from her home.

The Mexican consul had heard about the arrests and called the new detainees at Eloy to give what help he could. Agustín and Arturo wanted him to call their families, but "I was so nervous I couldn't remember my number," Agustín said. They were issued prison uniforms colored green for the low level of their criminal offense: driving without a license and having a busted-up light over the license plate.

Luckily, the three Tenth Avenue detainees were locked up at Eloy only one night; immigrants without criminal records are nowadays freed more quickly than they used to be. On Thursday, bond was set at $1,500 apiece. Corazón de

Tucson stepped up to pay; the group regularly fundraised for just such emergencies as this. Raúl Alcaraz Ochoa and Eleazar Castellanos, Rosa's husband, drove to Eloy to pay the bonds for Rosa and Agustín; Arturo's family managed to find the money for his. The trio got out at 6:00 p.m. after nearly forty-eight hours in custody.

It was *triste* in Eloy, Agustín said a week later. Sad. He'd seen Guatemalan women being herded together for a deportation flight to their homelands, and he wished he'd had money to give all his fellow prisoners who would soon follow them into exile. He offered what he could. "I gave a pair of shoes to a guy who was going to be deported," he said, and he helped others after he got home. "When they heard I was being released, people asked me to call their families in Central America, Ecuador, and New York." He sighed. "We're all in the same situation. We have the same *necesidades.*" The same needs. "I have to help."

Ramón was *feliz* now. "He's proud and happy his father is out," Agustín said, but seeing his father arrested had changed the boy. "He's getting more involved. He is committed to religion and the church and to serving the cause. I advise my son: get educated, to understand the separation of families."

Agustín would be receiving a notice for a court date soon, and he'd already made an appointment with a lawyer. Reflecting on his case, he said he'd been in the United States seventeen years. His whole family lived in Tucson. "My mom is here too. My brother has been here twenty years," and his son had been born in America. Agustín was a hard worker and, save for the episode of the burned-out light, he'd never been in trouble with the law. He prayed that the United States would allow him to stay. "I've been here since the age of twenty-two," he said. "I'm too old to start over. Everything is here."

CHAPTER TEN

Streamline

Culpable. *Guilty.*

—Vicente Javier, Streamline defendant entering plea

Just after dawn, the old El Hoyo neighborhood south of downtown Tucson was quiet. The early-morning sun lit up A Mountain in the distance, but there were still deep shadows in the barrio. El Hoyo ("the hole") was a tangle of streets and old adobes that sloped downward from El Tiradito Wishing Shrine on Main Street—where an adulterous anti-saint was said to grant favors to prayerful petitioners—past the whitewashed San Cosmé Chapel. It ended at the freeway frontage road.

Now prized by gentrifiers, the barrio's old Mexican-style houses, brightly colored and decked with flowers, had once been part of a much bigger neighborhood, Tucson's oldest, that stretched north a mile or more. A voracious urban-renewal project had sliced through the neighborhood in the late 1960s, knocking down historic houses and uprooting some eleven hundred people, many of them descendants of the city's original Mexican residents. More than 260 old houses and stores were bulldozed to make way for new government towers, a convention center, and, eventually, in 2000, the Evo A. DeConcini Federal Courthouse.[1]

The courthouse built on the site of demolished Mexican houses was best known nowadays for Streamline, its daily fast-track proceedings against Latino immigrants. Each weekday afternoon, up to seventy defendants, mostly from Mexico and Guatemala, shuffled in shackles and chains into an upstairs courtroom. Inside, the prisoners participated in a mass hearing before a federal judge, answering to criminal charges of crossing the border into the United States. Almost invariably, each defendant pled guilty, was sentenced to up to six months in jail, and then ordered deported. The hearings almost never lasted more than an hour and a half.

On this Friday morning in October 2013, hours before the Streamline proceedings were about to start, a few strollers could be seen on the streets of El Hoyo, a half mile from the courthouse. I got a glimpse of John Heid, of Casa Mariposa, walking west on West Eighteenth Street toward the I-10 frontage road. Paula Miller of Casa was somewhere in the winding *calles* and so were Carlos Garcia and Sandra Castro Solis of Puente Arizona, a Phoenix activist group that had been fighting hard against Sheriff Arpaio's raids and the fallout of SB 1070. A white van loaded with other people was parked near the San Cosmé Chapel. Three more stood waiting on the corner of Simpson and the frontage road.

None of them attracted any notice from the El Hoyo neighbors, or even from a Tucson Police Department vehicle that pulled out of a maintenance garage and drove leisurely toward downtown. But the people walking the streets and waiting in the van had an ambitious—and tightly choreographed—plan: they aimed to do nothing less than shut down Streamline.

———

The activists knew that early each weekday, two buses loaded with migrants would pass by this spot on their way to the courthouse from Border Patrol headquarters. The drivers always took the back way around, skirting the neighborhood and driving north up the frontage road. As expected, at precisely 7:55 a.m., two white buses crammed with prisoners pulled into view. When the vehicles got close to Simpson, the protesters pounced. At least eighteen people ran into the frontage road. Three darted in front of the first bus and held up signs that read, "Stop the Buses. People Under Tires. We Mean No Harm." The driver slammed on the brakes, and the second driver followed suit. In that instant a dozen people chained themselves to the tires.

The drivers grabbed their phones to call for help, but the buses were trapped. They wouldn't roll again for more than four hours.

Within minutes, supporters arrived with media-ready posters. A couple of people sprinted to the first bus with a giant banner that proclaimed, "End Streamline. Not One More Deportation." They tried to put it on the windshield, but the driver thwarted them; he turned on the wipers and swished the sign aside. The sign carriers capitulated and instead held the banner aloft with their hands. The buses had dark, tinted windows, and the migrants stuck inside could be seen only in shadowy outlines. Masked "angels" turned up with large signs meant to reassure them they were not in danger. "Querer una vida mejor no es un crimen," read one. *Wanting a better life is not a crime.*

Over on the tarmac, Angie Loreto, a thirty-one-year-old mother of two, had chained herself to the front wheels of the first bus. The day was turning hot, and she was sitting in the full blast of the now-strong morning sun. Angie was proudly "Tucson born and raised," she told me, and she had planted herself on the street to make sure that justice was properly carried out in her hometown.

"Streamline is an unjust way to prosecute," she said. "We're using our bodies to bring awareness to Streamline. We want to feel what the migrants feel." And, she added, "We are prepared to be arrested."

The arrests weren't going to happen anytime soon. Angie and the other protesters weren't just chained to the bus tires: they were chained to each other. They'd linked themselves together in groups of three around the tires, using so-called dragon sleeves to fasten their arms together. Made of nearly impregnable PVC piping, the dragon sleeves were designed to make it impossible for police to pull the protesters apart— and difficult to cut the chains that bound them. (In addition to the twelve surrounding the buses, six more protesters had dragon-sleeved themselves across the entrance to the driveway of the federal courthouse several blocks away.)

Sixty-eight-year-old Steve Johnston was chained to the wheel on the shady side of the bus, opposite Angie. Steve had been a mainstay of the No More Deaths desert camp for years, camping out for weeks on end and hiking out into the wilderness to help migrants. Now he was lying on asphalt in the city, underneath a hot bus. Yet he was exuberant as he looked up and spoke to me. "Streamline is a travesty of justice," he declared. "Everyone in Tucson should know about it. Over seventy thousand people have been run through this kangaroo court since 2008. Seventy people every day are convicted and sentenced in less than two hours.

"The immediate goal is to shut it down today. We want people to know the travesty of justice that takes place every working day in this town."

Nicknamed Deportation Court by a Tucson immigration attorney with a black sense of humor, Operation Streamline had started in Del Rio, Texas, in 2005. A component of the Bush administration's new "zero tolerance" policy on unauthorized immigration, the program barreled into Tucson three years later. By the end of 2013, some 73,900 migrants had made the harrowing Streamline trudge through a DeConcini courtroom. Streamline was meant to counteract "catch and release" programs that allowed captured border crossers to be quickly recycled across the line. The idea was that charging and jailing even a small sampling of migrants, randomly selected from among those arrested each day, would deter more would-be crossers from coming. Now bearing criminal records, they'd face increasingly steeper punishments if they tried to come back. To its critics, it was the criminalization of migration.

I'd been to see the Streamline spectacle a number of times; I'd last visited in July 2013, a few months before the bus protest. That time, sixty-nine migrants had been hauled into the courtroom in the usual shackles and chains. Most of them were dark-skinned *indígenas*. They were chained hand and foot, their wrist and their hands attached to still another chain that encircled the waist. (A University of Arizona study found that Streamliners were chained up to six hours on average; the US marshals guarding the court insisted that the chains were the only possible way to manage seventy prisoners at a time.)[2]

Just a few prisoners were women. They were seated on a bench in front of the judge, while the dozens of men sat in rows and rows along one wall.

All of the accused had been in the Border Patrol holding pen for a few days, where there were no showers to be had, and they were still dusty from the desert. The smell of their sweat permeated the courtroom. Because they were facing criminal charges, each of the migrant defendants was entitled to a free, court-appointed attorney. A small army of fifteen lawyers stood near the judge; each of them was representing four or five clients.

Another time when I dropped in, Judge Bernardo Velasco

was on the bench. Famed for being the speediest of the Streamline justices, he zipped through the hearing so rapidly I could barely take notes. He'd once boasted that his shortest hearing had taken a mere thirty minutes—to run through the cases of seventy people.[3] His fast pace lent ammunition to critics who called Streamline assembly-line justice. On my July visit, Judge Charles Pyle was presiding, and by comparison, his ninety minutes of court time, devoted to sixty-nine defendants, unfolded in slow motion.

Judge Pyle called seven defendants at a time to the bench, and they walked awkwardly, their dragging chains making a racket as loud and unnerving as the chains of Marley's ghost. One of the accused, Vicente Javier, hopped on one shackled foot as he approached, his other foot still lame from an injury sustained in the desert. Judge Pyle called for a chair and Vicente sat down. With an interpreter translating into Spanish, the judge asked Vicente a series of questions. Was he a citizen of Mexico? *Sí*. Had anyone forced him to plead guilty? *No*. Had he spent time speaking with his lawyer? *Sí*. He was charged, the judge said, with the felony of reentering the United States illegally, on June 24, near Nogales.

"The government will dismiss the felony charge if you plead guilty to a misdemeanor and agree to one hundred eight days in prison," Judge Pyle explained. "How do you plead?" Vicente didn't hesitate. "Culpable," he said, giving the word the Spanish pronunciation, *cul-PAH-blay*. *Guilty*.

In the early years of the program, most Streamline prisoners were charged with first-time entry, a less-serious offense, and sentenced to time served. Now the government —and Streamline in particular—was cracking down on repeat border crossers, and all sixty-nine of the defendants this day were charged with reentry, a felony. If they pled guilty, the government would make them a deal: the felony would be reduced to a misdemeanor.

Every single one of the sixty-nine agreed to the plea bargain, and the Vicente scenario was repeated again and again. Charges were read, questions were asked, answers given, guilty pleas were entered. *Culpable. Culpable. Culpable.*

One defendant's request for asylum broke the monotony. The man had a "credible fear" for his safety, the lawyer said. No matter. The man had to go to prison anyway and file his claim there. If he did, he'd get an interview with an ICE asylum officer, and he might, just might, escape deportation. But he still had to serve his time.

Now burdened with a criminal record, the prisoners would be in even greater trouble if they tried to cross the border again. All sixty-nine *culpables* were led to the exit, still in shackles, Vicente once again precariously hopping. Outside they'd be loaded onto buses and driven to the private CCA prison in Florence or another prison elsewhere. They were criminals now, and they'd be going to criminal prisons, not immigration detention centers. After they served their time—sentences varied from about 30 days to 160—they'd be deported.

If their deportation destination was Nogales, they'd complete a circle of DeConcini connections. The Streamline courthouse where they'd just been sentenced was named for the late Evo DeConcini, a former Arizona Supreme Court justice. The DeConcini port of entry at Nogales was named for Evo's son Dennis DeConcini, a former Arizona senator. Dennis DeConcini had still another link to immigration: he was a longtime member of the board of the for-profit Corrections Corporation of America, a major imprisoner of Streamliners across the Southwest.

Dan Anderson, a Tucson lawyer in private practice, spent one day most weeks working Streamline as a court-appointed attorney. He liked to go to El Minuto Mexican restaurant after court, and he met me there one afternoon to explain the nuts and bolts of the hearings. Located right next door to the shrine of El Tiradito in El Hoyo, near where the Streamline siege would later unfold, El Minuto had bright saguaro cacti painted on the Spanish arch around the doorway. Inside, the norteño music of the borderlands played on the radio. Dan was a regular, a favorite customer who spoke with the staff in his fluent Spanish, and the waiters razzed him good-naturedly. "Hola, abogado!" one called out. *Hi, lawyer!* "Send anyone to jail today?"

Dan had once upon a time worked for Pima County as a public defender. His old boss, Isabel Garcia, was an outspoken immigrant-rights activist and opponent of Streamline, and she had called upon lawyers like Dan to refuse to participate in the operation.

"Isabel tried to get me to promise not to do Streamline," Dan said, but he saw no reason to stop. He said he worked as hard for his Streamline clients as he did for the other poor people he represented: when he wasn't doing Streamline, he was a court-appointed attorney in the regular criminal courts. "I'm a defense lawyer. I'm looking for grounds for defense. I ask questions. I look for anything I can fish with."

On his Streamline days, he spent three hours in the courtroom in the morning, devoting a half hour or so speaking to each of his clients. Sometimes he found his angle when he discovered that a client spoke one of the many indigenous languages of Mexico or Guatemala, Zapotec, say, or Mam, and could understand very little Spanish. In those cases, he could usually get the charges dismissed, on the grounds that the client couldn't understand the court's Spanish translations well enough to meet the legal standard of participating meaningfully in the hearing.

"If they don't speak enough Spanish to have a fair trial, they just get dismissed. They get sent to the border. They'll have an arrest record"—but they don't have to go to jail.

Dan had once sent an investigator to Mexico to look into

a Streamline client's claim to "derivative citizenship." The woman's grandparents, he'd learned, were US citizens who long ago had moved to Mexico; thus the woman's mother, though born in Mexico, was an American citizen. If the mother had ever lived in the United States, that would give her Mexican-born daughter, the Streamline defendant, a claim to citizenship as well. As a bonus, Dan's client had US-citizen children of her own. The woman was jailed while Dan's investigator looked into the case.

Despite the money and time put into the investigation, it didn't pan out. The defendant's mother had lived her whole life in Mexico. The case fell apart and the woman was deported. Ironically, she was the only one in a family of four generations *not* entitled to American citizenship.

Most of the cases were simpler: the clients were citizens of another country who were accused of crossing the border, twice. Dan would lay out the plea deal the American government was offering them.

"I explain that there are two charges: one, a felony for reentry after deportation, and two, misdemeanor for illegal entry." If clients took the deal and pled guilty to the misdemeanor, the maximum sentence they'd get would be six months.

If they were to fight their case, first they'd have to wait a minimum of three and half months in jail before their regular jury trial began. And at trial, they'd be facing the felony charge. If they were found guilty, they'd have to wait two to three months more before they were sentenced. Then they'd be looking at doing much more time than Streamline's maximum of six months. "I go over the choices," Dan said. "I say, 'You can do all that or take the plea.' I just say, 'Which sounds better?' Most of them will say, 'The plea looks better.' To accept the misdemeanor is to get home much sooner."

Dan understood that the masses of prisoners in chains in the Streamline courtroom offended Americans' sense of justice. But he wished that the Streamline critics would also look into how badly indigent defendants are treated in regular criminal courts. "Why aren't all these observers going to city court, to justice court, to see the injustice there? Go to any misdemeanor court—people get ramrodded through. It's all about poverty and racism."

The Streamline sentences varied depending on the client's history. Harsh treatment was meted out to anyone who'd been "A-Tepped," deported through the Border Patrol's Alien Transfer Exit Program, and then caught coming back. ATEP is meant to disrupt human smuggling networks, to separate border crossers from their coyotes. Picked up in one location, the Tucson Sector, say, they're deported out of another, maybe the McAllen Sector in South Texas. With rival cartels operating in different parts of northern Mexico, "it's dangerous for people from Sonora and Sinaloa to be deported out of Texas into Tamaulipas or Nuevo León," Dan said. "We clearly don't take into account the danger of the places we release them."

And if the A-Tepped deportees fled these violent locations, slipped back into the States, and got arrested through Streamline, "they give them an extra thirty days because they didn't learn their lesson."

The court reserved even greater wrath for defendants who'd been deported through Streamline before—and then got caught up in Streamline again when trying to cross the line once more. These double-timers who've defied the United States could get five to six months in jail.

When the Streamline lawyers like Dan met with their clients for the first time the morning of their hearings, they sat down to talk at tables and chairs temporarily set up in the courtroom. There might be seventy captured immigrants in the room, fifteen attorneys, teams of US marshals, and a couple of Border Patrol agents. The utter lack of privacy, attorney Heather Williams told a congressional subcommittee in 2008, compromised the whole operation from the get-go.

"Confidentiality of information must be guaranteed between client and lawyer" by law, she said in a written statement. Many of the migrants had been picked up in groups; a coyote might hear what one of his customers told an attorney, with possible consequences for the migrant's safety in the future. Williams, then an assistant federal public defender, ticked off a host of other concerns. The defendants were held by Border Patrol for forty-eight hours or more before an initial court appearance, a possible violation of the Fifth Amendment right to due process. Once they were in the rush of the fast-track proceedings, exculpatory issues "can be and have been missed," she said. Clients might have a mental illness or be under the influence, or be so exhausted or hungry that they were in no condition to give assent. And attorneys, no matter how hardworking, had inadequate prep time.[4]

Critics contend that the quickie hearings for the immigrants fall far short of the standards guaranteed by the Fifth Amendment. And that amendment doesn't limit those constitutional rights to citizens. It reads, "Nor shall any person ... be deprived of life, liberty, or property, without due process of law."[5]

Sixty percent of deported Streamliners in the University of Arizona study told interviewers that their appointed lawyers did not explain their legal rights; 40 percent said that their lawyer simply told them to plead guilty and to sign their order of deportation.[6] Scholar Hailey Anne Sheldon argues that "illegal entry is a highly defensible crime. It is the burden of government to prove the defendant knowingly crossed." The nearly universal guilty pleas raise the suspicion that lawyers are not adequately pushing the government to prove its case.[7]

Prosecutors complain that illegal-entry cases have so clogged the docket in federal courts that they have diverted money and staff away from the pursuit of serious criminal cases. As immigration prosecutions have risen, UC Berkeley law professor Joanna Lydgate writes, "white-collar prosecutions, organized crime prosecutions, public corruption prosecutions and drug prosecutions" have dropped.[8]

After the Streamline hearing I attended in March 2013, Judge Velasco came out to speak to Samaritans and a student group gathered in the back of his courtroom. Fully 40 percent of the cases heard at DeConcini were now immigration-related, Streamline and otherwise, he told them.

And the price tag for Streamline is staggering. Politicians on both sides of the aisle complain that numbers are hard to come by. No More Deaths calculates the annual costs of the Tucson Streamline apparatus alone at $120 million in court costs, including fees of $100 an hour and up for private court-appointed attorneys like Dan Anderson. The costs of imprisonment of Tucson's Streamline convicts run to $50 million annually.[9] Those costs are multiplied across Streamline proceedings all along the Southwest border.

Judge Velasco noted that the failed 2013 immigration-reform bill, with its emphasis on security, would have tripled the number of migrants sent through Streamline in Tucson. (And their criminal convictions would have denied them any relief offered by immigration reform.) A sharp rise in the Streamline census would have provided more work for lawyers, more jobs for US marshals to guard defendants, and maybe even more gigs for construction workers to build new courtrooms. Plus, Judge Velasco said, the higher numbers would have enriched the for-profit prisons where most of the Streamline defendants across the Southwest were held.

"The private prisons are pushing for 'reform,' meaning incarceration," he said. "They're pushing to make sure reform has a high"—and profitable—"security component."

———

Streamline is touted as a deterrent. The jail time that Streamliners serve, the reasoning goes, makes them think twice
about coming back. And friends and family back in Mexico
or Central America might reconsider coming too, if they
knew that prison was a real possibility. A 2013 report from
the Congressional Research Service provided some evidence
that the program was working as intended. In the 2012 fiscal
year, only about 10 percent of deported Streamliners tried
their luck crossing again, compared to 27 percent of immigrants who had been "voluntarily returned" without consequences.[10] But Customs and Border Patrol figures show a
smaller disparity. According to the CBP numbers, 10 percent
of Streamliners cross the border again—the same propor-
tion that the congressional researchers found—but the re-
try rate for all returnees is just 17 percent. That makes for a
divide between Streamline convicts and other deportees of
just 7 percent.[11] Border Patrol nevertheless points to lower
apprehensions along the border in recent years as evidence
that Streamline is working. Critics view that conclusion as
simplistic.

"It is impossible to isolate the relative success of Operation Streamline as compared with . . . other recent enforcement efforts," contends Lydgate.[12] The Streamline years
coincided with the construction of more and bigger walls
along the border, more Border Patrol boots on the ground,
and the devastating economic recession. All of these devel-
opments played a part in persuading more would-be migrants to stay home. The team of researchers from the Center for Latin American Studies at the University of Arizona
interviewed more than eleven hundred deportees who'd been
sent back to six different Mexican cities along the border,
between 2010 and 2012. They found that deportees' decisions
on whether or not to return to the United States depended

far more on whether they had family *al Norte* and far less on whether they stood to be punished severely if they returned.

"People that have established lives in this country will do just about anything possible to be reunited with their family members in the United States," wrote study coauthor Daniel E. Martínez, now an assistant professor at George Washington University. "When family is the main motivation for migration, many people will cross again and again regardless of the punishments handed down."[13] Of the deportees who told the researchers their home was in the United States, fully 70 percent said they would go north again.

Public defenders report seeing more and more second-timers back in Streamline, and Streamline convicts frequently turn up at the aid stations in Nogales. They readily admit that they'll slip across the border again: they're desperate to return to their families in the States or they need to work and send money back home to families in Mexico. Ted Robbins of NPR sat at the Kino comedor for two days straight in 2010 and questioned the ninety-six deportees who came to eat. Though they didn't all know the term "Streamline," thirty-five told Ted they had pled guilty to a criminal charge of entering unlawfully; thirty of those convicts said they intended to reenter the United States. Only one of the Streamliners said he'd stay in Mexico for fear of a lengthier prison term.[14]

Samaritan Bob Kee once ran into a Streamline convict walking north through Arizona's Tumacacori Highlands. "He told me, 'I was in Streamline,'" Bob said. The man's reasons for coming back were more powerful than the threat of more criminal penalties. He had a wife and child in Tucson.

No More Deaths has argued that Streamline makes the journey north more dangerous. Convicted Streamliners, fearful of even greater punishment if they get caught coming back, are more likely to take ever riskier wilderness routes.

A staffer in the Mexican Consulate in Tucson told me that at least one Streamline convict had paid the ultimate price. The man had talked to the consular officer before he was deported, and he was distraught that he was being sent back to Mexico, far from his wife and children.

Months later, the man turned up on the lists of the desert's dead. In October 2013, the same month as the Streamline protest, he perished in the southern Arizona wilderness, on his way home.

Back at the bus confrontation on that bright October day, the first two Tucson Police Department cars arrived at 8:08 a.m. and blockaded the road. By midmorning I counted at least a hundred law enforcement officers on the scene: Border Patrol agents, some in their regular green uniforms, others in desert camouflage; Tucson cops, many in riot helmets and carrying billy clubs; Tucson firefighters; federal marshals; state Department of Public Safety officers.

Tucson Police Department chief Roberto Villaseñor got there early on. It was three days after the showdown on Tenth Avenue, and this time the chief was going to make sure that everything was done by the book. And there were plenty of people watching. The news of the bus captures had spread rapidly, and dozens of reporters flooded the street; social media types were livestreaming the action. Legal observers, including Isabel Garcia, had arrived to monitor the situation.

Protesters shouted and sang. "Obama, *escucha: Estamos en la lucha*," they chanted. *Obama, listen: We're in the fight.*

The morning grew hotter—the temperature shot up into the 80s—and there was little shade. Volunteers gave sips of water to the chained activists; a Border Patrol agent climbed onto the buses to hand out water bottles to the prisoners. Angie Loreto, sitting on the sunny east side of the bus, was suffering in the heat; the fire department medics questioned her carefully and checked on her regularly.

Shortly before 11:00 a.m., the police announced that people who didn't leave the vicinity of the buses would be arrested. Eighteen cops in riot gear moved in; six took positions at the head of the first bus and twelve along the side, facing the chanting protesters. Some of the unchained supporters retreated; others remained by the buses with plans to be arrested. Among them were Paula Miller and John Heid of Casa Mariposa. Paula was one of the first to be taken, and John soon followed. Both went along quietly without resisting; they were cuffed, patted down, and loaded into a police wagon.

Once the street was clear, seven Border Patrol agents in desert camouflage and floppy hats rolled a big black case over to the first bus. They pulled out a hacksaw attached to an orange electrical cord. By 11:20 a.m. they were noisily sawing through the dragon sleeves of Maryada Vallet, a longtime No More Deaths volunteer. After minutes of careful work, they extricated first one arm, then the other. Maryada let her body go limp. The officers lifted her up and maneuvered her over to the police van.

"We got your back, Maryada," the crowd chanted. "You shut down Streamline, Maryada."

It was true, more or less. Late in the morning, the presiding judge of the federal court canceled Streamline for the day, a first. It was too late for the defendants to have their allotted morning time with their lawyers, and without those consultations, the hearings would have been illegal. A cheer went up through the crowd. With every arrest, they congratulated the protester by name.

"You shut down Streamline, Steve."

"You shut down Streamline, Angie."

When Angie was sawed out of her dragon sleeves, she was taken first to the firefighters' emergency van to be examined and treated and was then put into the police wagon. Steve, the oldest of the protesters, grinned broadly as he was led away. The unchained Carlos Garcia and Sandra Castro were plucked from the crowd and arrested as well. In all, eighteen were arrested at the bus protest and six others at the courthouse. They spent most of the evening in the Pima County Jail, singing in their cells.

"Most fun I've had since the civil rights movement," Steve said later.

The participants in the bus blockade were originally slapped with a felony charge of hindering prosecution and misdemeanor failure to obey an order to disperse. Later those charges were knocked down to a host of state misdemeanors: blocking a road, trespassing, resisting arrest, public nuisance, disturbing the peace, and misdemeanor hindering prosecution. The dragon-sleeved six who blocked the driveway to the courthouse were treated more leniently, dealt federal misdemeanor charges of disorderly conduct and failure to follow the directions of federal officers.

By 12:30 p.m. the day of the siege, the human barricades were fully dismantled and the traffic barriers were down. The two buses pulled swiftly into gear and zoomed away. The would-be Streamliners who had spent the morning in a captive bus were driven back to Border Patrol. Yet they were spared a criminal charge, spared the Streamline hearing, and spared a prison sentence.

Instead of spending months locked up in Florence, most of them were taken back to the border, unshackled, and deported back to Mexico.

CHAPTER ELEVEN

Dreaming

I have suffered for what my daughter has gone through. She blamed us. She said, "I'm not from here or there." She doesn't feel she has an identity. She has no country of her own.

—*Arely Gonzalez, mother of a Dreamer*

What I wanted to accomplish was coming back home.

—*Adriana Díaz, Dreamer*

For years, Arely Gonzalez never went anywhere in Tucson without first doing a car check.

"I made sure everything was good in my car," she said firmly. "No flat tires." No broken taillights. And no burned-out bulb over the license plate. She limited the places she drove: she avoided stores where Mexican immigrants shopped and bypassed the neighborhoods where they lived.

"I didn't go to the Harkins shopping center," she said in Spanish. "I didn't go to South Tucson. I didn't go on the freeway." Tucson, she added, was "mi carcel." *My prison.*

When Arely and her husband, Jorge, looked for a house, they considered only neighborhoods where they wouldn't attract attention from the police, the sheriff's deputies, or the

Border Patrol. They didn't even look at the Mexican barrios south of downtown. Instead, they'd settled on a modest red-brick house on the far Eastside, eight miles from South Tucson. It was conservative out here; dotted with Christian and Mormon churches, it was one of the few parts of the city that reliably voted Republican. There were some Mexican American families, but the district was majority white.

"I tried to be safer and live in a mixed neighborhood," Arely told me on a sunny September afternoon in 2013, sitting in her immaculate living room. Her strategies for living under the radar had paid off. She and Jorge were undocumented immigrants from Guaymas, Sonora, a seaside city six hours south of Tucson, and "we never had problems with *la migra*." They'd lived in the United States nearly twenty-five years without undergoing a single immigration stop.

"My daughters had a happy, normal childhood. I see other Mexicans with many problems, with the police or in detention, and I'm grateful for our good fortune." She paused. "Arizona has become very hard toward immigrants." *Se puso muy duro.*

That new harshness had begun to affect Arely's family as their daughters grew older. The older girl, her namesake, Arely, had been born in Mexico, in Sinaloa, and brought to the United States as a one-year-old. Three years later, her sister, Silvia, was born in Los Angeles. Silvia's American citizenship gave her prospects in life that were markedly better than her sister's. Silvia had just graduated from the University of Arizona; a photo of her smiling in her cap and gown, flanked by her proud parents, hung on the living room wall.

"She graduated in December 2012 with two majors, linguistics and speech therapy, with a minor in French," her mom said. As an American citizen and graduate of an Arizona high school, Silvia was eligible for in-state tuition—$9,114 her last year of college. Arely had graduated from the same college prep high school as her sister, but the state denied in-state tuition benefits to undocumented students. She was free to apply to the UA, but if she enrolled, she would have had to pay out-of-state tuition. In 2006, the year she got her high school diploma, that would have been $13,682, a big jump up from that year's in-state tuition of $4,498.

"Arely couldn't go to the university," her mother said. "We couldn't pay so much money."

Instead Arely settled on Pima Community College, an associate's degree, and diminished career prospects.

When the girls were little, their unequal status didn't seem to matter. The elder Arely was a university graduate—she'd studied dentistry at the University of Guadalajara—and she made sure her daughters attended good public schools. Both were active kids who excelled at their studies. Young Arely only gradually became aware that she was different from her friends. "When she couldn't drive it really hit home; it was really upsetting," her mom said. "Her friends were learning to drive." The undocumented can't legally drive but Arely couldn't bring herself to explain to the other kids why she couldn't get a permit. It was even more embarrassing a few years later when her little sister got her license and climbed behind the wheel of the family car.

The two girls both went to Basis, a nationally ranked charter high school famed for its rigorous college-prep program. "At Basis, they want all the students to go straight to the university," Arely said. Her daughter "didn't want to tell them her situation. She said, 'I'll go to Pima.' The teachers would get upset and say, 'No, why don't you go to the university?'" She had done as well at school as friends who went on to the UA or to elite private schools, but community college was her only option.

By law, even at Pima she had to pay out-of-state tuition. But Pima was cheaper overall than the UA, and the tab for undocumented students was about $6,000 a year. The community college was welcoming to all students, but its five campuses were scattered around the city, a set-up that posed transportation problems for the undocumented. Students typically rocketed around by car from campus to campus to get to their classes; there wasn't time to take the slow-moving bus all the way across town. Arely couldn't drive herself, so her family pitched in. It was hard to say which was more humiliating, being driven to college by her little sister or by her mom. Her mother didn't have a driver's license either, but she willingly risked her own arrest to protect her daughter.

Arely studied art and earned an associate's, the only degree available in Pima's two-year programs. Her mom had carefully framed her daughter's college artwork and exhibited it in every room of the house. I was struck by two pieces in the living room. One was a deftly painted Arizona desert landscape; the other was an exquisite pencil drawing of Jorge's dad as a young man on a horse on his family's *ranchita* in Mexico. One honored the homeland Arely didn't remember, and the other celebrated the only home she knew.

Now Arely was twenty-five and working as a waitress. Silvia, twenty-two, had gotten a great job in her field after college; she was working with a doctor in a language-pathology clinic.

"I have suffered for what my daughter's gone through," Arely lamented. "She blamed us. She said, 'I'm not from here or there.' She doesn't feel she has an identity. She has no country of her own." Immigration had been tough on the elder Arely too. At fifty-one, she hadn't been home to Guaymas in years; she was from a large family of eight children and she missed her siblings. Her mother had died the year before, and Arely grieved that she hadn't been able to go to her deathbed; she comforted herself that her mother had made a final visit to Tucson on a tourist visa not long before she died. For Jorge, it was a little different. Some of his nephews had moved up to Tucson, and he was satisfied with his job doing asbestos removal. Arely had been a dentist in Mexico, and she'd had to give up her profession. Now she worked cleaning houses.

With all the heartbreak immigration had caused her, "I ask myself sometimes, why do we live here?" she said. "But to go back would be difficult now."

There'd been some big improvements in the last year. When Silvia turned twenty-one, she petitioned for legal status for her parents. "Jorge now has a green card," Arely said happily. "I have a work permit." She couldn't use it to leave the country and get back in—the card was marked with a warning: "Not valid for re-entry to U.S." But she felt free at last. She could even drive legally.

"When we were undocumented, we were nervous, fearful, afraid to drive. I got the card in April. Now I go everywhere!"

Yet young Arely once again was excluded. The law didn't allow her sister to include a sibling on the petition; it applied only to parents. But as a Dreamer, brought to the United States as a child and as a graduate of a US high school, she did qualify for DACA, Deferred Action for Childhood Arrivals. DACA status would give her permission to be in the country for two years, the right to renew it for another two years, and even the right to work. DACA dreamers in other states were able to get driver's licenses, but Arizona governor Jan Brewer had issued an executive order prohibiting DACA young adults from getting an Arizona driver's license. (Nebraska was the only other state with a similar ban.) So even with DACA, Arely wouldn't be able to drive. Nor could she complete her education. And she knew that coming forward to apply carried some risk; a future administration might revoke the program, and immigration authorities would have all the information they needed to find her and deport her. She decided to apply anyway. As she told her mother, "I want to get something."

Now she had been awarded the DACA waiver. "She can work. She feels a little better," her mom said with relief. "I think it will turn out," she added fervently. "I think things will get better for her."

The next year, Arely's new DACA status came under attack. The Republican-led Congress voted in August 2014 to end the program. In theory, the measure they passed would have permitted the deportation of all 643,000 of the young graduates who'd won DACA. It had no chance of becoming law at that time—it was doomed in the Senate and would have been vetoed by Obama—but it was a shadow on Arely's future. It was just what she had feared.[1]

That same summer brought a flip-flop on DACA in Arizona. In July a federal appeals court overturned Governor Brewer's ban on driver's licenses for the young immigrants. For a brief, happy moment, it seemed that Arely could at last learn to drive. But that hope quickly dissolved. The governor appealed, and for the time being the ban remained in effect.

Instead of getting behind the wheel and striking out on her own, Arely had to climb back onto the bus.

Arely Gonzalez was by no means the only undocumented immigrant who worked hard to stay under the radar. Corazón de Tucson and Las Promotoras, support groups whose members had borne witness at the arrests of Arturo and Agustín, trained immigrants in the basics that Arely had figured out on her own: how not to get arrested, how not to be detained. Some Promotoras women described their strategies in voiceover interviews in *Dreams and Silhouettes*, a multimedia theater production staged in South Tucson in 2014. In the era of SB 1070, one of the interviewees, Alejandra, said she did whatever she could to avoid detection. First she turned to God.

"I'm always praying, 'Please, God, allow me to end this

day, to go and pick up my kids from school,'" without getting arrested. Like Arely, Alejandra had rules about driving. She made sure everything in her car was in order. She didn't drive at night, even if she needed medicine from the pharmacy, knowing that's when cops often pounced on the undocumented for minor traffic infractions and then called Border Patrol.

"Sometimes they stop people because they're changing lanes, sometimes they stop people because of a taillight, or you know that small light in the license plate," she said. "When I drive I risk my freedom, my mental health. After SB 1070, well, months before that, wow, it was like a different world . . . with all the detentions and all the profiling, I just stopped. I stopped being me. Alejandra died."

Another woman was tormented by the same problem that Arely had. "I have two children. One is a citizen and the other is not. It is very hard . . . to know that one will be able to do what he wants, that he can go anywhere he wants, and my other child cannot do the same."[2]

Younger undocumented immigrants, including would-be Dreamers, grew tired of living in the shadows that the older generation had tolerated. They were galvanized in part by the repeated failure of the Dream Act to become law. First introduced in 2001, the Dream Act (its name is an acronym for Development, Relief, and Education for Alien Minors) would have provided a path to citizenship for young immigrants who'd been brought to the country as children and who had grown up in the United States. The bill had various incarnations, but all required potential young Dreamers to meet certain conditions: they had to have graduated from a US high school, earned a GED, or served in the military. At first the measure seemed like a slam dunk, but despite being brought to Congress in 2001, 2009, 2010, and 2011, it failed to become law. The failure ignited many young would-be Dreamers into action. Adept at social media, they began to make their voices heard, bearing witness to arrests, marching in protests, jumping into the new wave of activism that was rolling across the country.

In 2010 Mohammad Abdollahi won national attention for an imaginative action in Tucson. A young adult who had been brought without papers to the United States from Iran at the age of three, Mohammad was gay. If he were deported back to his native country, he could be persecuted for his homosexuality, or even face a possible death sentence. Mohammad and two other undocumented Dreamers—wearing their graduation caps and gowns—staged a sit-in in Senator John McCain's Tucson office to demand that McCain support the Dream Act.

All three protesters were arrested; having openly declared their undocumented status, they were detained by ICE, but only briefly. Now they risked deportation. The boldness of their action electrified other young immigrants. They dreamed up a forceful new rallying cry: "Sin Papeles, Sin Miedo"—*Undocumented, Unafraid.*

Eventually, Mohammad enlisted Adriana Diaz—the would-be Dreamer who'd been working at Albergue San Juan Bosco—into an action that was far more defiant and riskier than the McCain office sit-in. In the summer of 2013, along with eight other Dreamers, Adriana presented herself at the port of entry in Nogales and asked the United States to let her back in.

Adriana had entered the United States as a baby. She was only four months old when her mom, María Antonia Díaz Rodriguez, brought her to Phoenix from Mexico. As a child she'd had no clue that she was undocumented. She only gradually began to understand. "I was older, fifth or sixth grade, about to finish elementary," Adriana told me one spring evening at the albergue, when she was still trapped in

Nogales, Sonora. "Friends would go on vacation in the summer, go camping. I would ask my mom to go to Disneyland."

There was a reason her mother never took her anywhere special. María had no driver's license; she drove only in Phoenix and only where she had to go. She was afraid that if she drove out of town she'd get stopped on the highway by Immigration. Adriana realized, "I couldn't do things other kids could do." And watching the TV coverage of Sheriff Joe Arpaio's immigration raids as a kid, she began to understand the danger she and her mother were in.

She excelled at her charter high school, Crestview College Preparatory, where she specialized in art, graphic design, and computers. "I liked it a lot," she told me, lighting up. As the top student in the senior class, she was named valedictorian. Adriana had always planned to go to college, but Arizona's laws denying in-state tuition to the undocumented stymied that ambition. Even the out-of-state tuition at her local community college, Paradise Valley, was out of reach. She didn't have the resources that Arely Gonzalez had. María was a single mom, and the tightening noose of anti-immigration laws had triggered financial problems for the family. After E-Verify came in, María lost her job at Goodwill.

Mother and daughter, on the foolhardy advice of the school principal, decided to self-deport. They had family in Mexico City, and they figured the high-achieving Adriana could go to one of the excellent universities in the capital. She had her eye on the prestigious National Autonomous University of Mexico (UNAM). She and María sold all that they had and rode by bus to Mexico City in spring 2012. The scheme was a disaster. One college after another, including UNAM, refused to allow Adriana to apply; her school records were all in Phoenix, and universities required her to get her transcript and paperwork notarized in person—in Arizona, a place she couldn't go. The bureaucracy permitted no way around the rules.

Mexico City was dangerous too, Adriana said, marred by corruption and kidnappings. Nor did the locals take kindly to a hybrid American/Mexican like Adriana. Worst of all, in June, when they'd been in Mexico just three months, President Obama announced the DACA plan—but it applied only to young Dreamers who could prove that they were physically present in the United States on June 15, 2012. On that day, Adriana was still futilely knocking on college doors in Mexico City. Otherwise she met all the requirements: she could easily prove that she'd been brought to Phoenix as a baby, gone all through school there, and graduated from high school, at the top of her class, no less. But Adriana's departure from the country rendered her ineligible. There was no arguing the point. She had missed an important opportunity back home, while chasing a hopeless dream in Mexico.

Overwhelmed by sadness at the failure of their journey, Adriana and María decided to go back north, to the Sonoran border town of Nogales, the closest they could get to the home they missed in Phoenix. Things had gotten so bad that they had to borrow the price of their bus fare.

Adriana and María got room and board for their labor at Albergue San Juan Bosco, for cooking up big meals and for comforting migrants, but they had no money. Adriana searched diligently for months for work in Nogales, but she found nothing. She tried the dentists' offices, thinking her excellent English would serve their American patients well; she tried fast-food joints, but there was no work to be had. "I see why so many people want to leave," she said. "I see all these people here in the shelter and hear their stories. Now I say, I know. I understand."

In the summer of 2013, their friend Bob Kee persuaded Adriana and María to move to the Mexican seaside resort of Rosarito, near Tijuana. They could stay at the home of the mother of one of his friends; surely a tourist town catering to Americans could use a worker with Adriana's English skills. And Adriana swiftly got a job as a hotel clerk, after dazzling an interviewer with her bilingualism. But three weeks in, something bigger came along: an invitation from the activist group National Immigrant Youth Alliance to present herself at the border for admission.

Mohammad Abdollahi brainstormed the plan: a whole troupe of immigrant young people who'd been raised in the United States would march boldly up to the gates and announce their desire to come back. Three of the participants were taking an especially risky step. They had already been safely in the United States—one was about to start law school that fall—but they crossed over into Mexico to challenge the laws that marginalized them. Mohammad wasn't going himself, but in a reprise of his debut in the public eye at McCain's office, he would arrange for all the petitioners to wear their high school graduation gowns.

Adriana wanted in. "I wasn't really happy," she told me months later. The hotel job was pleasant enough; she'd easily won over guests with the same wide smile that had endeared her to desperate deportees at the albergue. But Rosarito wasn't home.

"Mohammad told me straight out of the risks. There were no guarantees we'd get back." They were pretty sure that they'd be locked up in detention for a while, and they knew that they could be formally and permanently deported.

On July 22, 2013, Adriana and the rest of the "Dream Nine," all of them graduates of American high schools, put on their gowns—hers was black—and paraded several blocks through Nogales. Supporters and media were there in abundance. Adriana had had a tearful good-bye with María. "I hugged my mom. We both were crying."

Approaching Morley Gate at 11:00 a.m., they chanted, "Undocumented, unafraid. Sin papeles, sin miedo." Like anyone else crossing through the border port, they had to wait in a long line. Lawyers Margo Cowan and Kit Sinclair from Tucson were with them, and a local religious leader accompanied each of the petitioners. When Adriana stepped up to the booth, she told the customs agent, "I am requesting humanitarian parole." The agent told her to "step aside." "After that, we were in their hands."

Each of the Dreamers was interviewed at length, telling of their childhoods in the United States and their travails in Mexico. They were denied humanitarian parole, so they asked for asylum. All nine were held in Nogales for hours. In the evening, they were handcuffed and locked into a freezing van and taken to Florence for processing. It was midnight by the time they arrived and were assigned bunk beds to sleep in. By then they had already been in custody twelve hours.

The next morning, they were driven to Eloy. "I was a little more nervous," Adriana said. "Eloy is the real deal. I always heard how it was horrible, humiliating."

They went through the usual procedures at the giant private prison—a whirl of showers, photos, fingerprinting, medical screening, and document signing. The five Dreamer women were put together in Charlie pod and given uniforms in green.

Adriana found Eloy to be as loathsome as its reputation. "The clothes smelled nasty, like plastic. We hated the food. The oatmeal was an insult to oatmeal. It was like glue. It tasted disgusting." Though ICE denied to the media that the Dreamers' phone calls had been restricted, the nine found they couldn't return phone calls from reporters on the phones hanging on the pod's walls; nor could they talk to their relatives. They staged a hunger strike in response. "I only lasted two days," Adriana said; others stuck it out longer. Some of the Dreamers were proselytizing among the other detainees, explaining their legal rights, and two, María Peniche and Lulu Martinez, organized a protest in the lunchroom.

"María stood up on a stool, and Lulu got the other girls to make a lot of noise. We were all yelling. The guards freaked out" and called for backup. María and Lulu were tossed into solitary for eight days as punishment, each locked up, alone, for twenty-three hours at a stretch.

"I was seventeen days in Eloy," Adriana said. "It felt like a year. I was trying to hang in. The last couple of days I was getting anxious."

Media attention on the Dream Nine was intense; articles ran in the major national media, and Mohammad kept the story humming on social media. Protests were triggered around the country, and thirty-three congressional representatives, including Raúl Grijalva of southern Arizona's Third District, personally championed their case in a letter to Obama. With their original petition for humanitarian parole denied, lawyer Margo Cowan submitted briefs for asylum. Adriana's case detailed the dangers of Mexico and the discrimination she had experienced there. She was taken to Florence for an asylum interview. The female interviewer was respectful, she said, but "it was difficult, with an emotional side. You had to bring up everything that you've lived, bad things that you try to put in the furthest part of your mind. Then you have to bring it up."

On August 6, asylum officers made their ruling: all nine were to be set free. They'd been found to have a "credible fear" of returning to Mexico and a right to present their case to an immigration judge. They could still be deported one day, but not now. It could be years before their hearings came up; meantime, they could live lawfully on the outside, in their American homes.

All nine were released from Eloy on August 7 and delivered to the Greyhound bus station in Tucson. The male Dreamers didn't dress up again, but Adriana and the four other women stepped off the bus triumphantly in their graduation regalia, their gowns billowing in the hot breeze. A crowd of well-wishers whooped and cheered.

Adriana went back to Phoenix to live with her older brother. His wife and two daughters were American citizens, and he was in the process of getting his legal residency; in five years, he'd be able to petition to bring María home from Mexico. María was still living in deportation exile in Nogales, but she was thrilled for her daughter. "Now that I've made it, she's really happy," Adriana said.

Her new life wasn't perfect, though. She didn't have to live in fear anymore, but like Arely she still couldn't afford to get an education. She wasn't eligible for DACA and she was still forbidden to drive. To get to the babysitting jobs she took on, she traveled around the city by bus.

Some pro-immigrant activists had criticized the Dream Nine for taking such a provocative action at a time when immigration reform was being seriously discussed in the halls of government. But Adriana didn't regret any of it, not marching back to the United States so publicly nor taking the risk of being imprisoned in Eloy for a long time, or facing possible deportation. She was proud that the Dream Nine had brought so much attention to the plight of young immigrants. "We were representing not only ourselves, but our families and our stories," she said, helping Americans understand what it meant to be young and undocumented.

Mostly she was happy she had met her goal. She missed her mom, but she was back in Phoenix, living in the only city she had ever really known.

"What I wanted to accomplish," she said, "was coming back home."

Epilogue

On a lazy Memorial Day, early in the evening, the phone rang. Casa Mariposa volunteer Laurie Melrood was on the line.

"You have to come down to Greyhound," she told me. "There are seventy-five to eighty women and children here."

I went. The station in downtown Tucson was pure pandemonium. Little kids were racing around, in between the chairs, darting to the vending machines and back. Mothers were everywhere, sitting wherever they could, in the metal seats, on the floor, nursing their babies, trying to keep an eye on the bigger kids. One baby was sick and crying uncontrollably. There were so many migrants the bus station couldn't hold them all. Some had spilled outside. Women were plopped down on the sloping ramp that led to the front door, sitting on the concrete.

Yesenia Flores slouched against the ramp's metal poles, and her fourteen-year-old son leaned against her. They both looked exhausted. They had fled the slaughter in Honduras.

"Three of my family members were murdered," she told me, "three of my husband's brothers."

Her husband feared that he was next, and their son was of a prime age to be coerced into one of the rampant drug gangs. So the family departed for America and safety, but they'd been caught. The husband had been sent to detention, and Yesenia and her son had been released to the bus station. They were under strict instructions to report to ICE in Fairfax, Virginia, in two weeks. Now she was trying to figure out how to pay for two bus tickets to Hyattsville, Maryland, where still another brother-in-law lived.

Nearby, eighteen-month-old Dimas was rolling around on his mother's outstretched legs, drinking from a bottle. Paula Briseño Rodriguez had come with the child from Huehuetenango, in Guatemala, where she'd been abandoned by her husband. She had seven other children back home. She was headed to Florida, where her sister lived, in hopes of finding work to support them all.

Now she'd lost her sister's two little daughters. They'd started the journey with her, and Paula was supposed to deliver them to her sister. But the US authorities had taken them away. Paula was family, but she wasn't the mother.

Guatemalan women and children like Paula and Dimas had been getting dropped off by ICE at Greyhound in Tucson for eight months. Usually there were ten, or twenty, or even thirty migrant travelers brought to the station, but seventy-five or eighty was on a whole other scale. And now in addition to the Guatemalans there were Salvadoreños and Hondurans, all of them escaping poverty-stricken places racked by gang and drug violence and government corruption.

And there was something else new. No one here had been picked up in the Arizona desert. Every single person in this throng of nearly one hundred people had been flown to Tucson from Texas. For months, Texas had been seeing an ever-increasing number of migrant women and children—as well as unaccompanied minors. Central Americans were taking the shortest route to the United States, up through eastern Mexico and into the southernmost tip of Texas. But so many crossed the Rio Grande on Memorial Day weekend 2014 that the Border Patrol hit its breaking point.

Over the course of several days, four hundred women and children were flown to Tucson. They'd all spent several days freezing in the Border Patrol icebox before being dropped at Greyhound.

Yesenia's and Paula's sons were lucky to be with their mothers. The unaccompanied Central American children who'd come north, riding atop the dangerous trains, were separated out from the family groups. (The numbers of these kids would reach sixty-three thousand by August in fiscal year 2014.) A 2008 law gave children traveling alone certain protections: they were to be taken out of Border Patrol custody within seventy-two hours and handed over to the federal Office of Refugee Resettlement. The agency's social workers would search for the family members the kids had been trying to reach in the United States—like the parents of Paula's nieces.

For the short term, the strapped government began placing hundreds of children into hastily repurposed military barracks. More airplanes flew to Arizona bearing nothing but kids. By early June, eleven hundred teens and children and teen mothers with babies had been taken to Nogales to be housed temporarily in a warehouse retrofitted with steel fences and barbed wire. They were kept isolated from community members who wanted to help. Even Father Sean Carroll of Kino Border Initiative was not permitted to make pastoral visits.

The news from Texas and Tucson—and news photos of kids crossing the border—set off a firestorm that summer of 2014. Anti-immigrant politicians railed against the "invasion." Politicians on both sides of the aisle demanded that the 2008 child-protection law be watered down so the children could be easily deported. Texas senator Ted Cruz declared that the travelers were motivated by Obama's DACA program, and he vowed to end it. Governor Rick Perry took to a helicopter to monitor the Lone Star State's defenses against the children. He had himself photographed aiming a machine gun at the border below.

In Arizona, the word went out that the children were carrying diseases. Resurrecting nineteenth-century fears of pestilential immigrants, a prominent Tucson doctor warned publicly that the children could soon infect American citizens. A friendly Jehovah's Witness who came to my door one morning was alarmed. "I just heard on the radio that they have diseases," she said, clucking disapprovingly. The idea gained such traction that the Pima County chief medical officer felt obliged to take to the airwaves to refute it.

And in neighboring Pinal County—where residents had benefited for years from the plentiful jobs at the detention centers—the anti-immigration sheriff Paul Babeu alerted constituents that on an upcoming morning, Central American minors were to be bused to a boarding school in the small town of Oracle. Loyal citizens, some raising the disease alarm, lined the roadway with hand-lettered signs warning, "Go Back to Your Own Country." But the children never showed up. In the end the Oracle protesters terrorized only a busload of local kids on their way to day camp.

Americans didn't know their own history: the United States shared plenty of blame for the families showing up on its doorstep. During the Cold War, Uncle Sam had propped up murderous military dictatorships in Guatemala, El Salvador, and Honduras, and the region had collapsed into brutal civil wars in the 1970s and '80s. The CAFTA free trade agreement had worsened poverty by displacing campesinos from their lands, and the stepped-up deportations after IIRIRA had transplanted violent Los Angeles gangs into El Salvador and Honduras. Since 2008 the United States had showered all three countries with billions of dollars to fight the drug wars. The money armed and trained police forces and national armies, and the violence and corruption only escalated.

Many of the women and children I saw at Greyhound that night were refugees, fleeing for their lives.

The Casa Mariposa volunteers did what they could to help these traumatized travelers. On that first chaotic Memorial Day night, they worked the phones, trying to get people on a limited number of buses. Concerned Greyhound workers called corporate; it was a holiday, but the company managed to scare up an extra bus and driver so that more of the stranded could get out of town that night.

Meantime, the children and moms were half-starved. It was the usual story. A young Guatemalan mother, Concepción Gonzalez, told me that she and her two young daughters had gotten barely any food all weekend at the freezing Border Patrol headquarters. Concepción was wrapped now in a warm jacket, but the agents had confiscated it in the holding pen, leaving her to shiver for days in a tank top and jeans.

One of the volunteers went out to get boxes of fast-food chicken; someone else bought up a supermarket's entire supply of child-size bottles of milk. When volunteer Margie King began to hand out the provisions, the place went into a feeding frenzy.

Margie brought Concepción and the kids home that night, and Paula and Dimas went to Casa Mariposa. But as the days wore on, bringing busload after busload of the desperate, the volunteers struggled, wearied, and wore out. At long last the community responded to the endless tragedy of the bus station. Catholic Community Services stepped in and took over from Casa, efficiently deploying its resources to care for the travelers and house them. Tucsonans were invited to contribute what Casa had been providing on its own: food, jackets, diapers. Border Patrol agreed to give the travelers sack lunches when they were released. And after the protests broke out in Oracle and elsewhere—and one local TV station published an aerial map of Greyhound's location online—Catholic Community Services wisely plotted with ICE to have the families dropped off at a private, undisclosed location.

Greyhound's stint as a refugee center ended, and Casa Mariposa brought its longtime ministry to immigrant bus travelers to a close.

A month into the crisis, stung by criticism that moms like Yesenia and Paula had been let go, Obama opened two refurbished centers to detain the mothers and their children, one in New Mexico, one in Texas. Not all the families still coming were locked up. Others were allowed to continue their travels to family across the country; the selection seemed as random as Streamline. Critics charged that the detention centers were nothing more than fast-track deportation depots. The ACLU soon filed suit, charging that the setup made it impossible for the women to get judicious review of their asylum claims, as demanded by both US and international law.

The new family detention centers were gussied up with toys and bright colors, and teachers were scheduled to be brought in. But nothing could conceal the fact that these were places of incarceration, or that America was now detaining small children. The youngest of the nation's newly detained were babies just a few months old.

Acknowledgments

Thanks first and foremost to the detainees and deportees who so generously shared their painful stories with me. Among many others whom I met behind the bars of detention centers or trapped behind the border wall in Nogales, Sonora, I am especially grateful to Yolanda Fontes, Elena Santiago, Marco Galdino, and Adriana Diaz. Mariana Rodriguez, María Antonia Díaz Rodriguez, and Alma Hernandez Rodriguez graciously recounted their grim sojourns after they were liberated.

Numerous human rights workers led me into these shadow worlds, including Laurie Melrood, Marjorie King, Rachel Winch, Bob Kee, Dorothy Chao, and Scott Nicholson. Nina Rabin, Charles Vernon, Cindy Schlosser, and Dan Anderson patiently tried to help me understand the complex legal dimensions of detention and deportation, and Will Gosner deployed his formidable research and editing skills on the text. All mistakes that remain are, of course, my own. At Beacon Press, I give all thanks and praise to my editor, Gayatri Patnaik; Rachael Marks; Caitlin Meyer; Tom Hallock; Helene Atwan; Susan Lumenello, and Beth Collins. The talented young Samantha Sais contributed a perfect photo; Andy Mosier made the elegant map; Michael Brescia vetted the Spanish; and my pal Ellen Foos volunteered to proofread. Portions of the prologue first appeared in the *Tucson Weekly* in a somewhat different form.

As I wrote this book, its dark subject matter was lightened by the support of good friends: Jay Rochlin, Cynthia Clinch, Carolyn Cooper, Jacqueline Bland, Steve Cox, Barbara Kremer, and all the Musettes; Eileen Devlin, Anne and John Gerbner, Tom Miller, Tim Vanderpool, Matt Rosney, and Brian Byrne; and the Hill Hall gang, Sally Immerman, Marsha Kalman, Rhonda Friedman, and Margaret Stern.

In writing this book about family separation, I thought often about the endurance of family bonds. My Tucson-bred children are grown and gone, and my big, extended Philadelphia family is likewise blown to the four winds. I'm grateful that barricaded international borders don't prevent our reunions, and family remains my strength. Love and gratitude always to my sibling supporters, Mary, Billy, Anne Marie, Eileen, Michael, Paul, and Jimmy Regan; my in-laws, Pam Gosner, Marilou Regan, Doug Magee, Tim Smith, Patricia Regan, Mark Brack, Sandra Riley, and the late Alice Swaboski; the tribe of grown nieces and nephews; Gabriel and Natalie Regan, the newest (and most adorable) members of the expanding clan; and my beloved parents, the late William and Mary Regan, whose remarkable blend of skepticism and compassion helped shape my work.

I dedicate this book to the southwest branch of this oversized family tree: my daughter, Linda Gosner, now a globe-tripping archaeologist, who delights me with her zest for what's underground and her adventurous spirit (she's digging in Sardinia as I write); my son, Will Gosner, a writer and musician in Chicago, who touches me with his lyricism, his way around the guitar, and his kindness; and my husband, Kevin Gosner, still at my side in Tucson, who's notable for his selflessness, his editorial acuity, and especially for the calm he displays in the fiercest of writer's storms.

Notes

PROLOGUE

1. Margaret Regan, "Barrier Rebuilt: As a New Wall Is Built Through Nogales, Well-Known Art Is Being Relocated or Destroyed," *Tucson Weekly*, June 23, 2011, http://www.tucsonweekly.com/tucson/barrier-rebuilt/Content?oid=3028495.

INTRODUCTION

1. Department of Homeland Security, *Immigration Enforcement Actions: 2012*, annual report, December 2013, http://www.dhs.gov/sites/default/files/publications/ois_enforcement_ar_2012_1.pdf.
2. Global Detention Project, "United States Detention Profile," updated March 2009, http://www.globaldetentionproject.org/countries/americas/united-states/introduction.html.
3. Department of Homeland Security, *Immigration Enforcement Actions: 2012*.
4. Coalición de Derechos Humanos, Missing Migrant Project, http://www.derechoshumanosaz.net/projects/arizona-recovered-bodies-project/; US Border Patrol, "Total Illegal Alien Apprehensions by Fiscal Year," http://www.cbp.gov/sites/default/files/documents/U.S.%20Border%20Patrol%20Fiscal%20Year%20Apprehension%20Statistics%20by%20sector%20and%20border%20area.pdf.

5. Leng May Ma v. Barber, 357 U.S. 185 (1958), *Justia*, http://su preme.justia.com/cases/federal/us/357/185/case.html.

6. I am indebted to Arthur C. Helton for his history of immigration detention. "The Imprisonment of Refugees in the United States," in *In Defense of the Alien*, vol. 9 (New York: Center for Migration Studies of New York, 1986), 130–37.

7. Gretchen Gavett, "Map: The U.S. Immigration Detention Boom," *Frontline*, "Lost in Detention," PBS website, October 18, 2011, http://www.pbs.org/wgbh/pages/frontline/race-multi cultural/lost-in-detention/map-the-u-s-immigration-deten tion-boom/.

8. Todd Miller, *Border Patrol Nation: Dispatches from the Front Lines of Homeland Security* (San Francisco: City Lights, 2010).

9. David Bornstein, "Immigrants Welcome Here," *New York Times*, February 19, 2014, http://opinionator.blogs.nytimes .com/2014/02/19/immigrants-welcome-here/?_php=true& _type=blogs&_r=oreference.

10. Gavett, "Map."

11. Carl Hulse, "Immigrant Surge Rooted in Law to Curb Child Trafficking," *New York Times*, July 7, 2014, http://www.nytimes .com/2014/07/08/us/immigrant-surge-rooted-in-law-to-curb -child-trafficking.html.

12. Homeland Security, *Yearbook of Immigration Statistics: 2012*, Table 39, "Aliens Removed or Returned: Fiscal Years 1892 to 2012," http://www.dhs.gov/yearbook-immigration-statistics -2012-enforcement-actions.

CHAPTER ONE: YOLANDA IN LIMBO

1. Byrd H. Granger, *Arizona's Names: X Marks the Place* (Arizona: Falconer, 1983), 226.

2. Yolanda's last name has been changed to a pseudonym at her request for privacy and protection.

3. Nina Rabin, "Disappearing Parents: Immigration Enforcement and the Child Welfare System," *Connecticut Law Review* 44 (2011): 99; Nina Rabin, "Unseen Prisoners: A Report on Women in Immigration Detention Facilities in Arizona," *Georgetown Immigration Law Journal* 23 (2009): 695, http://papers.ssrn.com /sol3/papers.cfm?abstract_id=1327841.

4. The names of Yolanda Fontes's family members have been changed to protect their privacy.

5. This account of Yolanda Fontes's life, especially the details of her legal issues and her employment with the brothel, draws on Nina Rabin, "Victims or Criminals? Discretion, Sorting, and Bureaucratic Culture in the U.S. Immigration System," *Southern California Review of Law and Social Justice* 23 (2014): 195. Additional personal material relies on two interviews of Yolanda Fontes by the author, by phone on March 27, 2012, and in person on April 1, 2012.

6. William Selway and Margaret Newkirk, "Congress Mandates Jail Beds for 34,000 Immigrants as Private Prisons Profit," *Bloomberg News*, September 23, 2013, http://www.bloomberg .com/news/2013–09–24/congress-fuels-private-jails-detaining -34–000-immigrants.html.

7. National Immigration Forum, *The Math of Immigration Detention: Runaway Costs for Immigration Detention Do Not Add Up to Sensible Policies*, August 2013, www.immigrationforum.org.

8. Ibid.

9. "Eloy, Arizona," City-Data.com, http://www.city-data.com /city/Eloy-Arizona.html#ixzz2tLCuCZec. Population figures: Google Public Data Explorer (source: US Census Bureau), last updated September 25, 2013, https://www.google.com/public data/explore?ds=kf7tggr1uo9ude_&met_y=population&hl=en& dl=en&idim=place:0422360.

10. Rabin, "Victims or Criminals?"

11. TRAC Immigration, "Judge-by-Judge Asylum Decisions in Immigration Courts FY 2007-2012," *Graphical Highlights: Immigration*, 2013, http://trac.syr.edu/immigration/reports/306 /include/denialrates.html.

12. Rabin, "Victims or Criminals?"

CHAPTER TWO: SUICIDE

1. US Immigration and Customs Enforcement, "ICE Detainee Passes Away at Eloy Detention Center," press release, April 30, 2013, http://www.ice.gov/news/releases/1304/130430phoenix.htm.

2. Lindsay Marshall (Florence Project), "It's Surprising That More Immigrants Don't Commit Suicide in Jail," *Arizona*

Republic, May 16, 2013, http://www.azcentral.com/opinions /articles/20130515marshall-its-time-look-human-cost-immigra tion-system.html.

3. US Department of State, US Passports and International Travel, "Honduras Travel Warning," December 24, 2013 (up-dated June 24, 2014), http://travel.state.gov/content/passports /english/alertswarnings/honduras-travel-warning.html.

4. US Immigration and Customs Enforcement, "List of Deaths in ICE Custody: October 2003–December 2, 2013," http://www .ice.gov/doclib/foia/reports/detaineedeaths2003-present.pdf.

5. Nina Bernstein, "Hurdles Shown in Detention Reform," *New York Times,* August 20, 2009, http://www.nytimes.com /2009/08/21/nyregion/21detain.html?pagewanted=all&_r=0.

6. J. J. Hensley, "ICE to Probe 2 Inmate Suicides at Eloy Deten-tion Center," *Arizona Republic,* May 2, 2013, http://www.az central.com/news/arizona/articles/20130502ice-probe-inmate -suicides-eloy.html; US Immigration and Customs Enforce-ment, *2011 Operations Manual ICE Performance-Based Na-tional Detention Standards,* https://www.ice.gov/detention-stan dards/2011/.

7. US Immigration and Customs Enforcement, "ICE Detainee Under Criminal Investigation Passes Away at Eloy Detention Center," press release, May 2, 2013, http://www.ice.gov/news /releases/1305/130502phoenix.htm.

8. Ian Urbina and Catherine Rentz, "Immigrants Held in Soli-tary Cells, Often for Weeks," *New York Times,* March 23, 2013, http://www.nytimes.com/2013/03/24/us/immigrants-held-in -solitary-cells-often-for-weeks.html?pagewanted=all.

9. Ian Urbina, "Using Jailed Migrants as a Pool of Cheap La-bor," *New York Times,* May 24, 2014; http://www.nytimes .com/2014/05/25/us/using-jailed-migrants-as-a-pool-of-cheap -labor.html.

CHAPTER THREE: PURGATORIO ARPAIO

1. Sari Horwitz, "U.S. Sues Arizona Sheriff over Alleged Vio-lations of Hispanics' Civil Rights," *Washington Post,* May 10, 2012, http://www.washingtonpost.com/politics/justice-to-sue -arizona-sheriff-joe-arpaio-saying-he-violated-hispanics-civil

-rights/2012/05/10/gIQAYfFwFU_story.html. See also Edward Barraza, "Guadalupe Residents Forced Arpaio to Move Command Center," April 3 and 4, 2008, http://eduardobarraza.photo shelter.com/image/Io00062QDg6BpLVc.

2. Horwitz, "U.S. Sues Arizona Sheriff"; ACLU, "Ortega Melendres, et al. v. Arpaio, et al.," October 4, 2013, https://www.aclu .org/immigrants-rights-racial-justice/ortega-melendres-et-al -v-arpaio-et-al.

3. Howard Fischer, "Appeals Ruling Says Arpaio Jail Menu 'Inedible,'" Capitol Media Services, *Verde Independent*, October 14, 2010, http://verdenews.com/main.asp?SectionID=1&SubSec tionID=1189&ArticleID=38751.

4. Stephen Lemons, "Bill Montgomery's Smoking Gun: ICE PowerPoint Shows Monty's Minions How to Deport More Immigrants," *Phoenix New Times*, *Feathered Bastard* blog, February 15, 2013, http://blogs.phoenixnewtimes.com/bastard/2013 /02/bill_montgomerys_smoking_gun_i.php.

5. Jacques Billeaud, "Arizona Upholds Immigrant Smuggling Law," Associated Press, *Washington Post*, June 9, 2006, http:// www.washingtonpost.com/wp-dyn/content/article/2006 /06/09/AR2006060901492.html.

CHAPTER FOUR: A TALE OF TWO TOWNS

1. Pinal County Historical Society, *Florence*, Images of America series (Charleston, SC: Arcadia Publishing, 2007), 93.

2. Lynh Bui, "Marking 100 Years of Incarceration: Prison in Florence Will Celebrate with Anniversary Bash," *Arizona Republic*, July 12, 2008, http://www.azcentral.com/news/articles/2008/07 /12/20080712prisonparty0712.html#ixzz334qTwyfo.

3. "Immigrants in Solitary," editorial, *New York Times*, April 1, 2013, http://www.nytimes.com/2013/04/02/opinion/immigrants-in -solitary.html.

4. Gregory Pratt, "Immigrants Who Fight Deportation Are Packed into Federal Gulags for Months or Years Before Their Cases Are Heard," *Phoenix New Times*, June 23, 2011, http:// www.phoenixnewtimes.com/2011-06-23/news/immigrants -who-fight-deportation-are-packed-into-federal-gulags-for -months-and-years-before-their-cases-are-heard/.

5. Detention Watch Network et al., letter to President Obama, November 18, 2014, http://www.detentionwatchnetwork.org /sites/detentionwatchnetwork.org/files/ec-obamaletter.pdf.

6. Detention Watch Network, *Pinal County Jail Arizona: Expose and Close* (Washington, DC: Detention Watch Network, 2012), http://www.detentionwatchnetwork.org/sites/detentionwatch network.org/files/ExposeClose/Expose-Pinal11-13.pdf.

7. Esther Yu-Hsi Lee, "The Government Spent About $406K to Detain This Immigrant," *Think Progress*, May 8, 2014, http://thinkprogress.org/immigration/2014/05/08/3435069 /marco-galdino-detention-quota/.

8. Will Coley, "Detention Watch Network Applauds End of ICE Contract with Pinal County Jail in Arizona," Detention Watch Network, July 22, 2014, http://detentionwatchnetwork.word press.com/2014/07/22/detention-watch-network-applauds -end-of-ice-contract-with-pinal-county-jail-in-arizona/.

9. Will Coley, "The Jena Times: LaSalle Detention Facility Immediately Downsizing Operation in Louisiana," Detention Watch Network, January 13, 2010, http://detentionwatchnet work.wordpress.com/2010/01/13/the-jena-times-lasalle-deten tion-facility-immediately-downsizing-operation-in-louisiana/.

CHAPTER FIVE: GREYHOUND

1. Margaret Regan, "Border Art and Song: A Visual Artist and a Singer Explore the Tragedies that Spur Migrants to Come to the U.S.," *Tucson Weekly*, March 14, 2013, http://www.tucsonweekly .com/tucson/border-art-and-song/Content?oid=3663049.

2. Julia Preston, "Hoping for Asylum, Migrants Strain U.S. Border," *New York Times*, April 10, 2014, http://www.nytimes .com/2014/04/11/us/poverty-and-violence-push-new-wave-of -migrants-toward-us.html.

CHAPTER SIX: WOMAN WITHOUT A COUNTRY

1. Elena Santiago, Luis, and Camila are pseudonyms; their real names have been changed for their privacy and protection.

2. Seth Freed Wessler, "Nearly 205K Deportations of Parents of U.S. Citizens in Just Over Two Years," *Colorlines*, December 17,

2012, http://colorlines.com/archives/2012/12/us_deports_more
_than_200k_parents.html.

3. Cited in Victoria Kline, *Where Do We Go from Here? Challenges Facing Transnational Migrant Families Between the U.S. and Mexico* (Mexico City: IMUMI, October 2013), http://uf.imumi.org/recursos/challenges_summary.pdf.

4. Seth Freed Wessler, *Shattered Families: The Perilous Intersection of Immigration Enforcement and the Child Welfare System* (New York: Applied Research Center, November 2011).

5. Bob Christie, "Arizona Gov. Jan Brewer Dissolves State Child Welfare Agency," Associated Press, *Christian Science Monitor*, January 14, 2014, http://www.csmonitor.com/The-Culture/Family/2014/0114/Arizona-Gov.-Jan-Brewer-dissolves-state-child-welfare-agency.

6. National Migration Institute numbers from Murphy Woodhouse and Sam McNeil, "U.S. Policies Separate Families, Kill the Sick and Create Havoc on the Mexican Border," *Truthout*, May 30, 2012, http://truth-out.org/news/item/9349-los-deportados.

7. Seth Freed Wessler, "'I'm Here, My Children Are Over There': Immigration and Its Impact on Families," *Elle*, August 27, 2013, http://www.elle.com/life-love/society-career/immigration-families-4.

CHAPTER SEVEN: IN THE CITY OF THE DEPORTED

1. Dylan Smith, "Tucson's Hot Streak Ends; 39 Consecutive 100-Degree Days," *Tucson Sentinel*, July 10, 2013, http://www.tucsonsentinel.com/local/report/071013_hot_streak/tucsons-hot-streak-ends-39-consecutive-100-degree-days/.

2. La Roca shelter shut down in July 2014 when the family who operated it fled Nogales. Father Sean Carroll reported in the Kino Border Initiative newsletter of August 1, 2014, that the Sonoran State Police had raided La Roca on July 10 and robbed and threatened the family and the migrants sheltering there.

3. Perla Trevizo, "Criminal Prosecution of Border Crossers at All-Time High," *Arizona Daily Star*, December 7, 2013, http://tucson.com/news/criminal-prosecution-of-border-crossers-at-all-time-high/article_cd6e5255-a3ac-52ca-8951-fdd3b74f0fff.html.

4. Gerardo, "35 Zetas Executed in Boca del Rio, Veracuz," *Borderland Beat*, September 20, 2011, http://www.borderlandbeat .com/2011/09/35-zetas-executed-in-boca-del-rio.html.

5. Gustavo Sanchez reappeared at the comedor in 2014 and told a slightly different tale to another reporter. Melinda Henneberger, "Cardinal O'Malley: Immigrant Outreach on Mexican Border Inspired by Pope Francis," *Washington Post*, April 1, 2014, http://www.washingtonpost.com/local/2014/04/01/55456b74 -b91e-11e3-899e-bb708e3539dd_story.html.

CHAPTER EIGHT: ALBERGUE EVENING

1. Perla Trevino, "Labor of Love Keeps Immigrant Shelter Open 31 Years," *Arizona Daily Star*, February 2, 2013, http://www .highbeam.com/doc/1P2-34721511.html.

2. Jo Tuckman, "El Chapo Guzmán: Mexico's Most Wanted Drug Kingpin Arrested," *Guardian/Observer*, February 22, 2014, http://www.theguardian.com/world/2014/feb/22/joaquin -guzman-mexico-drugs-arrested.

CHAPTER NINE: SHOWDOWN ON TENTH AVENUE

1. Samaritans Kathryn Ferguson, Norma A. Price, and Ted Parks published *Crossing with the Virgin: Stories from the Migrant Trail* (Tucson: University of Arizona Press, 2010).

2. Hipolito Corella, "Dozens Confront Border Patrol Agents During Tucson Traffic Stop," *Arizona Daily Star*, October 9, 2013, http://tucson.com/news/local/border/dozens-confront-border -patrol-agents-during-tucson-traffic-stop/article_977b6e76 -309d-11e3-b3be-001a4bcf887a.html. Photo by Perla Trevizo.

3. Valerie Cavazos and Marcelino Benito, "Routine Traffic Stop Leads to Protest, Pepper Spray," KGUN9-TV video, October 8, 2013, http://www.jrn.com/kgun9/news/Routine-traffic-stop -leads-to-protest-pepper-spray-227010991.html.

4. Perla Trevizo and Carli Brosseau, "State of Confusion: Enforcement of Immigration Law Varies Widely About Immigration Checks in Tucson," *Arizona Daily Star*, March 3, 2014, http://tucson.com/special-section/sb1070/.

5. A portion of the video appears in Fernanda Santos, "Border Patrol Scrutiny Stirs Anger in Arizona Town," *New York Times*,

June 27, 2014, http://www.nytimes.com/2014/06/28/us/border
-patrol-scrutiny-stirs-anger-in-arizona-town.html.

6. Bob Ortega and Rob O'Dell, "Deadly Border Agent Incidents
   Cloaked in Silence," *Arizona Republic*, December 16, 2013, http://
   www.azcentral.com/news/politics/articles/20131212arizona
   -border-patrol-deadly-force-investigation.html.

7. Brian Bennett, "Border Patrol's Use of Deadly Force Criticized
   in Report," *Los Angeles Times*, February 27, 2014, http://www
   .latimes.com/nation/la-na-border-killings-20140227,0,2649003
   .story#ixzz2vlhbAkH6.

8. Roque Planas, "Mother Sues Border Patrol over Death of
   Child Shot Multiple Times," *Huffington Post*, July 29, 2014,
   http://www.huffingtonpost.com/2014/07/29/jose-antonio
   -elena-rodriguez-lawsuit_n_5631071.html.

9. Damien Cave, "Complaints of Abuse by Border Agents Often
   Ignored, Records Show," *New York Times*, May 5, 2014, http://
   www.nytimes.com/2014/05/06/us/complaints-of-abuse-by
   -border-agents-often-ignored-records-show.html?emc.

10. Andrew Becker, "Ousted Chief Accuses Border Agency of
    Shooting Cover-ups, Corruption," Center for Investigative
    Reporting, August 14, 2014, https://beta.cironline.org/reports
    /ousted-chief-accuses-border-agency-of-shooting-cover-ups
    -corruption/.

11. *A Culture of Cruelty: Abuse and Impunity in Short-Term U.S.
    Border Patrol Custody* (Tucson: No More Deaths/No Más
    Muertes, 2011), http://www.nomoredeathsvolunteers.org/Print
    %20Resources/Abuse%20Doc%20Reports/Culture%20of%20
    Cruelty/CultureofCrueltyFinal.pdf.

CHAPTER TEN: STREAMLINE

1. Margaret Regan, "There Goes the Neighborhood: The Down-
   fall of Downtown," *Tucson Weekly*, March 6, 1997, http://www
   .tucsonweekly.com/tw/03-06-97/cover.htm.

2. Jeremy Slack et al., *In the Shadow of the Wall: Family Separation, Immigration Enforcement and Security* (Tucson: Center for
   Latin American Studies, University of Arizona, March 2013),
   http://las.arizona.edu/sites/las.arizona.edu/files/UA_Immi
   gration_Report2013web.pdf.

3. Fernanda Santos, "Detainees Sentenced in Seconds in 'Streamline' Justice on Border," *New York Times*, February 11, 2014, http://www.nytimes.com/2014/02/12/us/split-second-justice-as-us-cracks-down-on-border-crossers.html.

4. "Heather E. Williams, Amended Written Statement of Heather E. Williams, First Assistant Public Defender, District of Arizona–Tucson, before the United States House of Representatives, Subcommittee of Commercial and Administrative Law, Oversight Hearing on the 'Executive Office for United States Attorneys,'" June 25, 2008, http://judiciary.house.gov/_files/hearings/pdf/Williams080625.pdf.

5. Stephen Lemons, "Grinding Justice: Operation Streamline Costs Millions, Tramples the Constitution, Treats Migrants Like Cattle, and Doesn't Work," *Phoenix New Times*, October 21, 2010, http://www.phoenixnewtimes.com/2010–10–21/news/grinding-justice-operation-streamline-costs-millions-tramples-the-constitution-treats-migrants-like-cattle-and-doesn-t-work/.

6. Slack et al., *In the Shadow of the Wall*.

7. Hailey Anne Sheldon, "Operation Streamline: The Border Patrol Prosecutions Initiative," *Public Purpose* 11 (Spring 2013): 105.

8. Joanna Lydgate, *Assembly-Line Justice: A Review of Operation Streamline*, policy brief (Berkeley: Chief Justice Earl Warren Institute on Race, Ethnicity and Diversity, University of California, Berkeley Law School, January 2010), www.law.berkeley.edu/files/Operation_Streamline_Policy_Brief.pdf.

9. No More Deaths, "Fact Sheet: Operation Streamline," March 2012, http://www.cultureofcruelty.org/content/uploads/2012/03/nmd_fact_sheet_operation_streamline.pdf.

10. Marc R. Rosenblum, "Border Security: Immigration Enforcement Between Ports of Entry," Congressional Research Service Report to Congress, May 3, 2013, http://fas.org/sgp/crs/homesec/R42138.pdf.

11. Perla Trevizo, "'Operation Streamline' Takes Hard Line on Illegal Crossers," *Arizona Daily Star*, March 24, 2013, http://azstarnet.com/news/local/border/operation-streamline-takes-hard-line-on-illegal-border-crossers/article_35cb6dc5–45e3–55e5-b471-c1dd2a72bc31.html.

12. Lydgate, *Assembly-Line Justice*.

13. Slack et al., *In the Shadow of the Wall*.

14. Ted Robbins, "Claims of Border Program Success Are Unproven," NPR, September 13, 2010, http://www.npr.org/tem plates/story/story.php?storyId=129827870.

CHAPTER ELEVEN: DREAMING

1. Elise Foley, "House Votes to Strip Deportation Relief from Dreamers," August 1, 2014, http://www.huffingtonpost.com /2014/08/01/house-bill-daca_n_5643287.html.

2. *Dreams and Silhouettes/Sueños y Silhuetas*, a theater piece put together by performance artist Denise Uyehara, filmmaker Jason Aragón, and video artist Adam Cooper-Terán, was based on interviews with undocumented women in Las Promotoras. Performed January 25, 2014, at the Global Justice Center, Tucson; http://vimeo.com/87735280.